FREEDOM OF
CONSCIENCE AND RELIGION

Other books in the *Essentials of Canadian Law* series

ESSENTIALS OF
CANADIAN LAW

FREEDOM OF CONSCIENCE AND RELIGION

RICHARD MOON
Faculty of Law, University of Windsor

IRWIN
LAW

Freedom of Conscience and Religion

Published in 2014 by

Irwin Law Inc
14 Duncan Street
Suite 206
Toronto, ON
M5H 3G8

www.irwinlaw.com

ISBN: 978-1-55221-364-3
e-book ISBN: 978-1-55221-365-0

Cataloguing in Publication available from Library and Archives Canada

The publisher acknowledges the financial support of the Government of Canada through the Canada Book Fund for its publishing activities.

We acknowledge the assistance of the OMDC Book Fund, an initiative of Ontario Media Development Corporation.

Printed and bound in Canada.

1 2 3 4 5   18 17 16 15 14

SUMMARY
TABLE OF CONTENTS

DETAILED
TABLE OF CONTENTS

CHAPTER 3:
THE RESTRICTION AND ACCOMMODATION OF RELIGIOUS PRACTICES   66

CHAPTER 4:
THE AUTONOMY OF RELIGIOUS ORGANIZATIONS   139

PREFACE

When the *Canadian Charter of Rights and Freedoms*[1] was enacted in 1982, the first of its fundamental freedoms seemed less significant and less interesting than many of its other rights. Religion in Canada was generally regarded as a private matter, with little visible presence in the country's political life. There were, of course, individuals and groups who were motivated by a religious commitment to take political action, but their objectives were almost always civic — to eradicate poverty, or ban land-mines, or prohibit abortion — and not to advance the particular practices of their faith. Indeed, political actors seldom spoke publicly about their faith and did not justify their public actions explicitly on religious grounds. Some of the early support for a charter of rights in Canada had been a reaction to acts of state suppression of religious and cultural practice, such as the "war without mercy" against the proselytizing activities of the Jehovah's Witness community in 1950s Quebec.[2] But by 1982, the state seemed to be no longer engaged in the direct suppression of religious practice.

Yet in 1982 there were also several reasons to think that issues of religious freedom might again become significant. Those who had predicted the ineluctable decline of religious belief had begun to rethink

---

1 *Canadian Charter of Rights and Freedoms*, Part 1 of the *Constitution Act, 1982*, being Schedule B to the *Canada Act 1982* (UK), 1982, c 11 [*Charter*].

2 Maurice Duplessis quoted in William Kaplan, *State and Salvation: The Jehovah's Witnesses and Their Fight for Civil Rights* (Toronto: University of Toronto Press, 1989) at 230.

this assumption. Religious commitment seemed not only to be stubbornly persistent, but indeed, to be experiencing a revival in evangelical, fundamentalist, and spiritualist forms. Even if most religious adherents accepted that religion and politics should remain separate, they did not always agree about where the line between private spirituality and public secularism should be drawn. As well, immigration in the later part of the twentieth century had significantly added to the religious diversity of the country. The number of adherents to non-Christian belief systems, including Sikhism, Islam, and Hinduism, grew significantly in this period. This growth in diversity raised questions about the historic ordering of public life on the basis of Christian practices. Even if the majority in the country saw the imprint of Christian practice on public life as "just the way things were," or as cultural rather than religious in character, other religious groups viewed the public traces of Christian practice differently. In the freedom of religion cases that arose in the first decades of the *Charter*, the courts and other state actors were asked to remove the vestiges of Christian practice from the public sphere (for example, saying the Lord's Prayer in the public schools or Sunday closing laws) or to exempt religious minority group members from legal standards that privileged mainstream Christian practice and failed to take account of minority practices (such as the RCMP uniform requirement or statutory holidays). These issues, though, seemed manageable, requiring only minor adjustments to existing practices. They could be, and generally were, worked out in particular settings by the affected parties.

However, the Salman Rushdie affair, the 9/11 attacks, and later the publication of the "Danish Cartoons" helped to move religion or religious difference to the forefront of public consciousness. These events seemed to confirm that religion, or at least particular religions, represented a threat to the values of liberal-democratic society. They contributed to the idea that different religious world views were so fundamentally at odds that coexistence, if possible, was bound to be difficult. Religious freedom issues that may have been minor and easily resolved "on the ground" were increasingly seen through this lens of intractable conflict, and as opening the door to a broader threat to Western democracy. In Canada, anxiety about religion has been far less acute than in Europe, where it is perceived as an internal threat to liberal-democratic values, or in the United States, where the threat is understood as external. Nevertheless, concern about the character of religion has shaped the public reaction to religious diversity and freedom. This has been most powerfully so in Quebec where, as in Europe, national identity remains a concern, and the political role of the Catholic church in the recent past has caused many to be wary of the visibility of religion in the public sphere.

The introductory chapter of the book sets out the basic history of religious freedom in Canada and the general claims about the freedom that are developed in later chapters. A central theme of this book, which is introduced in Chapter 1, is the shift in the courts' conception of religious freedom from a liberty to an equality-based right. In their early *Charter* judgments, the courts describe religious freedom as a liberty that has two dimensions—the freedom to engage in religious practice without state restriction (unless necessary to advance the public interest) and the freedom from state compulsion to engage in a religious practice. However, in later cases, the courts seem to say that the freedom does not simply prohibit state coercion in matters of religion or conscience, but requires also that the state treat religious belief systems or communities in an equal or even-handed manner—that it remain neutral in religious matters. The state must not support or prefer the practices of one religious group over those of another (religion, or at least religious contest, should be excluded from politics) and it must not restrict the practices of a religious group, unless this is necessary to protect a compelling public interest (religion should be insulated from politics). This shift in the courts' understanding of the freedom's justification from a liberty to an equality right has been accompanied by a narrowing of the freedom's scope or focus. Despite the apparent breadth of section 2(a), and the courts' formal acknowledgment that freedom of conscience and religion protects both religious and nonreligious (fundamental) beliefs, the former have been at the centre of the freedom of religion/conscience cases. The protection of nonreligious beliefs and practices (the freedom of conscience component of section 2(a)) appears to be limited to practices that resemble in content and structure familiar religious practices.

Yet the neutrality requirement has not been consistently enforced by the courts. The problem is not only that religious beliefs involve claims about what is true and right, which must be viewed as a matter of judgment (rather than cultural practice) and must be open to debate in the public sphere. The more fundamental difficulty with the requirement of state neutrality is that religious beliefs sometimes have public implications. State neutrality is possible only if religion can be treated as simply a private matter. Because religious beliefs sometimes address civic concerns and are often difficult to distinguish from nonreligious beliefs, they cannot be fully excluded or insulated from political decision making. And, indeed, the courts have applied the neutrality requirement selectively; sometimes treating religion as a cultural identity towards which the state should remain neutral, and other times (when it touches upon or addresses civic matters) as a political or moral judgment by the individual that should be subject to the give-and-take of politics.

Behind the courts' uneven application of the religious neutrality requirement lies a complex conception of religious commitment in which religion is viewed as both an aspect of the individual's identity and as a set of judgments or beliefs made by the individual about truth and right. The challenge for the courts is to find a way to fit this complex conception of religious commitment (as deeply held or foundational) and its value (as a source of meaning, purpose, and identity for the individual and group) into a constitutional framework that relies on a distinction between individual choices or commitments that should be protected as a matter of liberty, and individual attributes or traits that should be respected as a matter of equality. The constitutional framework (and perhaps more deeply, our conception of rights) imposes this distinction, between judgment and identity, on the rich and complex experience of religious commitment.

Chapter 2 considers the issue of state support for religion, including the place of religious practices and symbols in public institutions and the role of religious values in public decision making. While the courts have said that the state should remain neutral in matters of religion and should not support or favour the practices of a particular religion, they have not interpreted section 2(a) as excluding religion entirely from the political sphere. First, the courts have said that the state may support religious practices and institutions provided it does so in an even-handed way, and (in the case of schools and other services) ensures the availability of a nonreligious option. Second, the courts have not demanded that governments (literally or metaphorically) sandblast religious symbols or practices from social and physical structures, some of which were constructed long ago. Religious practices have shaped the traditions and rituals of the community and cannot simply be erased from the public sphere or ignored in the formulation of public policy. As long as religion remains part of private life, it will affect the shape of public action. Third, the courts have said that while the state must not support or prefer the *practices* of a particular religious belief system, it is not precluded from relying on religious *values* when making political decisions. Religious values that address worldly concerns or civic issues cannot simply be excluded from political decision making, but must be debated on their merits—on their conception of human good or public welfare. However, the line between the "civic" and "spiritual" elements of a religious belief system (between religious values and religious practices) will depend on the courts' views about the ordinary forms of religious worship, the nature of human welfare, and the proper scope of political action.

Chapter 3 addresses the other dimension of religious freedom, the restriction or accommodation of religious practices by state action. According to the courts, the *Charter* right to freedom of religion is breached any time the state restricts a religious practice in a nontrivial way. Even when a law advances a legitimate public purpose, such as the prevention of drug use or cruelty to animals, the state must justify, under section 1, the law's nontrivial interference with a religious practice. The state must sometimes compromise its policies, at least to some degree, to make space for such a practice. Yet despite the courts' formal declaration that the state must justify any nontrivial restriction of a religious practice (or reasonably accommodate the practice), they have given this requirement little substance. The courts appear willing to uphold a legal restriction, if it has a legitimate objective (that is, an objective other than the suppression of an erroneous religious practice) that would be noticeably compromised if an exception were made. In other words, even though the courts have structured their approach to section 2(a) so that it has the form of an equality right (that draws on human rights code and *Charter* equality jurisprudence), they have adopted in practice a very weak standard of justification under section 1, so that the right protects only a limited form of liberty. The courts' weak standard of justification for limits (their reluctance to exempt a religious practice from ordinary law), reflects their uncertainty about whether religious practices — which are based on contestable beliefs — are different from other practices in a way that justifies their insulation from otherwise legitimate political action.

While the courts do not engage in anything that could properly be described as the "balancing" of competing public and religious interests (in which the state's objectives might sometimes be subordinated to the claims of a religious community), they have sometimes sought to create space for religious practices at the margins of law by adjusting the boundary between private liberty and civic action. First, accommodation may sometimes be granted to religious practices that conflict indirectly with the law (that conflict not with the law's objective, but with the means chosen to advance that objective). In such a case, the court may require the state to compromise, in a minor way, its pursuit of a particular objective to make space for a religious practice. Second, in the case of a more direct conflict between a religious practice and a legal norm, the court will require the state to exempt (accommodate) a religious individual or group from the law only if the exempted activity is "self-regarding" and will have no significant impact on others in the community. In such a case, the practice will be treated as personal to the individual or internal to the group and insulated from the application of the law.

The next three chapters consider the issue of religious restriction in particular contexts. Chapter 4 discusses the autonomy of religious organizations from state regulation. When an individual believer seeks an exemption from the law for her religious practice, the key issue for the court is whether the exemption (the accommodation) will negatively affect the public interest or the rights of others. In some cases though, the accommodation claim is made not by an individual, who is seeking exemption for a specific practice, but by a religious organization or institution, which is seeking a degree of autonomy in the governance of its affairs — in the operation of its internal decision-making processes and the application of its own rules. In these institutional autonomy cases, the court must determine not only whether the exemption from state law will impact the rights and interests of others (whether the group's application of its own rules will negatively affect outsiders to the group), but also whether the members of the group should be protected by state law from internal rules that are unfair and contrary to public policy.

Chapter 5 addresses the issue of state support for religious schools. The courts have held that section 2(a) precludes the state from supporting the practices or institutions of a particular religion, but does not prevent the state from providing general support for religious practices or institutions. A province then may fund religious schools as long as it does so in an even-handed way. There is, however, a constitutional exception to the requirement of equal treatment. Section 93 of the *Constitution Act, 1867* protects the rights of "Separate" or "Dissentient" schools (principally Roman Catholic schools) that existed in a province at the time of Confederation or its entry into the union.[3] Many of the recent section 93 cases have been concerned with the right of separate schools to maintain their religious character, even when this involves adherence to values or practices that are at odds with public values such as sexual-orientation equality.

Chapter 6 considers freedom of religion in the context of the family, and in particular, the parent-child relationship. It is not surprising that some of the most contentious freedom of religion cases involve the claim of parents to make religiously-based decisions concerning their chil-

---

3   *Constitution Act, 1867* (UK), 30 & 31 Vict, c 3, reprinted in RSC 1985, App II, No 5. See also the *Saskatchewan Act*, SC 1905, c 42, s 17; *Alberta Act*, SC 1905, c 3, s 17.

dren. In these cases, the parents' claim to oversee the spiritual welfare of their children, and to transmit their faith to their children, is often pitted against their children's interest in developing as independent agents, capable of making their own judgments, including spiritual judgments, or the interest of the larger community in ensuring the development of children as citizens who are tolerant and able to contribute to society. In this way the debate about religious freedom in the family context exposes most starkly the central tension in the courts' understanding of religion, as both a personal commitment and a cultural identity, and of religious freedom as both the right of the individual to make spiritual choices, and the right of religious believers or communities to be treated with equal respect.

Finally, Chapter 7 looks at the freedom of conscience component of section 2(a). Despite the courts' formal definition of the scope of freedom of conscience and religion, as encompassing both religious and non-religious beliefs, religious beliefs have been at the centre of the section 2(a) jurisprudence. In their section 2(a) decisions, the courts seem to regard religious beliefs and practices as special or as different from other, nonreligious, beliefs and practices. Section 2(a) protects conscientious beliefs that seem to stand outside ordinary political debate—that are at odds with the most basic and widely held moral assumptions of the general community. This may be what is meant when these beliefs are described as "deeply held"—not just that they are fundamental to the individual, but that they are part of a distinctive worldview or moral framework. A conscientiously held belief may fall within the scope of section 2(a) when it resembles a paradigmatic religious belief or practice (a faith-based commitment) that is fundamental in significance, specific in content, peremptory in force, and perceived by non-believers as inaccessible or unconventional. A belief of this kind though, is less likely to be sustained outside a religious or cultural group. It is not an accident then that many nonreligious "conscientious" practices are historically linked to religious practices. Despite their formal claims, the courts have not done much to accommodate religious practices and, unsurprisingly, even less to accommodate nonreligious practices. A nonreligious belief or practice that is fundamental to the individual, does not directly address civic or public concerns, and rests on moral premises that are not widely shared in the community may be insulated from political action. It might then be said that when "religion" looks like civic morality, it will be subject to the give-and-take of ordinary politics; and when "conscience" (secular morality) looks like religion, it will fall within the protection of section 2(a).

ACKNOWLEDGMENTS

Early work on this book was supported by grants from the Social Sciences and Humanities Research Council of Canada and the Law Foundation of Ontario. The book draws on my earlier publications, including the following:

- "Liberty, Neutrality and Inclusion: Freedom of Religion under the *Canadian Charter of Rights*" (2003) 41 Brandeis LJ 563
- "From Liberty to Equal Respect: Religious Freedom under the *Canadian Charter of Rights and Freedoms*" in M Habibi et al, eds, *Theoretical Foundations of Human Rights* (Qom, Iran: Mofid University Publications, 2007)
- "Religious Commitment and Identity: *Syndicat Northcrest v. Amselem*" (2005) 29 Sup Ct L Rev (2d) 201
- "Government Support for Religious Practice" and "Introduction" in R Moon, ed, *Law and Religious Pluralism in Canada* (Vancouver: UBC Press, 2008)
- "Divorce and the Marriage of Law and Religion: Comment on *Bruker v. Marcovitz*" (2008) 42 Sup Ct L Rev (2d) 37
- "Accommodation without Compromise: Comment on *Alberta v. Hutterian Brethren of Wilson Colony*" (2010) 51 Sup Ct L Rev (2d) 95
- "The Supreme Court of Canada's Attempt to Reconcile Freedom of Religion and Sexual Orientation Equality in the Public Schools" in D Rayside & C Wilcox, eds, *Faith, Politics and Sexual Diversity* (Vancouver: UBC Press, 2011)

- "Christianity, Multiculturalism, and National Identity: A Canadian Comment on *Lautsi and Others v. Italy*" in Jeroen Temperman, ed, *The Lautsi Papers: Multidisciplinary Reflections on Religious Symbols in the Public School Classroom* (Leiden: Martinus Nijhoff, 2012)
- "Freedom of Religion under the *Charter of Rights*: The Limits of State Neutrality" (2012) 45 UBC L Rev 497
- "The Constitutional Protection of Religious Practices in Canada" in D Kirkham, ed, *State Responses to Minority Religions* (Farnham, Surrey, UK: Ashgate, 2013)
- "Freedom of Conscience and Religion" in S Beaulac & E Mendes, eds, *Canadian Charter of Rights and Freedoms* (5th ed) (Markham, ON: LexisNexis, 2013)

The chapter dealing with freedom of conscience was presented at the "Force of Laws Workshop," Centre for the Study of Religion, University of Toronto, in May 2011.

I want to give thanks to Alvin Esau, Shauna Van Praagh, Jean-François Gaudreault-DesBiens, Benjamin Berger, Janet Epp Buckingham, and Ronald Krotoszynski for their valuable comments on particular sections of the book, and to Max Rubin and Jessica Spina for last-minute research. Thanks are also owed to Audrey Macklin, who is the source of the book's better arguments. My children provided no help in the writing of this book, but still I want to thank them for being the wonderful people they are.

To Sibyl

CHAPTER 1

INTRODUCTION

A. RELIGIOUS TOLERANCE IN CANADA

Canada's early history as colony and nation was marked by periods of harsh religious suppression and moments of pragmatic religious tolerance.[1] The early efforts of European colonizers, first the French and later the British, to convert Aboriginal peoples to a version of Christianity sometimes involved the active suppression of spiritual practices. Cultural suppression became standard practice with the growth of European settlement and the extension of political control by colonial and Canadian authorities over lands occupied by Aboriginal peoples. Notably, in the late 1800s, spiritual practices, such as spirit dancing in the Prairies and the potlatch on the West Coast, were banned by the federal government. But perhaps the most significant program of cultural suppression was the residential school system, which involved the forcible removal of Aboriginal children from their families and communities and their placement in state-sanctioned residential Christian schools, where they were prevented from speaking their language and engaging in the practices of their culture. The residential school program, which began in the late 1800s and continued until the middle

---

1   For a helpful survey of some of this history, see Janet Epp Buckingham, *Fighting Over God: A Legal and Political History of Religious Freedom in Canada* (Montreal, QC; Kingston, ON: McGill-Queen's University Press, 2014).

of the 1900s, has been described by a former federal justice minister as "the single most harmful, disgraceful and racist act in our history."[2]

Yet the country's early history was also marked by significant acts of religious tolerance. With the conquest of Quebec by the British in the middle of the eighteenth century, a Protestant monarch came to rule over the colony's French Catholic population.[3] The practice, common at the time in which the conquering power imposed its faith on its new subjects, gave way to the practical necessities of government in colonial Canada. Under the *Treaty of Paris, 1763*,[4] which formally ended the Seven Years' War between Britain and France, the British government agreed that the French Catholic inhabitants of Canada would retain the right to practise their religion. Specifically, the treaty stated that "His Britannick Majesty, on his side, agrees to grant the liberty of the Catholick religion to the inhabitants of Canada: he will, in consequence, give the most precise and most effectual orders, that his new Roman Catholic subjects may profess the worship of their religion according to the rites of the Romish church, as far as the laws of Great Britain permit."[5] As MH Ogilvie notes, this concession was not free of ambiguity since at the time Roman Catholics in England were subject to a number of significant criminal restrictions.[6] However, the *Quebec Act, 1774* of the British Parliament formally extended to the colony's inhabitants the right to maintain the French language, the civil law system, and the Roman Catholic faith.[7] The British government's motives were entirely pragmatic: to en-

---

2   Irwin Cotler, justice minister in November 2005, when the federal government offered compensation to the victims of the residential school system, quoted in CBC News, "School abuse victims getting $1.9B" (23 November 2005), online: www.cbc.ca/news/canada/story/2005/11/23/residential-package051123.html.

3   The earliest settlers in New France included both Roman Catholics and Huguenots (French Protestants), although Huguenot immigration was subsequently halted, and the Huguenot settlers already residing in the colony came under significant restriction.

4   *Treaty of Paris, 1763*, France, Britain, and Spain, 10 February 1763.

5   *Ibid*, art IV. Acadia had been ceded to the British in 1713 by the *Treaty of Utrecht*, Britain and France, 11 April 1713. While this treaty included language similar to that in the *Treaty of Paris, 1763*, a very different strategy was employed following the British acquisition of Acadia. To ensure political stability, the British government in 1755 expelled a significant portion of the French-speaking population. The expelled Acadians either returned to France or resettled in Louisiana or the American colonies.

6   MH Ogilvie, *Religious Institutions and the Law in Canada*, 3d ed (Toronto: Irwin Law, 2010) at 34.

7   The *Quebec Act, 1774* (UK), 14 Geo III, c 83 [*Quebec Act*] provides the following:

V. And, for the more perfect Security and Ease of the Minds of the Inhabitants of the said Province, it is hereby declared, That his Majesty's Subjects, profess-

sure the stability of the Quebec colony and the loyalty of its inhabitants at a time when the American colonies were becoming disenchanted with British rule.

The growth of English-speaking, Protestant settlement in Lower and Upper Canada (later Canada East and Canada West, and then Quebec and Ontario) in the late 1700s and early 1800s (with Protestants soon forming the majority in Upper Canada) led to increasing conflict between Catholics and Protestants. During this period, the assumption of many English-speaking settlers, which was given expression in the *Durham Report* of 1839, was that continued immigration from Britain and the political unification of Canada East and West would result eventually in the assimilation of the "French race."[8] Nevertheless, the colonial government maintained its formal commitment to religious freedom. In 1851 the legislature for Canada East and West recognized the "legal equality among all religious denominations . . . [as a] principle of Colonial legislation" and "the free exercise and enjoyment of Religious Profession and Worship, without discrimination or preference . . . allowed to all Her Majesty's subjects . . . ."[9] In this period the most significant religious accommodation was the extension of support to minority Roman Catholic schools in Canada West, where the dominant school system was non-denominational Protestant, and to Protestant schools in Canada East, alongside the larger Roman Catholic system.[10]

The *Quebec Act* permitted the Roman Catholic church in Lower Canada (Canada East) to continue collecting tithes from parishioners, as provided for in the *Civil Code*.[11] During the early period of British rule

---

ing the Religion of the Church of Rome of and in the said Province of Quebec, may have, hold, and enjoy, the free Exercise of the Religion of the Church of Rome, subject to the King's Supremacy, declared and established by an Act, made in the first Year of the Reign of Queen Elizabeth, over all the Dominions and Countries which then did, or thereafter should belong, to the Imperial Crown of this Realm; and that the Clergy of the said Church may hold, receive, and enjoy, their accustomed Dues and Rights, with respect to such Persons only as shall profess the said Religion.

8   John George Lambton, Earl of Durham, *Report on the Affairs of British North America*, (London: Robert Stanton, 1839) [*Durham Report*], which followed the rebellions in Lower and Upper Canada, also recommended the establishment of a system of responsible government and the creation of a single legislature for Canada East and West (Lower and Upper Canada).

9   *An Act to Repeal so much of the Imperial Act 31, Geo III, c 31, as relates to Rectories, and the presentation of Incumbents to the same*, S Prov C 1851 (3 & 4 Vict), c 55.

10   *An Act to repeal certain Acts therein mentioned, and to make further provision for the establishment and maintenance of Common Schools throughout the Province*, S Prov C (4 & 5 Vict), c 18.

11   Above note 7 at V.

in Upper Canada, the Anglican church was also granted certain privileges reflecting its status as the established church in England. Most
significantly, the *Constitutional Act, 1791* required that a certain proportion of lands, designated as clergy reserves, be set aside for "the Maintenance and Support of a Protestant Clergy," which in practice meant
the Anglican clergy.[12] While the political elite in Upper Canada in the
early 1800s was composed principally of Anglicans, the largest part of
the population, particularly in rural areas, was composed of Methodists,
Baptists, Congregationalists, and Presbyterians, and pressure from these
groups led eventually to the ending of the clergy-reserve system in the
mid-1800s and with it any semblance of religious establishment. While
the Anglican church had been formally established by the colonial legislatures in Nova Scotia (1758), New Brunswick (1784), and Prince Edward Island (1802), the privileged status of the church in each of these
colonies came to an end in the mid-1800s.[13] Nevertheless, in each of the
colonies the ties between church(es) and state remained significant, particularly in the delivery of social services. What has been described as
a shadow establishment of the Roman Catholic Church in Quebec and
of non-denominational Protestantism in the other provinces continued
well into the twentieth century, manifested in the religious teaching and
ethos of the public or common schools as well as in public holidays and
public prayers.[14]

---

12 *Constitutional Act, 1791* (UK), 31 Geo III, c 31, s XXXV. The law also provided
    in section XXXV for the setting aside of special rectory land "according to the
    Establishment of the Church of England." See Alan Wilson, *The Clergy Reserves of
    Upper Canada*, Booklet #23 (Ottawa: Canadian Historical Association, 1969). The
    other established church in Great Britain, the Church of Scotland (the Presbyter-
    ian church), laid claim to a percentage of the reserves.

13 But as Ogilvie notes, above note 6 at 37–38:

> Since there would appear to be no legislation in these provinces disestablish-
> ing the Church of England, in legal theory at least, it is still the established
> church! However, legislation in each province dating from the late eighteenth
> century in relation to a variety of matters, from rights to conduct marriage,
> to vote, to hold property, and to hold military and civil office, among others,
> have resulted in complete equality before the law for all religious groups.

14 David Martin, "Canada in Comparative Perspective" in David Lyon & Marguerite
    Van Die, eds, *Rethinking Church, State, and Modernity: Canada between Europe and
    America* (Toronto: University of Toronto Press, 2000) 23 at 23. See also George
    Egerton, "Trudeau, God, and the Canadian Constitution: Religion, Human Rights,
    and Government Authority in the Making of the 1982 Constitution" in Lyon &
    Van Die, *ibid*, 90 at 92:

> Although the Canadian church-state relationship was distinct from the
> separationist model of America, the establishmentarianism of England, and
> the secularism of republican France, what the retreat from state confession-

Confederation in 1867 was an act of union, bringing together several of the British North American colonies (Canada East and West, New Brunswick, and Nova Scotia) but also an act of separation. Canada East and West, governed since 1842 by a single legislature, was split into two provinces, Quebec and Ontario, each with its own legislature. The *BNA Act, 1867* (*Constitution Act, 1867*) gave provincial governments the power to regulate cultural matters, family relationships, and civil obligations, and the federal government the power to establish and maintain a general economic infrastructure and to ensure public order and security.[15] In this way the federal system ensured the continuation and protection of a level of religious and cultural diversity in the country, at least at a regional level. The *BNA Act*, though, also provided some protection for religious diversity within the provinces, by establishing certain rights for minority religious schools. While section 93 of the *BNA Act* gave the provinces jurisdiction in relation to education, it also protected the rights of dissentient schools in Ontario (principally, Roman Catholic schools) and Protestant and Roman Catholic schools in Quebec that existed at the time of Confederation. The Supreme Court of Canada later described the constitutional protection of minority religious schools as a "bargain" that made Confederation possible.[16] The recognition of Roman Catholic school rights was also one of the terms of entry into the union of Manitoba in 1870 and Saskatchewan and Alberta in 1905.[17] However, anti-Catholic sentiment, which was prevalent in "Orange Ontario," not only contributed to significant local conflict in Ontario and the Western provinces but also surfaced at the national level in the Manitoba Schools Crisis in the 1890s, which led to the denial of Roman Catholic education rights in that province.[18]

The political accommodation between Roman Catholic and Protestant communities, while always imperfect and often precarious, shaped

---

alism amounted to was a quasi-establishment of the major denominations, or 'national churches', which, in the Canadian experience, included Roman Catholicism.

15 *Constitution Act, 1867* (UK), 30 & 31 Vict, c 3, ss 91 & 92, reprinted in RSC 1985, App II, No 5 [*BNA Act*].

16 *Reference re Bill 30, An Act to amend the Education Act (Ontario)*, [1987] 1 SCR 1148 at para 27, Wilson J [*Reference re Bill 30*]. The constitutional rights of dissentient schools are discussed more fully in Chapter 5.

17 Each of the provinces was formally subject to such a provision; however, the courts found that the provision had no application in many of the provinces because they did not have a legally established separate school system at the time they entered Confederation. For a more detailed account, see Chapter 5.

18 A political compromise brokered at the federal level permitted Roman Catholic instruction after regular school hours. See Ogilvie, above note 6 at 49.

the new country's response to the growth of religious plurality in the late nineteenth and early twentieth centuries.[19] This response involved the general protection of individual liberty in religious practice but also the pragmatic accommodation of certain minority group practices, within the context of a general public privileging of Christian or non-denominational Protestant practices. In the late 1800s and early 1900s, the Government of Canada, seeking to attract settlers to the western part of the country, agreed to exempt certain religious groups from public obligations that were inconsistent with the group's practices. For example, Anabaptist groups, such as the Mennonites and the Hutterites, were assured at the time of their arrival in Canada that they would be exempted from compulsory military service and standard schooling requirements.[20] Yet, despite the country's general commitment to religious liberty, the first half of the twentieth century was marred by a number of significant and traumatic acts of religious oppression by the state, including the banning of the Jehovah's Witness community during World War II[21] and the removal of children in the Doukhobor community from parents who refused to send them to public schools.[22] A number of these conflicts became the subject of litigation, and in the resulting judicial decisions a

---

19   See Mark Noll, "Constitutional Divides: North American Civil War and Religion in at Least Three Stories" in Marguerite Van Die, ed, *Religion and Public Life in Canada: Historical and Comparative Perspectives* (Toronto: University of Toronto Press, 2001) 153 at 157: "Canada . . . developed under the necessity of accommodating in one nation Quebec, a traditional Old World society with church and state linked together organically, and English-language societies in Upper Canada and the Atlantic provinces shaped by both British Protestant paternalism and the American separation of church and state."

20   In 1873 the federal government assured the Mennonites settling in Manitoba that they could operate their own schools. The government stated that "[t]he fullest privilege of exercising their religious principles is by law afforded the Mennonites without any kind of molestation or restriction whatever" (quoted in Frank H Epp, *Mennonites in Canada, 1786–1920: the History of a Separate People* (Toronto: Macmillan, 1974) at 338). The commitment regarding schools, though, was not binding on the provinces. Earlier in Upper Canada, the Quakers and Mennonites, who arrived as United Empire Loyalists, were exempted from military service under the *Militia Act, 1793* (UK), 33 Geo III, c 1. See William Janzen, *Limits on Liberty: The Experience of Mennonite, Hutterite, and Doukhobor Communities in Canada* (Toronto: University of Toronto Press, 1990) at 163.

21   For an account, see William Kaplan, *State and Salvation: The Jehovah's Witnesses and Their Fight for Civil Rights* (Toronto: University of Toronto Press, 1989) ch 4. The ban was lifted in 1943.

22   For an account of the seizure of Doukhobor children under child protection laws in British Columbia, see John McLaren, "The State, Child Snatching, and the Law: The Seizure and Indoctrination of Sons of Freedom Children in British Columbia, 1950–60" in Dorothy E Chunn, John McLaren, & Robert Menzies, eds,

public and principled conception of religious freedom began to emerge. Perhaps the most significant instance of religious oppression, at least in terms of its role in shaping the contemporary Canadian conception of religious freedom, was the suppression by the province of Quebec of the proselytizing activities of the Jehovah's Witness community in the 1950s.[23] Maurice Duplessis, the premier and also the attorney general of Quebec, conducted what he described as a "war without mercy" on the province's Jehovah's Witness community.[24]

B. A PRINCIPLED ACCOUNT OF RELIGIOUS FREEDOM

While much of Canada's early commitment to religious freedom was simply a pragmatic compromise to ensure social peace and political stability, the judgments of the Supreme Court of Canada in the postwar period, and in particular in the 1950s, sought to articulate a principled account of religious freedom. In *Saumur v City of Quebec*, the Supreme Court of Canada struck down a bylaw that forbade the distribution of literature in the streets of Quebec City without the prior consent of the chief of police—a bylaw that was understood by all as intended to limit the proselytizing activities of the Jehovah's Witness community.[25] After setting out some of the history of religious tolerance in Canada, Rand J in the *Saumur* decision observed that

> [f]rom 1760, therefore, to the present moment religious freedom has, in our legal system, been recognized as a principle of fundamental character; and although we have nothing in the nature of an established church, that the untrammelled affirmations of religious belief and its propagation, personal or institutional, remain as of the greatest constitutional significance throughout the Dominion is unquestionable.[26]

Justice Rand went on to hold that the provinces lacked the authority, under the constitutional division of powers, to restrict religious freedom and other fundamental rights—that "legislation 'in relation' to religion and its profession is not a local or private matter . . . ; the dimensions

---

Regulating Lives: Historical Essays on the State, Society, the Individual, and the Law (Vancouver: UBC Press, 2002) 259.

23   For an examination of the attempt to suppress Jehovah's Witness proselytization in Quebec during the 1950s, see Kaplan, above note 21, ch 8.

24   Quoted in Kaplan, *ibid* at 230.

25   [1953] 2 SCR 299 [*Saumur*].

26   *Ibid* at 327.

of this interest are nationwide; . . . it appertains to a boundless field of ideas, beliefs and faiths with the deepest roots and loyalties; a religious incident reverberates from one end of this country to the other . . . . "[27] He described religious freedom as one of the "original freedoms which are at once the necessary attributes and modes of self-expression of human beings and the primary conditions of their community life within a legal order."[28] In *Chaput v Romain*, the Quebec provincial police "broke up," without a warrant, an orderly religious meeting of Jehovah's Witnesses in a private home, seizing bibles and other religious literature.[29] The Supreme Court of Canada found that the police action breached the *Criminal Code* prohibition against obstructing a minister who is conducting a religious meeting. In reaching this conclusion, Taschereau J declared that in Canada there is no state religion and that all denominations enjoy the same freedom of speech and thought.[30]

The concern for the protection of rights that emerged in Europe and elsewhere following the atrocities of World War II found expression in international human rights treaties such as the *Universal Declaration of Human Rights*[31] and the *International Covenant on Civil and Political Rights*,[32] both of which gave protection to freedom of conscience and religion. In Canada, as in other countries, this concern led to the enactment of human rights code restrictions on discrimination, including discrimination based on religion or creed, beginning in the late 1940s,[33]

---

27   *Ibid* at 329.

28   *Ibid*.

29   [1955] SCR 834.

30   *Ibid* at 840:

> Dans notre pays, il n'existe pas de religion d'Etat. Personne n'est tenu d'adhérer à une croyance quelconque. Toutes les religions sont sur un pied d'égalité, et tous les catholiques comme d'ailleurs tous les protestants, les juifs, ou les autres adhérents des diverses dénominations religieuses, ont la plus entière liberté de penser comme ils le désirent. La conscience de chacun est une affaire personnelle, et l'affaire de nul autre. Il serait désolant de penser qu'une majorité puisse imposer ses vues religieuses à une minorité. Ce serait une erreur fâcheuse de croire qu'on sert son pays ou sa religion, en refusant dans une province, à une minorité, les mêmes droits que l'on revendique soi-même avec raison, dans une autre province.

31   GA Res 217(III), UNGAOR, 3d Sess, Supp No 13, UN Doc A/810, (1948) [*UDHR*], online: www.ohchr.org/EN/UDHR/Documents/UDHR_Translations/eng.pdf.

32   GA Res 2200A(XXI), 21 UNGAOR Supp (No 16) at 52, UN Doc A/6316 (1966) (entered into force 23 March 1976) [*ICCPR*], online: www.ohchr.org/en/professionalinterest/pages/ccpr.aspx.

33   See *The Saskatchewan Bill of Rights Act, 1947*, SS 1947, c 35.

to the passage of the *Canadian Bill of Rights* in 1960,[34] and eventually to the constitutional entrenchment of the *Canadian Charter of Rights and Freedoms* in 1982.[35] Section 2(a) of the *Charter*, which protects the fundamental right of "freedom of conscience and religion," is framed in terms similar to article 18 of the *UDHR*[36] (as well as other provisions derived from article 18 such as article 18 of the *ICCPR*[37] and article 9 of the *European Convention on Human Rights*[38]). Because section 2(a) uses language similar to that used in these other rights charters, was enacted

---

34   SC 1960, c 44, s 1, reprinted in RSC 1985, App III: "It is hereby recognized and declared that in Canada there have existed and shall continue to exist without discrimination by reason of race, national origin, colour, religion or sex, the following human rights and fundamental freedoms, namely, . . . (c) freedom of religion . . . ."

35   Part 1 of the *Constitution Act, 1982*, being Schedule B to the *Canada Act 1982* (UK), 1982, c 11 [*Charter*].

36   Above note 31: "Everyone has the right to freedom of thought, conscience and religion; this right includes freedom to change his religion or belief, and freedom, either alone or in community with others and in public or private, to manifest his religion or belief in teaching, practice, worship and observance."

37   Above note 32:

   1.   Everyone shall have the right to freedom of thought, conscience and religion. This right shall include freedom to have or to adopt a religion or belief of his choice, and freedom, either individually or in community with others and in public or private, to manifest his religion or belief in worship, observance, practice and teaching.

   2.   No one shall be subject to coercion which would impair his freedom to have or to adopt a religion or belief of his choice.

   3.   Freedom to manifest one's religion or beliefs may be subject only to such limitations as are prescribed by law and are necessary to protect public safety, order, health, or morals or the fundamental rights and freedoms of others.

   4.   The States Parties to the present Covenant undertake to have respect for the liberty of parents and, when applicable, legal guardians to ensure the religious and moral education of their children in conformity with their own convictions.

38   *Convention for the Protection of Human Rights and Fundamental Freedoms*, Rome, 4 November 1950 [*ECHR*], online: www.echr.coe.int/Documents/Convention_ENG. pdf:

   1.   Everyone has the right to freedom of thought, conscience and religion; this right includes freedom to change his religion or belief and freedom, either alone or in community with others and in public or private, to manifest his religion or belief, in worship, teaching, practice and observance.

   2.   Freedom to manifest one's religion or beliefs shall be subject only to such limitations as are prescribed by law and are necessary in a democratic society in the interests of public safety, for the protection of public order, health or morals, or for the protection of the rights and freedoms of others.

in the same historical context, and was inspired by the same concerns and events, it is not surprising that the Canadian courts' interpretation of section 2(a) is in many respects similar to the interpretation given to these other provisions. At the same time, though, the Canadian courts' understanding of the scope and limits of the section 2(a) right has been shaped by the particular history and circumstances of Canada—a country in which there has been no formal religious establishment similar to that in the United Kingdom and other European countries nor a historical resistance to state support for religion, as in the United States.

While religious tolerance in Canada may initially have been based on pragmatic considerations and conceived as a political strategy to ensure social peace or stability,[39] the protection of freedom of conscience and religion in the *Charter* is now generally regarded as a principled right—as an aspect of the individual's basic liberty and, more particularly, as the right to hold and live in accordance with fundamental spiritual or moral commitments. This principled reading of the right follows from its inclusion in the *Charter*, a constitutionally entrenched bill of rights that is interpreted and applied by the courts. The role of the courts is not to make strategic judgments about the most effective way to ensure social peace but instead to define and defend the basic rights of individuals or minority groups.[40] Yet the story of religious freedom in Canada may not be simply that of a linear progression from the pragmatic tolerance of religious minorities to the principled protection of the individual's religious freedom. The courts have come to understand religious freedom not simply as an individual liberty but also as a form of equality right that requires the equal treatment by the state of different religious belief systems or communities. This understanding of the right appears to be based on practical as well as principled concerns and to require the courts to make pragmatic and context-based trade-offs between spiritual claims and civic interests. And so the same concerns

---

39   This was itself a significant realization—that social stability might be more effectively achieved through religious tolerance rather than the enforcement of religious uniformity. But, as the recently proposed *Charter of Values* (Bill 60, *Charter affirming the values of State secularism and religious neutrality and of equality between women and men, and providing a framework for accommodation requests*, 1st Sess, 40th Leg, Quebec, 2013) in Quebec illustrates, this claim continues to be challenged as different political communities struggle with issues of identity and social cohesion. For a discussion of the Quebec *Charter of Values*, see Chapter 3.

40   The role of the courts as a "forum of principle" or protector of rights fits with its nonpolitical character. However, as I have noted elsewhere, few rights can be interpreted in a way that does not entangle the courts in complex socio-political issues. See Richard Moon, *The Constitutional Protection of Freedom of Expression*, (Toronto: University of Toronto Press, 2000).

about social peace that lay behind the earlier extension of religious tolerance in Canada continue to be important in the contemporary justification and interpretation of religious freedom.[41]

C. A JUSTIFICATION FOR RELIGIOUS FREEDOM

The story of religious freedom in the West begins with the religious wars that disrupted Europe in the sixteenth and early seventeenth centuries.[42] It was in this context that writers such as John Locke sought to develop a principled argument for religious tolerance.[43] They argued not just that religious tolerance (rather than state-enforced religious conformity) was the better route to social peace but that it was morally required. At the centre of their principled defence of religious tolerance was the claim that spiritual matters lay within the sphere of individual conscience — the individual's divinely endowed capacity to recognize spiritual truth.

John Locke's *Letter Concerning Toleration* is regarded as the seminal defence of religious tolerance and freedom in the West.[44] Indeed, as we shall soon see, his central arguments are referred to, and partly relied

---

41   The pragmatic character of the origins of religious tolerance in Canada survives in accommodations that were established at an earlier time, most obviously the rights of Roman Catholic schools in Ontario — rights that were based on historical compromise and have not been extended to other religious schools.

42   See Perez Zagorin, *How the Idea of Religious Toleration Came to the West* (Princeton, NJ: Princeton University Press, 2003) at xii:

The rationale of religious toleration and the theological, moral, and philosophical justification of religious freedom had their real beginning in the sixteenth century; they were forged in the bitter denominational conflicts, the continued struggle against persecution, and the fierce intellectual controversies arising out of the religious divisions created in Europe by the Protestant Reformation.

43   See Zagorin, *ibid*, for an examination of the various advocates of religious tolerance in this period.

44   John Locke, "Letter Concerning Toleration" in John Locke, *Treatise of Civil Government and a Letter Concerning Toleration* (1689; repr, New York: Irvington Publishers, 1979). This, of course, is not the only starting point for the Western story of religious freedom — just the standard one. As well, there are other stories of religious freedom or tolerance, including stories from the Islamic world and from the Indian subcontinent where Hinduism and Islam met. For a discussion of the former and its relevance today, see Anver M Emon, *Religious Pluralism and Islamic Law: Dhimmis and Others in the Empire of Law* (Oxford: Oxford University Press, 2012).

on, by the Supreme Court of Canada in *R v Big M Drug Mart*, the Court's first religious freedom decision under the *Charter*, a decision in which the Court sought to articulate the theoretical basis for the freedom.[45] Locke argues that it is essential "to distinguish exactly the business of civil government from that of religion and to settle the just bounds that lie between the one and the other."[46] He insists that the state should concern itself only with "civil interests" such as life, liberty, health, and property. The authority of the state, argues Locke, does not extend to spiritual matters — "the salvation of the soul" — which lies within the exclusive domain of the individual. This is so for several related reasons. The government, says Locke, ought not to concern itself with the individual's spiritual welfare, because it has not been given authority in this matter.[47] The individual is responsible for her own spiritual welfare and cannot delegate this responsibility to anyone else because religious belief depends on "inner persuasion":

> [N]o man can so far abandon the care of his own salvation as blindly to leave to the choice of any other, whether prince or subject, to prescribe to him what faith or worship he shall embrace. For no man can, if he would, conform his faith to the dictates of another. All the life and power of true religion consist in the inward and full persuasion of the mind; and faith is not faith without believing. Whatever profession we make, to whatever outward worship we conform, if we are not fully satisfied in our own mind that the one is true and the other well pleasing unto God, such profession and such practice, far from being any furtherance, are indeed great obstacles to our salvation. For in this manner, instead of expiating other sins by the exercise of religion, I say, in offering thus unto God Almighty such a worship as we esteem to be displeasing unto Him, we add unto the number of our other sins those also of hypocrisy and contempt of His Divine Majesty.[48]

Locke observes that the power of government is exercised through coercion. But coercive power, notes Locke, is ineffective in spiritual matters. A government can require its citizens to conform to certain standards in their outward behaviour, but it cannot compel them to embrace spiritual truth — to sincerely believe. According to Locke, "It is only light and evidence that can work a change in men's opinions":[49]

---

45   [1985] 1 SCR 295 [*Big M Drug Mart*].

46   Above note 44 at 171.

47   *Ibid* at 172: "The commonwealth seems to me to be a society of men constituted only for the procuring, preserving, and advancing their own civil interests."

48   *Ibid* at 173.

49   *Ibid* at 174.

. . . For laws are of no force at all without penalties, and penalties in this case are absolutely impertinent, because they are not proper to convince the mind. Neither the profession of any articles of faith, nor the conformity to any outward form of worship . . . can be available to the salvation of souls, unless the truth of the one and the acceptableness of the other unto God be thoroughly believed by those that so profess and practise. But penalties are no way capable to produce such belief.[50]

Indeed, Locke notes that it may be an offence to God when individuals worship him in the correct form without "inward sincerity."

Locke supplements this argument about the nature of religious commitment with other practical considerations. He notes that even if the government could change "mens' minds" through coercion, there would be no reason to think that the faith it imposed was the true one. While "princes" may have particular skill or knowledge in civil matters, their spiritual judgment is not superior to that of other persons. After all, there are many different "princes" (or governments) in Europe, and each seems to hold a different view about the true faith. They cannot all be right. Moreover, says Locke, while governments may often be able to correct their mistakes in civil matters, they have not the power to correct their spiritual mistakes. If the government forces the wrong religion onto its citizens, the otherworldly consequences of its error will be borne exclusively by its citizens, and the government will be able to do nothing to mitigate their spiritual loss or injury.

Locke's defence of religious tolerance raised a variety of issues, at least three of which persist in the contemporary debate about the justification and scope of religious freedom. The first concerns his conception of religious commitment. Locke's claim that state coercion will be at best ineffective and at worst blasphemous follows from his belief that religious commitment must be based on individual judgment. He thought that the individual would come to know religious truth through the reasoned assessment of evidence rather than blind obedience to author-

---

50   *Ibid.* See also *ibid* at 173:

> In the second place, the care of souls cannot belong to the civil magistrate, because his power consists only in outward force; but true and saving religion consists in the inward persuasion of the mind, without which nothing can be acceptable to God. And such is the nature of the understanding, that it cannot be compelled to the belief of anything by outward force. Confiscation of estate, imprisonment, torments, nothing of that nature can have any such efficacy as to make men change the inward judgement that they have framed of things.

And see also *ibid* at 192: "It is in vain for an unbeliever to take up the outward show of another man's profession. Faith only and inward sincerity are the things that procure acceptance with God."

ity and indeed that an individual's religious commitment would only be acceptable to God if it was the outcome of "inner persuasion."[51] Yet, religious commitment is not always viewed in this way. It is as often regarded as faith based or nonrational or as a matter of cultural identity rather than individual judgment.[52] If religion is understood in cultural terms or if, as I will later argue, it is seen through two lenses as both individual judgment and cultural identity, the argument for religious freedom must take a different form and involve not just respect for individual autonomy or conscience but also respect for cultural identity or religious diversity.

The second issue concerns Locke's exclusive focus on state coercion. Even if we agree with him that the state cannot compel its citizens to embrace the true faith, the state may advance the truth in other ways. The state, at least in the contemporary context, does not act exclusively through coercion. It supports a variety of values and goals using non-coercive means, such as subsidy and advocacy. Locke's argument against religious coercion does not justify the exclusion of the state from spiritual matters as long as it employs noncoercive measures.[53] A central

---

51 Many commentators have disputed this claim and argued that state coercion might well be effective in bringing the individual to "the truth" over time, or across generations. Locke assumes that the state should be prohibited not only from compelling religious practice but also from restricting practices it regards as erroneous (*ibid* at 197–98):

> As the magistrate has no power to impose by his laws the use of any rites and ceremonies in any Church, so neither has he any power to forbid the use of such rites and ceremonies as are already received, approved, and practised by any Church; because, if he did so, he would destroy the Church itself: the end of whose institution is only to worship God with freedom after its own manner.

But this may not follow from his argument about the ineffectiveness of compulsion. It might reasonably be claimed that the spiritual welfare of citizens is advanced when the state inhibits the practice and promotion of a "false" religion. Locke's rejection of state restriction of religious practice appears to be based either on a skepticism about the state's ability to determine spiritual truth or on a belief that spiritual matters are the exclusive concern of the individual—a matter of individual liberty.

52 See, for example, Timothy Macklem, "Faith as a Secular Value" (2000) 45 McGill LJ 1.

53 Locke seems to be aware that his argument does not preclude the state from supporting particular religious practices (above note 44 at 173):

> It may indeed be alleged that the magistrate may make use of arguments, and thereby draw the heterodox into the way of truth, and procure their salvation. I grant it; but this is common to him with other men. In teaching, instructing, and redressing the erroneous by reason, he may certainly do what becomes

issue in contemporary debates about the scope of religious freedom is whether the state is simply precluded from compelling or restricting religious practice or whether it is also required to remain neutral in spiritual matters.

The third issue is Locke's narrow, otherworldly understanding of religion as concerned with the salvation of the individual's soul. In his view spiritual salvation is distinct from the civil concerns addressed by the state and falls exclusively within the individual's domain. Yet the realization of this goal—the salvation of the soul—may depend on the individual's actions in the material world. More generally, religions often have something to say about how we should treat others and the kind of society we should work to create. Indeed, even though Locke believed that civil and spiritual matters were distinguishable and that the state should concern itself only with the former, he did not think that religiously based moral arguments should or could be excluded from political decision making, as some today argue. Locke took for granted that public morality was grounded in religion and dependent on a belief in God. It is worth recalling that Locke thought atheists ought not to be tolerated because without a belief in God and the after-life, there was nothing to bind their consciences in civil society. As Perez Zagorin observes:

> [The early defenders of religious tolerance] certainly did not intend to banish religion from the polity or common life. Such a thought could hardly have occurred to them, nor could they ever have imagined as a proper setting for religious freedom a completely secular society in which the Christian religion had ceased to be a dominant public pres-ence and a pervasive force in morals and conduct and was largely rel-egated to the realm of personal and private belief.[54]

---

any good man to do. Magistracy does not oblige him to cut off either human-ity or Christianity . . . .

For a discussion of this claim, see Rex Adhar & Ian Leigh, "Is Establishment Consistent with Religious Freedom?" (2004) 49 McGill LJ 635. Locke's statement can be reconciled with his claim that the spiritual and civil spheres are distinct only if he is referring to the magistrate in her personal capacity rather than as a lawmaker or state authority—a distinction that may depend on Locke's assump-tion that the state acts exclusively by coercive means.

54   Above note 42 at 289–90.

D. RELIGIOUS FREEDOM UNDER THE *CHARTER*

Locke's defence of religious tolerance is apparent in the Canadian courts' account of religious freedom under the *Charter*. In two ways, though, his argument is adapted to contemporary circumstances. The first is that the freedom's justification is now framed in secular terms. Locke's argument rested on a particular conception of religious truth and was directed at the realization of that truth.[55] He viewed human conscience as a divinely endowed capacity to recognize religious truth. However, in the contemporary context it is assumed that freedom of conscience and religion cannot be based on values that are tied to a particular religious belief system or to religion generally. Freedom of conscience and religion is no longer protected as the most effective way to discover spiritual truth or as necessary to the individual's meaningful commitment to that truth. The "secularized" argument for religious freedom focuses on the value of individual autonomy or liberty and links the freedom to other fundamental rights such as freedom of expression and freedom of association. Freedom of conscience and religion protects the individual's autonomous choices or judgments because it is through the exercise of choice or judgment that the individual lives an authentic life, a life that is her own.[56] The second adjustment to Locke's argument concerns the interests or values that the freedom is thought to protect. In the Canadian courts' section 2(a) cases, there has been a partial shift from liberty to equality as the interest protected by the freedom and from state coercion to state support for a particular religion as the wrong addressed by the freedom. This change is tied to an understanding of religion as a cultural practice rather than simply a personal commitment.

In *Big M Drug Mart*, the first section 2(a) case decided by the Supreme Court of Canada, Dickson CJ said that section 2(a) protects the

---

55   In his defence of religious tolerance, Locke frequently cites the example of Jesus, who sought to persuade rather than compel others.

56   On this account, an individual's religious beliefs and practices should be protected, not because they are true nor even because he must be given the freedom to judge, and possibly err, so that a meaningful or sincere commitment to the truth may be possible, but simply because he has chosen them or is committed to them. The religious adherent may view this understanding of the protection (or the civic value) of religion as trivializing her beliefs. Religious beliefs and practices matter to the adherent, not because she has chosen them or has a preference for them, but because they are true. But, of course, any account of the value of religious belief that is external to the belief system — that rests on values that lie outside the belief system itself — is bound to be seen as trivializing.

individual's freedom "to hold and to manifest whatever beliefs and opinions his or her conscience dictates, provided inter alia only that such manifestations do not injure his or her neighbours . . . ."[57] The freedom precludes the state from compelling an individual to engage in a religious practice and from restricting her religious practice without a legitimate public reason. According to Dickson CJ, the protection of freedom of religion rests on "the centrality of individual conscience and the inappropriateness of governmental intervention to compel or to constrain its manifestation."[58] The Chief Justice traced this understanding of religious freedom back to Locke and other post-Reformation writers who based their opposition to state coercion in religious matters on the perception that "belief . . . was not amenable to compulsion" and that "[a]ttempts to compel belief or practice denied the reality of individual conscience and dishonoured the God that had planted it in His creatures."[59] Chief Justice Dickson, though, framed the protection of individual conscience in secular terms, tying it to respect for "human dignity" or to "our democratic political tradition."[60] When section 2(a) is understood in this way, as based on a commitment to individual autonomy, its protection will extend to both religious and nonreligious beliefs.[61]

---

57 Above note 45 at para 123. He continued, "Religious belief and practice are historically prototypical and, in many ways, paradigmatic of conscientiously-held beliefs and manifestations and are therefore protected by the Charter. Equally protected, and for the same reasons, are expressions and manifestations of religious non-belief and refusals to participate in religious practice" (ibid). He also noted, "The essence of the concept of freedom of religion is the right to entertain such religious beliefs as a person chooses, the right to declare religious beliefs openly and without fear of hindrance or reprisal, and the right to manifest religious belief by worship and practice or by teaching and dissemination" (ibid at para 94).

58 Ibid at para 121. He went on to say that "the government may not coerce individuals to affirm a specific religious belief or to manifest a specific religious practice for a sectarian purpose" (ibid at para 123).

59 Ibid at para 120.

60 Ibid at para 122: "It should also be noted, however, that an emphasis on individual conscience and individual judgment also lies at the heart of our democratic political tradition. The ability of each citizen to make free and informed decisions is the absolute prerequisite for the legitimacy, acceptability, and efficacy of our system of self-government."

61 For a similar view regarding art 18 of the ICCPR, above note 32, see UN Human Rights Committee, CCPR General Comment No 22, Article 18 (Freedom of Thought, Conscience or Religion, 30 July 1993 (adopted at the Forty-eighth session of the Human Rights Committee), which provides that "[a]rticle 18 protects theistic, non-theistic and atheistic beliefs, as well as the right not to profess any religion or belief. The terms 'belief' and 'religion' are to be broadly construed. Article 18 is not limited in its application to traditional religions or to religions and beliefs

In *Big M Drug Mart*, the Supreme Court of Canada described freedom of conscience and religion as the liberty to hold, and live in accordance with, spiritual and other fundamental beliefs without state interference.[62] But, as I will discuss below, there is implicit in *Big M Drug Mart*
another understanding of religious freedom that becomes more explicit
in subsequent decisions.[63] According to the Canadian courts, the freedom does not simply prohibit state coercion in matters of religion or
conscience (state compulsion or restriction of a religious practice); it
requires also that the state treat religious belief systems or communities
in an equal or even-handed manner. The state must not support or prefer the practices of one religious group over those of another (religion,
or at least religious contest, should be excluded from politics), and the
state must not restrict the practices of a religious group unless this is
necessary to protect a compelling public interest (religion should be insulated from politics).[64] This shift in the courts' understanding of the
freedom's justification has been accompanied by a narrowing of the freedom's scope or focus. Despite the apparent breadth of section 2(a) and

---

with institutional characteristics or practices analogous to those of traditional
religions." See, online: www.refworld.org/docid/453883fb22.html.

62   Above note 45 at paras 94–95.

63   *Ibid* at para 134, Dickson CJ:

> In my view, however, as I read the Charter, it mandates that the legislative
> preservation of a Sunday day of rest should be secular, the diversity of belief
> and non-belief, the diverse socio-cultural backgrounds of Canadians make it
> constitutionally incompetent for the federal Parliament to provide legislative
> preference for any one religion at the expense of those of another religious
> persuasion.

Earlier (*ibid* at para 97) he stated:

> In proclaiming the standards of the Christian faith, the [Lord's Day] Act cre-
> ates a climate hostile to, and gives the appearance of discrimination against,
> non-Christian Canadians. It takes religious values rooted in Christian morality
> and, using the force of the state, translates them into a positive law binding
> on believers and non-believers alike. The theological content of the legislation
> remains as a subtle and constant reminder to religious minorities within the
> country of their differences with, and alienation from, the dominant religious
> culture.

I have described this shift from liberty to equality in Richard Moon, "Liberty,
Neutrality and Inclusion: Freedom of Religion under the *Canadian Charter of
Rights*" (2003) 41 Brandeis Law Review 563.

64   The ban on state support is sometimes explained on the basis of a broad understanding of coercion—that favouritism isolates or pressures individuals to conform to the preferred religion. But, as I will argue below, it seems more credibly
tied to a conception of religion as a cultural identity, and the view that to disfavour one religion is to suggest that it is less worthy or valuable than others.

the courts' formal acknowledgement that freedom of conscience and religion protects both religious and nonreligious (fundamental) values and beliefs, the former have been at the centre of the Canadian freedom of religion and conscience cases. The protection of nonreligious beliefs and practices (the freedom of conscience component of section 2(a)) appears to be limited to practices that resemble in content and structure familiar religious practices.

E. STATE NEUTRALITY AND ITS LIMITS

The requirement of state neutrality toward religion was affirmed by Deschamps J, writing for the majority of the Supreme Court of Canada in *SL v Commission scolaire des Chênes*: "Religious neutrality is now seen by many Western states as a legitimate means of creating a free space in which citizens of various beliefs can exercise their individual rights . . . ."[65] The concurring judgment of LeBel J in *SL* expressed a similar view: "Moreover, in the modern Canadian political system, the state in principle takes a position of neutrality. And it is barred from enacting private legislation that favours one religion over another . . . ."[66] While the courts have sometimes come close to saying that the state should not favour secular (nonreligious) over religious belief systems, they have generally confined the application of the neutrality requirement to religious belief systems—so that the state is precluded from favouring one religious belief system over another and religious beliefs over nonreligious beliefs.[67]

---

65 2012 SCC 7 at para 10 [*SL*]. Justice Deschamps observed that the "Canadian courts have held that state sponsorship of one religious tradition amounts to discrimination against others" (*ibid* at para 17). The commitment to the equal treatment of different religions, or state neutrality in religious matters, was earlier described by LeBel J in *Congrégation des témoins de Jéhovah de St-Jérôme-Lafontaine v Lafontaine (Village)*, 2004 SCC 48 at para 65: "This fundamental freedom imposes on the state and public authorities, in relation to all religions and citizens, a duty of religious neutrality that assures individual or collective tolerance, thereby safeguarding the dignity of every individual and ensuring equality for all."

66 *SL, ibid* at para 54.

67 As will be discussed later, the scope of the neutrality requirement has been a point of contention. It appears from the cases that the state is not precluded from favouring "secular" or nonreligious views over religious beliefs, although in the judgments there are moments of ambivalence about this. See, for example, the s 15 judgments of McLachlin and L'Heureux-Dubé JJ in *Adler v Ontario*, [1996] 3 SCR 609 [*Adler*], which are discussed in Chapter 5.

The requirement of state neutrality (that the state should take no position on religious issues) may be understood as simply a pragmatic recognition that religious issues are difficult to resolve within the political process and may generate significant social and political conflict and so are best removed from political contest. As the Supreme Court of Canada has recognized, even if religious beliefs are not immutable, it may be necessary sometimes to treat them as such in the political realm.[68] While individuals must be permitted to adopt and adhere to particular religious beliefs or practices, to associate with others who share their beliefs, and to reject and even criticize the beliefs of others, the state should remain neutral in these matters and not participate in the contest between different religious belief systems. The state should remain neutral not because religion — or the search for spiritual truth — is without value or because there is no religious truth, but instead because it will contribute to social stability or will limit the marginalization of particular "identity" groups in the community.

At a deeper level, though, the state neutrality requirement may be rooted in a particular conception of religious commitment or engagement. While religious commitment is sometimes described by the courts as a personal choice or judgment made by the individual that, although deeply held, is in theory revisable, it is also, or sometimes instead, described as a central element of the individual's identity. Religious belief orients the individual in the world, shapes her perception of the social and natural orders, and provides a moral framework for her actions. It gives meaning or purpose to her life. It ties the individual to a community of believers and is often the central or defining association in her life. The individual believer participates in a shared system of practices and values that may in some cases be described as "a way of life."

Freedom of religion, on this account, may be viewed as a form of equality right — a right to equal treatment or equal respect by the state without discrimination based on religious belief or association. If religious belief is central to the individual's identity, then a judgment by the state that his beliefs or practices are less important or less true than others may be experienced as a denial of his equal worth and not simply as a rejection of his views and values.[69] Or if religious association is an

---

68   See *Corbiere v Canada (Minister of Indian and Northern Affairs)*, [1999] 2 SCR 203 at para 13.

69   State compulsion to engage in a religious practice as well as the restriction of such a practice may also be seen as deeply invasive once we recognize the strong connection between the individual and her religious beliefs. For a discussion of an equality-based conception of religious freedom, see Bruce Ryder, "The Canadian Conception of Equal Religious Citizenship" in Richard Moon, ed, *Law and*

important part of the individual's identity, then we may be concerned about the exclusion or marginalization of religious groups because of the impact on the adherent's social standing or the disruption of social peace that may follow. The inclusion of religion as a ground of discrimination under section 15 of the *Charter* lends support to this idea of religion as identity.[70]

However, the neutrality requirement may also, or instead, be based on a more negative view of religion. In an increasingly skeptical and agnostic world, we are more likely to view religious belief as nonrational, as the outcome of cultural socialization rather than reasoned judgment. It is sometimes said that religious beliefs lie outside the scope of reasoned judgment and are inaccessible to non-believers, and so should play no role in political decision making. If religious belief is held on the basis of faith or custom rather than judgment, then any reliance on, or support for, a particular belief by the state may be experienced by non-believers as the imposition of religion—of the cultural identity of others. While it is easy to join these two views of religion (religion as deeply rooted and religion as nonrational) under the general idea of religion as identity, they raise different concerns. On the first view, which sees religion as valuable because of its deep significance to the individual, religion and politics should be separated to protect religion. The state should not interfere with the individual's religious practices and should treat different religious belief systems with equal respect. On the second view, because religion is irrational, it should be excluded from the sphere of political action. Religion and politics should be separated to protect politics. The emphasis of each may lead to different results: the first more sympathetic to religion, more open to its value or worth, and the second

---

Religious Pluralism in Canada (Vancouver: UBC Press, 2008) 91; and Carissima Mathen, "What Religious Freedom Jurisprudence Reveals about Equality" (2009) 6 JL & Equality 163. As noted earlier, this view of religion, as a matter of identity, is very different from the conception of religion that underlay the defence of religious freedom or tolerance in earlier times. Early defenders of religious tolerance or freedom in the West assumed the existence of religious truth, generally some form of Protestantism, and sought to protect the conditions necessary for the individual and collective realization of that truth.

70   But, of course, if section 2(a) is understood in this way, it will overlap significantly with section 15. This may explain why s 15 has played such a limited role in religion cases. As Sopinka J observed in *Adler*, above note 67 at para 166, "It is evident that there is some overlap between the claims based on s. 2(a) and s. 15 of the Charter . . . . During oral argument, it became increasingly difficult to identify whether a particular argument supported a claim under s. 2(a) or under s. 15." See also José Woehrling, "L'obligation d'accommodement raisonnable et l'adaptation de la société à la diversité religieuse" (1998) 43 McGill LJ 325.

more skeptical about the value of religion, but resigned to its continu-
ing role in the private lives of community members.

Neutrality between different faiths can be achieved in a variety of
ways. At an earlier time, it may have seemed possible to base public action on widely held religious beliefs and practices, although this "common religious ground" was bound to exclude some individuals or groups
from its scope.[71] In any event, with the growth of religious diversity
and the rise of agnosticism and spiritualism, state reliance on common
religious grounds, if it ever was an option, is no longer one. The state
may also achieve a degree of neutrality by providing even-handed support to the different religious practices or institutions in the community as well as to nonreligious alternatives. Indeed, the Canadian courts
have held that the *Charter* does not preclude the state from providing
financial support to religious schools or acknowledging the practices or
celebrations of different religious groups as long as it does so in an even-
handed way.[72] However, the commitment to state neutrality toward different religious belief systems is most often understood as requiring the
privatization of religion, both the exclusion and insulation of religion
from political decision making. The state, it is said, must advance civic
or "secular" rather than religious purposes, and it must not interfere
with religious practices unless this is necessary to the public interest.

Yet the courts have not consistently enforced the neutrality requirement. The problem is not only that religious beliefs involve claims about
what is true and right, which must be viewed as a matter of judgment
(rather than cultural practice) and open to contest within the public
sphere.[73] The more fundamental difficulty with the requirement of state
neutrality is that religious beliefs sometimes have public implications.
State neutrality is possible only if religion can be treated as simply a
private matter. Religious belief systems, however, often say something
about the way we should treat others and about the kind of society we
should work to create. Because religious beliefs sometimes address civic
concerns and are often difficult to distinguish from nonreligious beliefs,
they cannot be fully excluded or insulated from political decision making. And, indeed, the courts have applied the neutrality requirement se-

---

71   Generally speaking, freedom of religion, at this earlier time, was understood as a
     liberty, and did not require state neutrality.

72   See, for example, *Reference re Bill 30*, above note 16 at para 62. The case is exam-
     ined in Chapter 5.

73   For a discussion of some of the problems with approaching religion as an identity
     (and with identity politics more generally), including the risk of "essentializing"
     the group or its belief system, see Avigail Eisenberg, "Rights in the Age of Identity
     Politics" (2013) 50 Osgoode Hall LJ 609.

lectively, sometimes treating religion as a cultural identity toward which the state should remain neutral and other times (when it touches upon or addresses civic matters) as a political or moral judgment by the individual that should be subject to the give-and-take of politics.[74]

Behind the courts' uneven application of the religious neutrality requirement lies a complex conception of religious adherence in which religion is viewed as both a cultural practice that should (sometimes) be excluded and insulated from politics and a personal judgment about truth and right that cannot simply be removed from politics. This complex conception of religious adherence, as both personal commitment and cultural identity, is apparent in the courts' uncertainty about the nature of the wrong addressed by the freedom—whether the freedom simply prohibits coercive state action (state restriction of religious belief or practice and state compulsion to follow the practices of a particular faith) or whether it goes further and prohibits the state from supporting or favouring a particular religious belief system because religious preference by the state signals to the members of the nonfavoured religious groups that they do not deserve the same respect as others or are not fully part of the political community. It can also be seen in the weak or vague standards set for the accommodation of religious practices. The courts have said that the state must justify any restriction on religious practice under the terms of section 1 of the *Charter*. Yet they have been prepared to uphold a restriction on religious practice as long as it advances a legitimate public objective. As well, the courts' complex conception of religion shows itself in judicial uncertainty about the scope of the freedom—about whether the freedom protects all deeply held views or beliefs or whether it protects only, or principally, religious beliefs and practices, which are in some way different from other (nonreligious) beliefs and practices. Finally, it is apparent in the courts' uncertainty about the character of public secularism. While the courts have generally regarded *secularism* (understood as the exclusion of religion from politics) as a neutral ground that lies outside religious controversy (and provides the baseline against which religious restriction, compulsion, and inequality are measured), they have on occasion been receptive to the claim that secularism represents a partisan, nonreligious,

---

74   The idea of religion as a form of cultural identity (that the state should treat with equal respect) fits some religious traditions, and some elements of particular belief systems, better than others. The shift to an equality-based conception of religious freedom may be in tension with the growth of spiritualism, of more individualized "systems" of belief and practice concerning the supernatural.

or antispiritual perspective that is in competition with religious world views.[75]

The challenge for the courts is to find a way to fit this complex conception of religious commitment (as deeply held or foundational) and its value (as a source of meaning, purpose, and identity for the individual and group) into a constitutional framework that relies on a distinction between individual choices or commitments that should be protected as a matter of liberty and individual attributes or traits that should be respected as a matter of equality.[76] The constitutional framework (and perhaps more deeply our conception of rights) imposes this distinction, between judgment and identity, on the complex phenomenon of religious commitment.

---

75   Following common practice, I will use "secular" to refer to a form of separation between religion and politics. This "separation" can take many forms, and its shape is the subject of debate and indeed a central issue in this book. However, the term sometimes refers more generally to the absence of religion, not just in politics, but across society. For a discussion of the term, see Iain T Benson, "Notes Towards a (Re)Definition of the 'Secular'" (2000) 33 UBC L Rev 520.

76   The courts' uncertain or complex conception of religious commitment reflects larger questions about individual agency and the distinction often made between matters of identity, which are fixed or rooted, and matters of choice, which are revisable and not part of the individual's identity. This is also apparent in the courts' s 15 jurisprudence, in which all grounds of discrimination are, on the face of it, treated the same — on the model of race or skin colour — as immutable traits that are generally irrelevant in political decision making. But the reality is that many of these grounds are not simply immutable and are, in part, a matter of choice or culture. I suspect that the inconsistent results in cases involving citizenship and marital status as grounds of discrimination reflect the courts' ambivalence about these grounds and a recognition that they involve an element of choice or control for which the individual may sometimes be seen as responsible. See, for example, the Supreme Court of Canada's judgment in Lavoie v Canada, 2002 SCC 23 (citizenship), and in Quebec (AG) v A, 2013 SCC 5 (marital status).

CHAPTER 2

GOVERNMENT SUPPORT FOR RELIGION

A. SUPPORT FOR RELIGIOUS PRACTICE

Religious freedom is understood to have two dimensions: the freedom to practise religion without state interference and the freedom from state compulsion to participate in a religious practice. At an earlier time, when most individuals adhered to a particular religious belief system, these two dimensions were closely tied. In seeking to advance its conception of religious truth or to ensure social stability through religious conformity, a state might both compel the "correct" or dominant religious practice and prohibit "erroneous" practices. To the religious adherent, because belief and practice play such a significant role in her life, state compulsion to engage in other practices might seem deeply invasive and even an interference with her chosen practices.[1] In some cases, the adherent might even consider his formal (and compelled) participation in "erroneous" practices to be a form of blasphemy. However, the tie between these two dimensions of the freedom has been loosened with the expansion of nonreligious or agnostic perspectives in the community. Indeed, as we shall see, most of the recent challenges against state support for a religious practice have been brought by non-

---

1   See *Alberta v Hutterian Brethren of Wilson Colony*, 2009 SCC 37 at para 92, Mc-Lachlin J: "To compel religious practice by force of law deprives the individual of the fundamental right to choose his or her mode of religious experience, or lack thereof."

believers who object not to the preference of one religion over another but instead to any form of state support for religion. Yet there may be other links, in the contemporary context, between the two dimensions of religious freedom. For example, the modern view that religion is a private matter may support not just the exclusion of religion from political decision making but also its insulation from state regulation. We may be concerned that if religion lies outside the scope of politics, the state may fail to take adequate account of the way that law and other state action may affect (private) religious practices, particularly those of minority groups.

In *R v Big M Drug Mart*,[2] the Supreme Court of Canada said that the test for determining whether section 2(a) has been breached is whether the state act in question amounts to "coercion" of the conscience. According to Dickson CJ, no one should "be forced to act in a way contrary to his beliefs or his conscience" except when necessary to protect important public interests or individual rights.[3] The individual must be free to practise her religion, and she must not be compelled to engage in other religious practices. The issue in *Big M Drug Mart* was whether the federal *Lord's Day Act*,[4] which prohibited a variety of commercial activities on Sundays, breached section 2(a) of the *Charter*[5] and, if it did, whether this breach could be justified under section 1, the limitations provision of the *Charter*. Chief Justice Dickson said that, in deciding whether the law breached section 2(a), the Court had to consider not just the law's effect but also its purpose. He found that the *Lord's Day Act* breached section 2(a) because its "true purpose" was to compel a religious practice—"the observance of the Christian Sabbath."[6]

In defending the Act, the government had argued that the purpose of the Sunday ban, at least in the contemporary context, was to create a common pause day for workers. Chief Justice Dickson, though, noted that the purpose of the law, at the time of its enactment, was to compel or support Sabbath observance. In his view, the law's "[p]urpose is a function of the intent of those who drafted and enacted the legislation at the time, and not of any shifting variable," and so the *Lord's Day Act* could not be found to have a secular purpose based on changes in the social context.[7] Before the enactment of the *Charter*, the *Lord's Day Act*

2   [1985] 1 SCR 295 [*Big M Drug Mart*].

3   *Ibid* at para 95.

4   *Lord's Day Act*, RSC 1970, c L-13, as repealed by SI/88-227, 12 December 1988.

5   *Canadian Charter of Rights and Freedoms*, Part 1 of the *Constitution Act, 1982*, being Schedule B to the *Canada Act 1982* (UK), 1982, c 11 [*Charter*].

6   Above note 2 at para 136.

7   *Ibid* at para 91.

had been viewed as a valid exercise of the federal government's power to enact criminal laws under section 91 of the *Constitution Act, 1867*.[8] However, the law's validity under the federal criminal law power was based on its religious purpose—and in particular its enforcement of the Sabbath. Since the provinces have exclusive jurisdiction under the Constitution to enact laws regulating business and trade activities within their territories, any attempt by the federal government to defend the law under the *Charter* on the basis that it advances a secular purpose, such as the creation of a common pause day for workers, would undermine its constitutionality under the federal division of powers.

The Chief Justice went on to find that the law could not be sustained under section 1, because its purpose was religious rather than secular: "The characterization of the purpose of the Act as one which compels religious observance renders it unnecessary to decide the question of whether s. 1 could validate such legislation whose purpose was otherwise . . . ."[9] A "religious" purpose, it seemed, could not be regarded as pressing and substantial, and so it was unnecessary for the Court to address the other elements of the section 1 test, as set out in *R v Oakes*.[10] The consequence of this finding may be that section 1 has no role in those section 2(a) cases in which the breach is based on state compulsion of (or support for) religion.

While the Court in *Big M Drug Mart* formally described the wrong addressed by section 2(a) as coercion in spiritual matters, the Court's finding that the *Lord's Day Act* breached section 2(a) seemed to rest on a different understanding of the wrong. The Act did not require anyone to honour the Sabbath, by attending church or reading the Bible or reflecting upon their spiritual commitments. It prevented individuals from working but did not require that they worship or even rest.[11] Chief Justice Dickson, though, adopted a broad view of religious compulsion:

---

8   (UK), 30 & 31 Vict, c 3, reprinted in RSC 1985, App II, No 5.

9   Above note 2 at para 142.

10   [1986] 1 SCR 103 [*Oakes*]. The *Oakes* test has several elements. A restriction on a right or freedom must have a substantial and pressing purpose. The restriction must be rationally connected to that purpose, and it must restrict the right or freedom no more than is necessary to advance that purpose. And, finally, the actual costs of the restriction to the right or freedom must not outweigh its benefits. A law that advantages the practices of one religious group, even if not intended to support or prefer that group, may sometimes be viewed as a restriction on the practices of other groups—a burden on their religious practice. See, for example, *R v Edwards Books and Art Ltd*, [1986] 2 SCR 713 [*Edwards Books*], which is discussed in Chapter 3.

11   This was the view of the majority of the Supreme Court of Canada in *Robertson and Rosetanni v The Queen*, [1963] SCR 651, a *Canadian Bill of Rights* case that

In my view, the guarantee of freedom of conscience and religion prevents the government from compelling individuals to perform or abstain from performing otherwise harmless acts because of the religious significance of those acts to others. The element of religious compulsion is perhaps somewhat more difficult to perceive (especially for those whose beliefs are being enforced) when, as here, it is non-action rather than action that is being decreed, but in my view compulsion is nevertheless what it amounts to.[12]

The Chief Justice recognized that the law did not compel the individual to perform a particular religious act but, instead, required that she refrain from performing an otherwise lawful activity.

The purpose of the law might have been simply to support those who wished to keep the Sunday Sabbath, by removing the economic costs that would result from not working on Sunday, when other people (and, more particularly, other retailers) were prepared to treat it as another business day. Or its purpose might have been to encourage all individuals to keep the Sunday Sabbath, without actually requiring anyone to do so. The Court, though, seemed prepared to find a breach of religious freedom simply because the law had a purpose that was religious

---

considered whether the *Lord's Day Act* breached religious freedom. Justice Ritchie wrote at 657–58 (quoted by Dickson CJ in *Big M Drug Mart* at para 69):

> My own view is that the *effect* of the Lord's Day Act rather than its *purpose* must be looked to in order to determine whether its application involves the abrogation, abridgment or infringement of religious freedom, and I can see nothing in that statute which in any way affects the liberty of religious thought and practice of any citizen of this country . . . .
>
> The practical result of this law on those whose religion requires them to observe a day of rest other than Sunday, is a purely secular and financial one in that they are required to refrain from carrying on or conducting their business on Sunday as well as on their own day of rest. In some cases this is no doubt a business inconvenience, but it is neither an abrogation nor an abridgment nor an infringement of religious freedom, and the fact that it has been brought about by reason of the existence of a statute enacted for the purpose of preserving the sanctity of Sunday, cannot, in my view, be construed as attaching some religious significance to an effect which is purely secular in so far as non-Christians are concerned. [emphasis added]

12   Above note 2 at para 133. In *S v Lawrence; S v Negal; S v Solberg*, 1997 (10) BCLR 1348 (CC), a majority of the South African Constitutional Court upheld a ban on the sale of liquor on Sundays and statutory holidays. The judges divided on the question of whether the constitutional protection of freedom of religion simply prohibited state compulsion to engage in a religious practice or whether it also precluded the state from supporting the practices of a particular religion.

in character.[13] And so the Court's objection to the *Lord's Day Act* may not have been that it compelled, or was intended to compel, individuals to keep the Sabbath but, instead, that it supported or favoured the practices of the dominant religious group. Indeed, near the end of his judgment, Dickson CJ indicated that it was "constitutionally incompetent for the federal Parliament to provide legislative preference for any one religion at the expense of those of another religious persuasion."[14] More specifically, about the law at issue in this case, he said:

> To the extent that it binds all to a sectarian Christian ideal, the *Lord's Day Act* works a form of coercion inimical to the spirit of the Charter and the dignity of all non-Christians. In proclaiming the standards of the Christian faith, the Act creates a climate hostile to, and gives the appearance of discrimination against, non-Christian Canadians. It takes religious values rooted in Christian morality and, using the force of the state, translates them into a positive law binding on believers and non-believers alike. The theological content of the legislation remains as a subtle and constant reminder to religious minorities within the country of their differences with, and alienation from, the dominant religious culture.[15]

In the later decision of *SL v Commission scolaire des Chênes*, the Supreme Court of Canada confirmed that the judgment in *Big M Drug Mart* was based on the requirement that the state remain neutral in religious matters. Referring to *Big M Drug Mart* and other cases, Deschamps J observed that "Canadian courts have held that state sponsorship of one religious tradition amounts to discrimination against others."[16]

In *R v Edwards Books and Art Ltd*, the Supreme Court of Canada held that a provincial law establishing a common pause day for retail workers had a secular purpose and so did not compel a religious practice contrary to section 2(a).[17] Chief Justice Dickson thought that

> [religious freedom] is not necessarily impaired by legislation which requires conduct consistent with the religious beliefs of another person.

---

13   See Shannon Ishiyama Smithey, "Religious Freedom and Equality Concerns under the Canadian Charter of Rights and Freedoms" (2001) 34 Canadian Journal of Political Science 85 at 93.

14   Above note 2 at para 134. Section 15, the equality rights provision of the *Charter*, did not come into force until 1985, three years after the enactment of the *Charter*. Because its challenge was initiated before this date, the respondent in *Big M Drug Mart* was unable to make a direct equality rights claim.

15   *Ibid* at para 97.

16   2012 SCC 7 at para 17 [*SL*].

17   Above note 10.

One is not being compelled to engage in religious practices merely because a statutory obligation coincides with the dictates of a particular religion. I cannot accept, for example, that a legislative prohibition of criminal conduct such as theft and murder is a state-enforced compulsion to conform to religious practices, merely because some religions enjoin their members not to steal or kill. Reasonable citizens do not perceive the legislation as requiring them to pay homage to religious doctrine.[18]

As discussed in Chapter 3, the Court in *Edwards Books* went on to find that even though the provincial Sunday closing law did not compel Sunday Sabbath observance, it had the effect of indirectly restricting the religious practice of those who kept a day other than Sunday as the Sabbath. The Court, though, found that this restriction on religious practice was justified under section 1.[19]

---

18   *Ibid* at para 99. Chief Justice Dickson's assumption is that the establishment of a common pause day does not breach s 2(a) if the reason or motivation behind it is not religious. He noted that the bans on murder and theft might coincide with the religious views of some, but this does not mean that their enforcement is a form of religious compulsion. What if the lawmakers thought that murder should be banned because it is forbidden by God or because life is a sacred gift from God? As I will argue later in this chapter, this ban does not breach s 2(a), even if some or many of those who support it do so for religious reasons. The courts have made a distinction between religious practices, which the state must not support (or at least not prefer), and religious values, which address civic concerns and may play a role in political decision making.

19   The US courts have similarly upheld Sunday closing laws on the basis that their purpose was no longer religious. In *McGowan v Maryland*, 366 US 420 (1961) at 450, the US Supreme Court found that the purpose of a Maryland Sunday closing law was "to set one day apart from all others as a day of rest, repose, recreation and tranquility . . . ." The Court noted that "[p]eople of all religions and people with no religion regard Sunday as a time for family activity, for visiting friends and relatives, for late sleeping, for passive and active entertainments, for dining out, and the like" (*ibid* at 451–52). The reason for this, said the Court, is now "irrelevant" and "[i]t would seem unrealistic for enforcement purposes and perhaps detrimental to the general welfare to require a State to choose a common day of rest other than that which most persons would select of their own accord" (*ibid* at 452). The Court concluded that the statute at issue was not a law "respecting an establishment of religion" (*ibid*). In *Braunfeld v Brown*, 366 US 599 (1961), the US Supreme Court held that if enacted for a secular purpose, a Sunday closing law did not breach either the establishment clause or the free exercise clause of the First Amendment.

B. RELIGIOUS PRACTICES IN THE SCHOOLS AND OTHER CIVIC FORUMS

In *Zylberberg v Sudbury Board of Education*, the Ontario Court of Appeal ruled that the inclusion of the Lord's Prayer in the opening exercises of public schools in Ontario was contrary to section 2(a) of the *Charter* and could not be justified under section 1.[20] This was the case even though students could opt out of the practice, either by remaining silent or withdrawing from the classroom during the recitation of the prayer. The court in *Zylberberg* found that the *purpose* of the state action was religious and, following the Supreme Court of Canada in *Big M Drug Mart*, concluded that it breached section 2(a). Yet the religious purpose of the law may not have been to compel or pressure students to engage in a religious practice but may instead have been simply to give students, who wished, the opportunity to participate in an important religious practice. However, the court also found that the *effect* of the practice was to compel students to participate in a religious practice. The court recognized that in the public school context, children would feel pressure from their peers to recite the prayer — that nonparticipants would feel isolated or stigmatized. In the court's view, this was enough for the prayer to be regarded as coercive, as state compulsion to engage in a religious practice. While the children had a formal right to opt out of the prayer, they would feel significant pressure to conform to the school-supported practices of the majority community.[21]

The Court of Appeal in *Zylberberg* went on to find that the law could not be justified under section 1, because its purpose was religious. Furthermore, said the court, even if the pressing and substantial purpose

---

20 [1988] OJ No 1488 (Ont CA) [*Zylberberg*]. The same conclusion was reached in *Russow v BC (AG)* (1989), 62 DLR (4th) 98 (BCSC), and in *Manitoba Assn for Rights and Liberties Inc v Manitoba (Minister of Education)* (1992), 94 DLR (4th) 678 (Man QB). Over the course of the twentieth century, the Protestant character of the public school system had gradually been eroded. Nevertheless, in 1982 at the time of the *Charter*'s introduction, many public schools still incorporated religious elements in the curriculum, as per provincial education policy. For a discussion, see RD Gidney and WPJ Millar, "The Christian Recessional in Ontario's Public Schools" in Marguerite Van Die, ed, *Religion and Public Life in Canada: Historical and Comparative Perspectives* (Toronto: University of Toronto Press, 2001) 275.

21 The majority judgment also thought it objectionable that students would have to identify themselves as different — as not part of the majority — to take advantage of the exemption. This objection, though, seemed to depend on the more fundamental claim that students should not be pressured to conform to the religious practices of the dominant group.

of the law was described in more general (nonreligious) terms, such as the affirmation of important values in the schools, the law did not interfere with section 2(a) rights as little as was necessary to advance this objective. The schools could advance this objective in ways other than a daily recitation of a Christian prayer. In holding that the law did not represent a minimal impairment of the religious freedom of non-Christians, the court referred to the practice of the Toronto School Board, which involved daily readings, on a rotating basis, from a book of materials that drew from a wide range of spiritual and philosophical traditions. The court did not decide that the Toronto School Board's practice was constitutional but only that it offered a less intrusive way to affirm public values in the schools than the practice of reciting the Lord's Prayer.[22]

In his dissenting judgment in *Zylberberg*, Lacourcière J noted the omission from the *Charter* of any provision resembling the establishment clause of the US Bill of Rights and argued that section 2(a) "does not prohibit all governmental aid to or advancement of religion per se."[23] In his view, the prayer was simply a "state-created opportunity to participate in . . . [a] religious activity . . . ."[24] According to Lacourcière J, it could not reasonably be said that either the purpose or the effect of the law was to compel participation in a religious practice given the broad exemption granted to dissenters. Yet, in the school context, the line between state compulsion of religion and state support for religion may be difficult to draw. As the majority recognized, school support for a particular religious practice may amount to compulsion or pressure because children are not yet independent agents and because the school represents a significant authority in their lives.

Justice Lacourcière went on to consider the application of section 15 of the *Charter* to both the provincial law and the practice of the Sudbury School Board of Education. He found that the provincial regulation, which required that the school day be opened or closed "with religious exercises consisting of the reading of the Scriptures or other

---

22 A system of rotating readings, drawn from different spiritual and moral traditions, might raise another problem. The use of different readings to create a moral or spiritual tone at the beginning of each school day could be seen as advancing a "relativistic" view of religion—that all traditions have merit. It does not appear that the roster of prayers and readings were being used to teach about religion, in a sociological sense, as occurred in the *SL* case, above note 16. For a discussion of the legislative response to this decision and some of the litigation that followed, see Robert Earl Charney, "The Limits of Religious Accommodation in Secular Public Schools" (2013) 7:2 Journal of Parliamentary and Political Law 247.

23 Above note 20 at para 113.

24 *Ibid* at para 78.

suitable readings and the repeating of the Lord's Prayer or other suitable prayers," did not breach section 15.[25] He could not imagine that the inclusive wording of the Lord's Prayer "could offend any religious group."[26] He added that even if the prayer (along with the reference to the Scriptures) was understood "to favour the Christian faith," the regulation permitted the use of other "suitable" prayers or readings.[27] However, Lacourcière J found that the particular practice of the Sudbury school board breached section 15. He noted that the board's practice "has been to formally open each school day by the singing of O Canada and the recitation of the Lord's Prayer, often followed by Scripture readings or Biblical stories, in order to encourage respect for the moral principles emphasized within the Judeo-Christian tradition."[28] This practice, he accepted, breached section 15 because "it gives preference to that tradition at the expense of all non-Christians" and could not be justified under section 1, because "there are other ways, which are less intrusive on the equality rights of religious minorities, to implement religious exercises which encourage respect for moral principles."[29]

In *Canadian Civil Liberties Assn v Ontario (Minister of Education)*, the Ontario Court of Appeal held that a provincial regulation requiring the public schools to devote two one-half hour periods each week to "religious education" had as its purpose the indoctrination of students into the Christian faith, and was therefore contrary to section 2(a) of the *Charter*, and could not be justified under section 1.[30] In reaching this conclusion, the court noted that the regulation permitted the delivery of the required religious education by clergymen even though uncertified instructors were not authorized to teach other parts of the school curriculum. The court thought that "in the absence of evidence that clergymen are better equipped to teach comparative religions than they are skilled at indoctrination, the conclusion has to be that the purpose was indoctrination."[31] The court also noted that the regulation referred to clergymen of "different denominations" rather than different religions, which suggested that the religious education was to be Christian in character. The regulation allowed students to be exempted from the religion classes, but the court thought that such an exemption would only be necessary if the instruction involved religious indoctrination. The court found that, as

---

25   *Ibid* at para 69.
26   *Ibid* at para 144.
27   *Ibid*.
28   *Ibid* at para 146.
29   *Ibid* at para 147.
30   [1990] OJ No 104.
31   *Ibid* at para 52.

in *Zylberberg*, the indoctrinating purpose or effect of the regulation was not altered by the fact that students who did not want to participate in the religious education classes could be granted an exemption. In the court's view, any students who requested an exemption would be stigmatized as "non-conformists" and set "apart from their fellow students who are members of the dominant religion."[32] The court also considered the constitutionality of the particular form of religious instruction provided by the Elgin County School Board. The court recognized that the line between religious indoctrination, which is contrary to section 2(a), and education about religion, which is compatible with religious freedom, may sometimes be difficult to draw. Nevertheless, based on the "general themes, lesson plans, teaching and resource materials and the manner of presentation of the course of study," the court concluded that the curriculum constituted religious indoctrination.[33] The assumption made by the court—reflecting a more general view about religion—is that to teach from a particular religious perspective, or to teach a particular religion as true, is to engage in religious indoctrination.

In *Freitag v Penetanguishene*, the Ontario Court of Appeal held that the practice of reciting the Lord's Prayer at the opening of town-council meetings violated the religious freedom of non-Christians.[34] The court found that the practice was coercive—that it pressured individuals to conform to the tenets of a particular faith—even though no one was directly required to recite the prayer, even though some individuals, including the complainant, chose not to participate, and even though the meeting was comprised of adults rather than children. The court acknowledged that "the nature and potential effect of the coercion are much different for an adult who wishes to attend Town Council meetings than for children, who are in the school environment all year with friends and teachers, and are subject to pressures that those important relations engender."[35] However, said the court, "[j]ust as children are

---

32   *Ibid* at para 21. The court observed at para 55 that

> [s]tate-authorized religious indoctrination amounts to the imposition of majoritarian religious beliefs on minorities. Although s. 2(a) of the Charter is not infringed merely because education may be consistent with the religious beliefs of the majority of Canadians . . . , teaching students Christian doctrine as if it were the exclusive means through which to develop moral thinking and behaviour amounts to religious coercion in the class-room. It creates a direct burden on religious minorities and non-believers who do not adhere to majoritarian beliefs . . . . [T]his amounts to violation of s. 2(a) of the Charter . . . .

33   *Ibid* at para 71.
34   (1999), 47 OR (3d) 301 [*Freitag*].
35   *Ibid* at para 33.

entitled to attend public school and be free from coercion or pressure to conform to the religious practices of the majority, so everyone is entitled to attend public local council meetings and to enjoy the same freedom."[36] The difficulty with this apparently reasonable assertion is that in *Zylberberg*, the school environment was critical to the court's conclusion that the recitation of the Lord's Prayer was coercive. The practice in *Zylberberg* was seen as coercive because it was imposed on children, who are vulnerable to peer pressure in a way that adults are not.

The court in *Freitag* found that the purpose of the practice was to "impose a specifically Christian moral tone on the deliberations of the Town Council," contrary to section 2(a).[37] Yet, it is unlikely that the council was trying to pressure non-Christians to say the prayer or adhere to the Christian faith. In all likelihood, the purpose was simply to signal the importance of the Christian faith in the community or to enable Christians attending the meeting to practice their faith. Nor is it even clear that a non-Christian adult attending the council meeting would experience the prayer as pressure to adopt the Christian faith and reject her own belief system. Recitation of the prayer may have caused the non-Christians present at the meeting to feel uncomfortable, embarrassed, and unfairly treated, but it put no tangible pressure on them. It appears that the real objection to opening a council meeting with a Christian prayer was that it excluded non-Christians from full participation in a public meeting. More generally, it signalled to non-Christians that they were not full members of the political community. The court in *Freitag* recognized this when it described the practice of saying the prayer as "exclusionary."[38] The court went on to say that "the appellant . . . feels intimidation when he attends the meeting of his local Town Council. This does not mean that he is so fearful that he does not participate. He does so, but as a citizen who is singled out as being not part of the majority recognized officially in the proceedings."[39] According to this view, state support for a religious practice is wrong because it sends an unacceptable message of exclusion to nonadherents or because it involves treating some individuals less favourably than others on the basis of their religious membership. Individuals may promote particular practices or beliefs (what they understand to be true), but the state is forbidden to do so.

---

36 *Ibid* at para 34.
37 *Ibid* at para 25.
38 *Ibid* at para 36.
39 *Ibid*. The evidence showed that Mr Freitag and others sat quietly during the recitation of the prayer.

C. LEGISLATIVE IMMUNITY

Despite the Canadian courts' determination that the recitation of Christian prayers in public schools or at municipal meetings breaches section 2(a) of the *Charter*, the daily session in several provincial legislatures still begins with the Lord's Prayer. The same Mr Freitag who had challenged the constitutionality of the recitation of the Lord's Prayer at Penetanguishene town-council meetings brought a complaint under the Ontario *Human Rights Code* against the Ontario legislature, which opens its daily session with the Lord's Prayer. In *Ontario (Speaker of the Legislative Assembly) v Ontario (HRC)*, the Ontario Court of Appeal held that the opening exercises of the provincial legislature, including the recitation of the prayer, were part of its internal operation and immune from *Charter*, and other forms of external, review.[40] According to the court:

> [M]atters relating to the internal workings of the House must be subject to the exclusive jurisdiction of the House, since control over such matters is necessary to the independent existence of the House. The House must be absolutely free to set its own guidelines for how its legislative sessions will be carried out and the Standing Orders that detail the operation of parliamentary procedure must be considered privileged and insulated from outside review. Having made this determination, it is not open to this Court, nor to any other body associated with the executive or judicial branches of government, to question an individual exercise of conduct that falls within the protected sphere. As the recitation of the prayers is called for by the Standing Orders, it is encompassed as part of the Assembly's privilege relating to control of its internal proceedings, and is not susceptible to outside challenge.[41]

It followed then that the Ontario Human Rights Commission had no jurisdiction to consider whether the practice of opening the daily session in the legislature with a recitation of the Lord's Prayer was contrary to the *Human Rights Code*.

In 2008 the premier of Ontario proposed that the legislature introduce a more inclusive opening to its daily session, involving a rotation of readings and recitations from different religious and other belief systems. The government, though, backed down from this plan following a public outcry. The Lord's Prayer continues to be part of the opening

---

40   [2001] OJ No 2180.
41   *Ibid* at para 48.

exercises of the Ontario legislature, although it is now supplemented with readings and prayers from other traditions. While the province of Quebec some time ago adopted a moment of silence in place of a Christian prayer in its opening exercises, a crucifix continues to hang in the legislative assembly. The recommendation of the Bouchard-Taylor commission that the crucifix be removed was rejected by all three parties sitting in the legislature.[42]

A related issue that has recently come to the fore in Canada is the right of civil servants to wear religious dress or symbols. The issue is sometimes presented as a tension or conflict between the two dimensions of religious freedom—the prohibition on state support for the practices of a particular religion and the right of the individual to practise her religion without state interference. This issue will be addressed in Chapter 3, which deals with state restrictions on religious practice.

D. IS SECULARISM NEUTRAL?

In *Allen v Renfrew (County)*, an Ontario judge held that a municipal council's practice of opening its meeting with an ecumenical prayer did not breach section 2(a).[43] The judge found that the prayer was not "in substance a religious observance, coercive or otherwise, and [did] not impose any burden on the applicant or any restriction on his exercise of his own beliefs."[44] Despite the mention of God, the prayer was described by the judge as "broadly inclusive" and "non-denominational."[45] Noting the reference to "supremacy of God" in the preamble of the *Constitution Act, 1982*, the judge declared that "it would be incongruous and contrary to the intent of the Charter to hold that the practice of offering a prayer to God per se is a violation of the religious freedom of non-believers."[46] Yet if a Christian prayer excludes non-Christians, does an ecumenical prayer that appeals explicitly to a divine creator not in the same way exclude nonreligious individuals (agnostics or atheists) or the followers of polytheistic or nontheistic belief systems? Is the state not favouring the practices of those who believe in a divine creator over those who do not? However, if a court were to decide that an ecumenical prayer was objectionable because it excluded non-believers (rath-

---

42   Gérard Bouchard & Charles Taylor, *Building the Future: A Time for Reconciliation* (Government of Quebec, 2008) at 152 [*Bouchard-Taylor Report*].

43   (2004), 69 OR (3d) 742 (SCJ) [*Renfrew (County)*].

44   *Ibid* at para 27.

45   *Ibid* at para 19.

46   *Ibid*.

er than simply those who adhere to a different set of spiritual beliefs), would the court then be favouring the beliefs or practices of agnostics and atheists over those of religious believers? In *Renfrew (County)* and other judgments, which are discussed later, the courts recognize that the spiritual commitments of public actors underpin their sense of ethical responsibility to the general public and so are reluctant to confine the spiritual entirely to the private sphere.

At an earlier time, when all or most community members adhered to some form of religion, it could be claimed that the exclusion of religious practice from the political sphere was neutral or even handed between different religious belief systems. (In practice, of course, an imperfect form of neutrality was achieved in most Western democracies not by excluding religious practices but rather by relying on "nonsectarian" or shared Christian practices). Secularism, understood as the ordering of public life (politics) on the basis of nonreligious beliefs or practices, is generally treated as a neutral ground that lies outside religious controversy. It provides the baseline for determining whether the state has compelled or restricted religious beliefs and practices or whether it has treated different religions unequally.

However, the complainants in most of the recent cases in which state support for religion has been challenged have been agnostics or atheists. Their complaint in these cases is not that the state is supporting one religion over another, the religion of the majority over a minority belief system, but rather that it is supporting religious belief or practice generally and sending a message of exclusion to citizens who are not religious, or imposing religion on them, or treating them unequally. If secularism is equated with agnosticism and understood as a position, world view, or cultural identity equivalent to religious belief, then its proponents may feel excluded or marginalized when the state supports even the most ecumenical forms of religious practice. But, by the same token, the complete removal of religion from the political sphere may be experienced by religious adherents as the exclusion of their world view and the affirmation of a nonreligious or "secular" perspective — the culture or identity of a particular segment of the community.[47] To religious adherents "secularism" may look less like a neutral or common ground that stands outside religious controversy and more like a particular world view that dominates the realm of politics simply because of the

---

47   The Supreme Court of Canada acknowledged but did not address this concern in *SL*, above note 16 at para 30: "We must recognize that trying to achieve religious neutrality in the public sphere is a major challenge for the state."

political power of its adherents.[48] Indeed, if the basis for excluding religious practice from the political sphere is that atheists or agnostics represent a group—a cultural identity group—that should be treated with equal respect, then excluding religion (even without an explicit denial of its truth) may be viewed as a preference for the beliefs or world view of the atheist or agnostic community.[49] Ironically, then, as the exclusion of religion from the political sphere, in the name of religious freedom and equality, becomes more complete, secular politics will appear less neutral and more partisan. Secularism is understood, then, not simply as a political doctrine (involving the separation of religion and politics) but as an agnostic or nonreligious world view. With the growth of agnosticism and atheism in the community, religious neutrality in the political sphere may have become impossible. What is for some the neutral ground upon which freedom of religion and conscience depends is for others a partisan, antispiritual perspective.

The courts, though, have not interpreted section 2(a) as excluding religion entirely from the political sphere. First, the courts have said that the state may support religious practices and institutions provided it does so in an even-handed way, and (in the case of schools and other services) ensures the availability of a nonreligious option. Second, as we shall see later in this chapter, the courts have said that while the state must not support or prefer the *practices* of a particular religious belief system, it is not precluded from relying on religious *values* when making political decisions. If the neutrality requirement applies only to religious practices ("private" worship) and not to religious values ("public" or civic concerns), then there is less force to the claim that "secularism," the exclusion of religious practices from the political sphere, marginalizes religious beliefs or communities and amounts to an affirmation of an agnostic world view. I will have more to say shortly about this distinction between practices and values—a distinction that is not without difficulty.

---

48 See Stanley Fish, "Mission Impossible: Settling the Just Bounds between Church and State" (1997) 97 Colum L Rev 2255.

49 See, for example, the recent decision of the Human Rights Tribunal of Ontario *RC and SC v District School Board of Niagara*, 2013 HRTO 1382, in which it was determined that "atheism" is a creed and that discrimination against atheists in the provision of services is prohibited under the Ontario *Human Rights Code*. The tribunal held that a school board policy that allowed the Gideon Society to distribute the Christian New Testament to grade five students in public schools but prevented the distribution of an atheist tract amounted to discrimination contrary to the *Code*.

E. RELIGIOUS SYMBOLS AND CULTURAL HISTORY

The Quebec Human Rights Tribunal in *Simoneau v Tremblay* held that the presence of a crucifix and a sacred heart statue in the town-hall meeting rooms of Ville de Saguenay—as well as the practice of opening town-council meetings with an ecumenical prayer—breached the right to freedom of conscience and religion in the Quebec *Charter of human rights and freedoms*.[50] The town appealed the decision to the Quebec Court of Appeal, which held that these practices were consistent with the town's obligation to remain neutral in religious matters.[51] Justice Gagnon found that the prayer recited at the town-council meetings (an active practice) did not breach religious freedom, because it was religiously inclusive. He noted the similarity between the Ville de Saguenay council's prayer, which referred to God but was not explicitly Christian, and the prayer that was challenged in the *Renfrew (County)* case. Regarding the crucifix, Gagnon J said that the town should be permitted to retain practices and symbols that reflect the community's cultural history. He based this conclusion, not on the long-standing presence of these symbols in the town hall (the crucifix had only been placed in the town hall in the 1980s), but rather on their significance as symbols of the historic role of the Roman Catholic faith in Quebec society. In the view of Gagnon J, the neutrality requirement does not preclude the state from preserving or acknowledging the province's cultural heritage or affirming widely held moral convictions. Yet, while it may be unreasonable to expect the state to remove a symbol of the community's religious and cultural heritage that has been in place for a long time (such as the cross on Mount Royal), the continued presence of a religious symbol such as a crucifix in a legislative chamber raises particular concerns about the link between religion and political membership. As the *Bouchard-Taylor Report* observes, "[i]t seems preferable for the very place where elected representatives deliberate and legislate not to be identified with a specific religion."[52]

In recent decisions, the Canadian courts have said more explicitly that section 2(a) prohibits the state from supporting or preferring the practices of one religion over those of another and religious practices over nonreligious practices.[53] This shift from a liberty- or autonomy-

---

50   [2011] QHRTJ No 1.

51   *Saguenay (Ville de) c Mouvement laïque québécois*, 2013 QCCA 936.

52   Above note 42 at 152.

53   See *SL*, above note 16.

based approach to religious freedom to an equality-based approach reflects a change in the courts' understanding of religion (and its value)—as a cultural identity rather than simply a personal commitment or choice. However, the prohibition on state support for religion may be difficult to apply consistently. Religious practices have shaped the traditions and rituals of the community and cannot simply be erased from the public sphere or ignored in the formulation of public policy. If a large part of the population is Christian, it is difficult to see how the state could not take into account the practices of this group when, for example, fixing holidays or establishing a "pause day" from work.[54] The public and private spheres of life are not so easily separated. As long as religion remains part of private life, it will affect the shape of public action. Sunday is, or at least was, the pause day in Canada because many in the community once regarded it as the Sabbath. It would seem to be impractical, even irrational, for the state to select another pause day (Tuesday, for example) simply to avoid the perception that Christianity is being favoured. The Canadian courts have not demanded that governments (literally or metaphorically) sandblast religious symbols and practices from physical and social structures, some of which were constructed long ago.[55] At the same time, though, the acknowledgement of the country's religious history—of the way in which public practices have been shaped by this history—or of the importance of religion in the private lives of citizens, should not be used by the state as an opportunity to affirm in the present the truth of a particular religious belief system.

---

54 See *Edwards Books*, above note 10. The decision in that case, which is discussed in the next chapter, reveals the Court's ambivalence about the legal recognition of religiously-based practices. The Supreme Court found that a provincial law restricting retail operations on Sunday was not intended to support the Sunday Sabbath and so did not amount to religious compulsion; however, the Court found that the law indirectly restricted the religious practices of those who regarded Saturday as the Sabbath. This conclusion, though, was based on a recognition that the law advantaged Sunday Sabbatarians over others. A majority of the Court went on to find that the law was a justified restriction on the s 2(a) right. See also *Islamic Schools Federation of Ontario v Ottawa Board of Education* (1997), 145 DLR (4th) 659, in which the Ontario Divisional Court found that public school holidays—which included a number of traditional Christian holidays—did not amount to religious support or favouritism by the state.

55 For a discussion of this point, see the *Bouchard-Taylor Report*, above note 42 at 152–53.

F. THE US ESTABLISHMENT CLAUSE: CEREMONIAL DEISM AND HISTORICAL TRADITION

While the Canadian courts have long accepted that the state may support religious practices and institutions provided it does so in an even-handed way, the US courts have only recently begun to move toward this position.[56] In *Everson v Board of Education*, the US Supreme Court said:

> The "establishment of religion" clause of the First Amendment means at least this: Neither a state nor the Federal Government can set up a church. Neither can pass laws which aid one religion, aid all religions, or prefer one religion over another. Neither can force nor influence a person to go to or to remain away from church against his will or force him to profess a belief or disbelief in any religion . . . . Neither a state nor the Federal Government can, openly or secretly, participate in the affairs of any religious organizations or groups, and vice versa. In the words of Jefferson, the clause against establishment of religion by law was intended to erect "a wall of separation between church and State."[57]

To be compatible with the establishment clause, a government action must have a secular purpose, its primary effect must not be to promote or inhibit the practice of a particular religion, and it must not cause the state to become "excessively entangled" with religion (the *Lemon* test).[58] In more recent cases, though, the US Supreme Court has held that the state may provide aid to a religious organization, such as a school, provided it does so as part of a more general or secular program that does not simply benefit religious organizations. For example, in *Agostini v Felton*, the Court held that a government program in which public school teachers delivered remedial education to disadvantaged children in private schools did not breach the First Amendment even though many of these schools were religious. Because the remedial education was secular and because it was provided to children in public and private, secular and religious schools, the program did not support

---

56   The relevant part of the First Amendment of the United States Constitution provides as follows: "Congress shall make no law respecting an establishment of religion, or prohibiting the free exercise thereof . . . ." The Bill of Rights is the collective name for the first ten amendments to the US Constitution.

57   330 US 1 at 15–16 (1947).

58   See *Lemon v Kurtzman*, 403 US 602 (1971) [*Lemon*], and *Agostini v Felton*, 521 US 203 (1997) [*Agostini*], in which the last two parts of the *Lemon* test were combined.

or advantage religion or religious schools.[59] As well, a state program that directs resources to third parties will not breach the establishment clause, even though religious groups or organizations indirectly benefit from the program as a result of choices made by the direct beneficiaries. In the case of *Zelman v Simmons-Harris*, the US Supreme Court upheld a voucher program in the City of Cleveland, which gave low-income parents an amount of money to be used to support their children's education costs.[60] Almost all of the money in this program was directed by parents to private religious schools.

Adhering to a version of the *Lemon* test and to the general principle of state neutrality, the US Supreme Court has prohibited the recitation of an ecumenical prayer as part of the opening exercises in the public schools[61] and the posting of the Ten Commandments on public school classroom walls.[62] More generally, the Court has held that the state cannot display a religious symbol on public property unless the display serves a secular purpose.[63] Supporters of the public display of the Ten Commandments (the Decalogue) argue that it is an important historical document that helped to shape contemporary Western law. They argue that the identity of the political community, even if now understood in "secular" terms, is tied to a religious history that ought to be acknowledged. There is something to this claim—that the political community has a history, which the members of the community should know something about, if only to understand better their current circumstance. However, the problem with this attempt to link the Ten Commandments to the contemporary legal order is that the former does not appear to have had either a unique or even a significant role in shaping contemporary Western law. The Ten Commandments includes several rules (the first four) that are exclusively about the duties of "man" to God. It also includes ideals that no legal system has sought to enforce, such as a ban on coveting the possessions of others. The few commandments that are included in modern legal systems, the bans on stealing and murder, are part of all moral and religious belief systems. There seems little doubt then, that those who advocate the posting of the Ten Commandments in public spaces wish to affirm the truth of the Ten Commandments as God's law—and to link the Christian (or Judeo-Christian tradition) to

---

59 *Agostini*, *ibid*. See also *Mitchell v Helms*, 530 US 793 (2000).

60 536 US 639 (2002).

61 *Engel v Vitale*, 370 US 421 (1962). See also *Abington Township v Schempp*, 374 US 203 (1963): Bible reading in the public schools.

62 *Stone v Graham*, 449 US 39 (1980).

63 *Van Orden v Perry*, 545 US 677 (2005); *McCreary County v ACLU of Kentucky*, 545 US 844 (2005); and *Salazar v Buono*, 559 US 700 (2010).

the US national identity. They recognize, though, that they must provide a "secular" reason for the posting if they are to avoid the strictures of the establishment clause. They regard the United States as a Christian nation and believe that its public institutions should reflect this, both symbolically and substantively. The US Supreme Court has recognized that this is often the motive behind the posting of the Decalogue and has been prepared to permit its posting in public buildings or on public grounds only if it is displayed along with other historically significant documents and is not given pride of place and (or instead) if the structure in which it is incorporated was installed some time ago and so can be seen as a historical piece.

The US courts have also accepted that references to God may be made during public events or processes provided they are simply ceremonial, adding to the solemnity of the occasion, without advancing a particular religious perspective. Justice O'Connor in *Elk Grove Unified School District v Newdow* described the religious elements in public rituals, such as the reference to God in the Pledge of Allegiance, as "ceremonial deism":

> Given the values that the Establishment Clause was meant to serve . . . I believe that government can, in a discrete category of cases, acknowledge or refer to the divine without offending the Constitution. This category of "ceremonial deism" most clearly encompasses such things as the national motto ("In God We Trust"), religious references in traditional patriotic songs such as The Star-Spangled Banner, and the words with which the Marshal of this Court opens each of its sessions ("God save the United States and this honorable Court"). These references are not minor trespasses upon the Establishment Clause to which I turn a blind eye. Instead, their history, character, and context prevent them from being constitutional violations at all.[64]

In *Marsh v Chambers*, the US Supreme Court held that the practice of opening the session of the state legislature with the recitation of an ecumenical prayer did not breach the First Amendment.[65]

---

[64]   542 US 1 at 37 (2004). A majority of the Court found that the plaintiff did not have standing and so did not express an opinion on the merits of the case.

[65]   463 US 783 (1983). The Court also upheld the constitutionality of the state's employment of the chaplain who led the prayer.

G. RELIGIOUS NEUTRALITY AND CHRISTIAN IDENTITY IN EUROPE

In several European countries, including the United Kingdom, there continues to be, at least formally, an established church. In *Darby v Sweden*, the European Commission of Human Rights noted that a state church system "exists in several Contracting states and existed when the [European] Convention [on Human Rights] was drafted" and accepted that such a system "cannot in itself be considered to violate article 9 of the Convention" provided its includes "specific safeguards for the individual's freedom of religion."[66] In many European countries, and not just those with an established church, religion—and Christianity in particular—is understood to be an important part of the country's national identity, not necessarily as a shared commitment to a set of spiritual truths but simply as a common cultural heritage.

This understanding of the role of religion seemed to underlie the judgment of the European Court of Human Rights in *Lautsi v Italy*, which concerned the practice of hanging crucifixes in public school classrooms.[67] At issue was whether this long-standing, legally established practice was consistent with freedom of religion under the *ECHR*. Article 9 of the *ECHR* protects "freedom of thought, conscience and religion," including the freedom to change one's religion and to manifest one's religion.[68] The court in *Lautsi* found that article 9 imposes on the state a "duty of neutrality and impartiality" toward different religious (and other) belief systems.[69] Yet, despite the court's formal commitment to neutrality,

---

66 Application no 11581/85, Commission Report, 9 May 1989, at para 45, online: www.strasbourgconsortium.org/common/document.view.php?docId=1960. See *Convention for the Protection of Human Rights and Fundamental Freedoms*, Rome, 4 November 1950 [*ECHR*], online: www.echr.coe.int/Documents/Convention_ENG.pdf.

67 Application no 30814/06, Eur Ct HR (Grand Chamber), 18 March 2011 [*Lautsi*]. The decision also considered art 2 of Protocol No 1 to the *ECHR*, above note 66, which protects the right to education and the right of parents "to ensure such education and teaching in conformity with their own religious and philosophical convictions." But see also the 12 May 1987 decision of the Federal Constitutional Court of Germany in *Crucifix Case (Classroom Crucifix Case)*, 1 BvR 1087/91 Kruzifix BVerfGE 93, in which the court held that crucifixes in the state schools of Bavaria breached art 4(1) of the German *Basic Law*.

68 *ECHR*, above note 66.

69 Above note 67 at paras 60 and 72. See also *Case of Manoussakis and Others v Greece*, Application no 18748/91, Eur Ct HR, 26 Sept 1996. For a brief discussion, see Malcolm D Evans, "Religious Symbols: An Introduction" in Silvio Ferrari &

when it considered whether the practice of hanging crucifixes in school classrooms was contrary to article 9, it appeared to apply a more limited test—asking not whether the state's display of the crucifix was religiously neutral but, instead, whether it coerced students to engage in a religious practice or indoctrinated them into a religious belief system.

The court acknowledged that "by prescribing the presence of crucifixes in State-school classrooms—a sign which, whether or not it is accorded in addition a secular symbolic value, undoubtedly refers to Christianity—the regulations confer on the country's majority religion preponderant visibility in the school environment."[70] But, in the court's view, this did not in itself amount to coercion or indoctrination contrary to article 9. In contrast to the recitation of a prayer or the teaching of scripture, the hanging of the crucifix did not compel or pressure students to participate in a religious practice and did not indoctrinate them into a particular belief system. According to the court, "a crucifix on a wall is an essentially passive symbol and . . . cannot be deemed to have an influence on pupils comparable to that of didactic speech or participation in religious activities."[71] Could it not be argued, though, that the "passive" nature of the symbol might actually contribute to its indoctrinating power? It is true that students are not required to participate in any ritual involving the crucifix, nor are they instructed about what it symbolizes. Instead, the crucifix is simply part of the environment within which students spend their days learning and interacting. It is an ordinary, natural, part of daily life. In this way, the passive presence of the crucifix affirms,

---

Rinaldo Cristofori, eds, *Law and Religion in the 21st Century* (Farnham, Surrey; Burlington, VT: Ashgate, 2010) 291 at 293–94.

70 *Lautsi*, above note 67 at para 71.

71 *Ibid* at para 72. The court added at para 74 that

> the presence of crucifixes is not associated with compulsory teaching about Christianity . . . . Italy opens up the school environment in parallel to other religions. The Government indicated in this connection that it was not forbidden for pupils to wear Islamic headscarves or other symbols or apparel having a religious connotation . . . . [T]here was nothing to suggest that the authorities were intolerant of pupils who believed in other religions, were non-believers or who held non-religious philosophical convictions.
>
> . . . [T]he applicants did not assert that the presence of the crucifix in classrooms had encouraged the development of teaching practices with a proselytising tendency, or claim that the second and third applicants had ever experienced a tendentious reference to that presence by a teacher in the exercise of his or her functions.

The court noted that it was presented with no evidence "that the display of a religious symbol on classroom walls may have an influence on pupils," and so it could not determine whether this "does or does not have an effect on young persons whose convictions are still in the process of being formed" (*ibid* at para 66).

without argument or assertion, the central place of the Roman Catholic faith in Italian society.

In deciding that the placement of crucifixes in public school classrooms does not breach the state-neutrality requirement, the court acquiesced in the Italian government's claim that the crucifix is a symbol of the national identity and Christian heritage of Italy and more substantially of the civic values of the Italian political community—values that the government claimed can be directly traced to Christian doctrine.[72] By tying religion and politics in this way, the government was able to make the crucifix into something more than a parochial symbol, something that transcends its religious origin. The crucifix in this context becomes a symbol of the culture or civic identity of Italy—a post-Christian political community.[73] It follows, then, that when the state hangs crucifixes in the schools, it is not favouring or supporting Christianity as the true faith but is simply recognizing the historical and conceptual link between Christian doctrine and the national identity and civic values of Italy. The court took the view "that the decision whether or not to perpetuate a tradition falls in principle within the margin of appreciation of the respondent State."[74]

This link between Christianity and politics, though, rests on the problematic claim that the values of democracy and tolerance emerged directly from Christianity (and are the logical, even necessary, outcome of Christian doctrine) and the disturbing claim that Christianity is

---

72 But see Ian Leigh & Rex Ahdar, "Post-Secularism and the European Court of Human Rights: Or How God Never Really Went Away" (2012) 75:6 Mod L Rev 1064, which argues that the removal of the crucifix would breach the neutrality requirement. This claim rests on a conception of neutrality that encompasses religious and nonreligious perspectives. The crucifix was placed in the classroom long ago. It is part of the *status quo*, and so its removal would be a positive, antireligious action.

73 It seems likely that many of the contemporary advocates of placing crucifixes in school classrooms believe that the crucifix symbolizes the sacrifice of Jesus and God's mercy and that these spiritual truths should be affirmed in the schools. Yet support for the practice seems also to come from those who no longer formally adhere to Catholic practice.

74 *Lautsi*, above note 67 at para 68. Additionally, the court said at para 67:

The Government, for their part, explained that the presence of crucifixes in State-school classrooms, being the result of Italy's historical development, a fact which gave it not only a religious connotation but also an identity-linked one, now corresponded to a tradition which they considered it important to perpetuate. They added that, beyond its religious meaning, the crucifix symbolised the principles and values which formed the foundation of democracy and western civilisation, and that its presence in classrooms was justifiable on that account.

uniquely tied to these values. The civic values of modern liberal democracies, such as Italy, have other, and more obvious, precursors. The
Italian government and courts conflate the plausible claim that certain
elements of Christian doctrine made possible the separation of church
and state in the West (the creation of a secular space) with the more
problematic claim that tolerance and democracy are Christian values or
values that arose directly or significantly from Christianity (and so may
be symbolized by the crucifix). Indeed, the claim made by the Italian
courts about Christianity, and more particularly Roman Catholicism, as
the foundation of these values seems remarkable in light of the church's
history and its relatively recent acceptance of religious tolerance.[75] In
making this claim about the link between Christianity and democratic
values, the Italian courts eschewed an external, objective position and
instead argued from a position within the faith community. According
to the Italian Administrative Court in *Lautsi*, Christianity is a religion of
inclusion "where it is properly understood, which of course has not always been and still is not always the case, not even thanks to those who
call themselves Christian."[76] This was an argument not about the historical impact of Christianity, or the Roman Catholic Church, but about
the proper understanding of the Christian faith, about the best reading
of Christian scripture or teaching. When the Italian courts argued that
there was a connection between Catholicism on the one hand and democracy and tolerance on the other and when they dismissed past justifi-
cations for religious oppression as erroneous, they wrote as Christians

---

75   The Administrative Court observed that "with the benefit of hindsight, it is easy
to identify in the constant central core of Christian faith, despite the inquisi-
tion, despite anti-Semitism and despite the crusades, the principles of human
dignity, tolerance and freedom, including religious freedom, and therefore, in
the last analysis, the foundations of the secular State" (quoted in *ibid* at para 15).
The Roman Catholic Church's "Declaration on Religious Freedom: *Dignitatis
Humanae*" was promulgated by His Holiness Pope Paul VI on 7 December 1965.
76   Quoted in *Lautsi, ibid.* Additionally, the Administrative Court wrote (quoted in
ibid):

> The logical mechanism of exclusion of the unbeliever is inherent in any
> religious conviction, even if those concerned are not aware of it, the sole ex-
> ception being Christianity—where it is properly understood, which of course
> has not always been and still is not always the case, not even thanks to those
> who call themselves Christian. In Christianity even the faith in an omniscient
> god is secondary in relation to charity, meaning respect for one's fellow human
> beings. It follows that the rejection of a non-Christian by a Christian implies a
> radical negation of Christianity itself, a substantive abjuration; but that is not
> true of other religious faiths, for which such an attitude amounts at most to
> the infringement of an important precept.

who were engaged in debate about the best or proper understanding of their faith.

The remarkable claim by the Italian courts that Christianity is uniquely tolerant and inclusive and lies at the foundation of the modern liberal and secular state is significantly a claim about other religions. The implicit message is that other religious traditions, most notably Islam, are incompatible with democratic values. Islam is marked off as un-Italian or undemocratic. Despite the large number of Muslims who live within democratic societies and are committed to liberal values and despite the growing literature that seeks to reconcile Islam with liberal-democratic principles, and more particularly with the separation of religion and politics, Islam is assumed to lack the doctrinal resources to embrace the values of liberty and democracy and indeed to be in irresolvable tension with these values. The further implication is that Muslims cannot be considered full members of the Italian civil and democratic community. The European Court of Human Rights' formal adherence to neutrality combined with its acceptance that Christianity is linked to the national identity and civic culture of Italy seemed to reflect European anxieties about Islam and to support a distinction between Christian secularism and political Islam.

Behind the claim that the crucifix is not simply a religious symbol but also a symbol of the Italian identity and political culture is the draw of a thicker or richer form of national identity than that offered by civic nationalism.[77] The assumption is that Italians are held together in a political community not simply by their shared commitment to liberal values or democratic institutions but by a common culture rooted in a religious tradition — if not exactly a civil religion, then at least a Christian-inspired public morality. Religion and politics are joined at the core of national identity and the root of political obligation. A Christian or post-Christian public morality may contribute to a richer or more substantial form of national identity than one that is based simply on a shared commitment to democratic principles. Yet, at the same time, the commitment to inclusion and religious neutrality — the separation of religion and politics — becomes a basis for excluding the members of other groups. The recognition of a link between Christianity and the identity and civic values of the Italian political community may serve to

---

77   See *ibid*, quoting from the decision of the Administrative Court: "Our era is marked by the ferment resulting from the meeting of different cultures with our own, and to prevent that meeting from turning into a collision it is indispensable to reaffirm our identity, even symbolically, especially as it is characterised precisely by the values of respect for the dignity of each human being and of universal solidarity . . . ."

strengthen the civic bond and to create a sense of identity and connection among many Italians, but it also serves to exclude some from that community.

The arguments made in support of the crucifix in Italian classrooms are similar to those used to justify the refusal to remove the crucifix that currently hangs in the Quebec legislature.[78] While history may justify the presence of a cross in Montreal's central public space, it cannot justify the continued presence of a cross in the Quebec legislature. This is not simply because the crucifix in the legislature was erected only seventy years ago while the cross on Mount Royal in Montreal was raised in 1924 to commemorate the cross first raised at the time of the city's founding in the seventeenth century. It is, as the *Bouchard-Taylor Report* notes,[79] because the legislative assembly is the centre of political decision making in the province and, as such, is meant to represent all of the province's citizens. Quebec was once a deeply Roman Catholic society; yet it is now the most "secular" or nonreligious part of Canada. There is no question that some of the support for the continued presence of the crucifix comes from practising Roman Catholics. However, as in Italy, resistance to the removal of the crucifix, which comes from both the political left and right in the province, seems to be motivated by anxieties about the growth of religious pluralism. The presence of the crucifix is not so much an affirmation of Roman Catholicism as it is a rejection of other religious commitments that are perceived to be incompatible with the province's post-Christian, secular culture. Significantly, the crucifix is understood to signify an ethnic identity that involves more than a shared commitment to democratic values—and more even than a common language.

These identity-based arguments seem unlikely to prevail in the Canadian courts.[80] Although religion sometimes intersects with politics in Canada, it no longer plays a role in the definition of the country's national identity. Canada some time ago embraced multiculturalism as the

---

78   The Government of Quebec has rejected calls to remove it, including a call from the Bouchard-Taylor commission, which had been mandated by the government to examine issues of religious diversity in the province. As noted earlier, the Canadian courts have held that the operation of the legislature is not subject to constitutional review, and so they have not addressed this particular issue.

79   Above note 42.

80   The Canadian courts' view of the crucifix would also be different. In a country such as Canada that has a significant Protestant community, the crucifix (rather than a bare cross) is viewed as a distinctly Roman Catholic symbol, and not as a "Christian" symbol. Crucifixes hang in separate schools (Roman Catholic schools) and are the most obvious marker of the distinction between these schools and public schools.

defining feature of its national identity and liberal-democratic values as its political bond. While there is no doubt that Canada's moral and social culture has been shaped in different ways by the Christian faith of earlier generations, any attempt to formally link Canadian national identity to a particular religious tradition would run against the country's self-conception as a multicultural (multifaith) society. The critical difference then between Italy and Canada (excluding Quebec, perhaps) is not that Canada has had to negotiate cultural, linguistic, and religious differences in a way that other countries have not. It is instead that Canada's identity has become tied to this diversity. Multiculturalism has become part of Canada's self-understanding—a constituent part of the Canadian identity. This is why no serious English-Canadian politicians would speak, as many European leaders have done recently, about the failure of multiculturalism. English-Canadian politicians may express concerns about religious accommodation going too far, but they will not be heard to question the basic commitment to religious and cultural pluralism.[81] The Canadian political community is bound not by a common language, culture, or religion but by a shared commitment to civic values such as tolerance, equality, and liberty.[82]

What is surprising about the *Lautsi* decision is not the result that crucifixes can hang in Italian school classrooms but rather the assumption that this practice is compatible with the principle of state neutrality. If the European Court of Human Rights accepted that it is legitimate for the Italian state to hang crucifixes in classrooms and, more broadly, to link Italian national identity to the society's Roman Catholic past, why did it (like most other Western courts) maintain a formal commitment to the "neutrality" requirement? Why does the court not instead present

---

81 While it is true that the claims about "going too far" might be seen as a challenge to multiculturalism, they are seldom framed in such terms. For example, the ban introduced by the current Canadian government on women wearing the niqab (face cover) when taking the citizenship oath is an act of religious exclusion (and an appeal to ignorance and fear) that the government formally defends as necessary to ensure that the oath is really being said. One of the many political purposes of the Quebec *Charter of Values* (which is discussed in Chapter 3) is to distinguish Quebec from English Canada and its commitment to multiculturalism.

82 I will not explore here the deficiencies and limitations of this "identity," and there are many. For example, it may be complained that the Canadian commitment to multiculturalism is superficial, that it rests on a form of liberal individualism and does not, and indeed cannot, respect deep diversity, or that a shared commitment to liberal-democratic values is too thin a basis to sustain national unity and political loyalty, as the ongoing Canadian existential crisis may demonstrate. The point here is simply that any attempt to *formally* link Canada's national identity to a particular religious tradition would be inconsistent with the core understanding of that identity—Canada as a multicultural political community.

religious freedom as a liberty, that is, as a ban on state coercion in religious matters? Behind the court's formal commitment to religious neutrality is the powerful idea in the West that religion should be removed from politics because it is a matter of group identity or is irrational or inaccessible. The *Lautsi* decision reflects the deep ambivalence in Western liberal democracies about religion and its relationship to politics. Like the Canadian courts, the European Court of Human Rights seems to recognize that religion and politics should be separated but that this separation cannot be complete. Where the European Court of Human Rights parts company with the Canadian courts is in its willingness to accept a formal link between religion, national identity, and political obligation. While both the European Court of Human Rights and the Supreme Court of Canada rely, at least formally, on a similar test for determining a breach of religious freedom, a test that emphasizes the state's obligation to remain neutral in spiritual matters, their application of the test is guided by different understandings of the public and political significance of religion and, more particularly, of the relationship between religion, civic values, and national identity.

H. RELIGIOUS VALUES IN PUBLIC DECISION MAKING

It is sometimes argued that religious values should be excluded from political decision making because state law must be based on reasons that are accessible to all members of the community.[83] Because religious beliefs rest on faith or familial and cultural socialization rather than reasoned judgment, they cannot provide a publicly acceptable basis for law making. To base state action on religious values would be to impose

---

83   This position is associated with John Rawls and his book *Political Liberalism* (New York: Columbia University Press, 1993), although Rawls's argument is simply that constitutional essentials should be based not on a comprehensive belief system but instead on an "overlapping consensus" among such systems. The "clash of civilizations" argument may be the Rawlsian argument stated in more general or regional terms. Both positions rest on the idea that engagement between the adherents of different belief systems must be limited because each system is fixed and impervious at a foundational level. Rawls's argument, in contrast to the "clash of civilizations" claim, is more optimistic about the possibility of agreement on principles of justice—an overlapping consensus—based on a coincidence of the political morality derived from different fundamental belief systems. Nevertheless, both arguments ignore the dynamic and evolving character of comprehensive belief systems.

the beliefs of some on others or to favour illegitimately the beliefs of some over those of others. Political actors, then, must base their actions on nonreligious values or must be able to defend their actions on nonreligious grounds, even if their deeper motives are religious in character. That, at least, is the familiar argument. The debate on this issue has been particularly vigorous in the United States, where personal religious engagement is significant and the political commitment to state neutrality in matters of religion is well-established.[84]

Two objections are often raised to the exclusion of religious values from political decision making. The first is that religious adherents should not be prevented from making political decisions based on their deeply held values and concerns because this will have the effect of excluding them from meaningful political participation. Because religion matters so deeply to its adherents and is often the foundation for their views about justice and the collective good, it may be unreasonable or unrealistic to expect them to leave their beliefs behind when they participate in public life.[85] The second and more substantial objection is that religious and secular values are not different in any way that can justify the exclusion of the former from political decision making.

The distinction between secular and spiritual values may be challenged from two directions. It is sometimes claimed that religious values (in either some or all cases) are not beyond reasoned debate and in this respect are like secular values. At the same time, it may be claimed that fundamental secular values, such as respect for human dignity or equality, rest, no less than religious values, on a basic acceptance of their truth and are the premises rather than the conclusions of reasoned political debate. Charles Taylor argues that there is no clear distinction "in

---

84   The literature on the issue is substantial, and I will make no attempt to address it directly. A sample of the different positions taken in the debate might include Robert Audi, *Religious Commitment and Secular Reason* (Cambridge, UK: Cambridge University Press, 2000); Christopher J Eberle, *Religious Conviction in Liberal Politics* (Cambridge, UK: Cambridge University Press, 2002); Kent Greenawalt, *Religious Convictions and Political Choice* (New York: Oxford University Press, 1988); and Michael J Perry, *Under God? Religious Faith and Liberal Democracy* (Cambridge, UK: Cambridge University Press, 2003).

85   See Benjamin Berger, "The Limits of Belief: Freedom of Religion, Secularism, and the Liberal State" (2002) 17 CJLS 39 at 67: "When religious conscience is properly understood as a pervasive claim upon the lives of believers, a liberalism that demands the severance of moral claims and political positions and a vision of secularism that requires an a-religious public space are irreconcilable with the freedom of the religion accorded by the *Charter*." See also David Blaikie & Diana Ginn, "Religious Discourse in the Public Square" (2006) 15:1 Const Forum Const 37.

rational credibility between religious and non-religious discourse . . . . If we take key statements of our contemporary political morality, such as those attributing rights to human beings as such, say the right to life, I cannot see how the fact that we are desiring/enjoying/suffering beings, or the perception that we are rational agents, should be any surer basis for this right than the fact that we are made in the image of God."[86] It may be that state enforcement of religious values can be viewed as objectionable (as compelling or imposing religion contrary to the constitutional commitment to freedom of religion) only if we believe that nonreligious values represent an alternative—accessible—basis for political action. However, if we view nonreligious values and practices instead as part of a "faith-based" world view, then state support for such values may also amount to (quasi-religious) compulsion or imposition on others who do not hold those values. Any reliance on fundamental values, religious or otherwise, would involve the imposition on others of a particular world view. This is the concern that lies behind the argument that political decision making, at least when it concerns fundamental issues, should be based on values that are part of an overlapping consensus and are not explicitly or exclusively tied to a particular comprehensive belief system.[87]

It is sometimes argued that an individual may draw on her religious values in political debate and decision making as long as she frames her argument in secular terms or there is a parallel secular argument that could be made to support her position. The presence of a parallel secular argument, though, may not fully address the problem of inaccessibility. While a religious adherent may be able to describe his values to others in nonreligious terms, his understanding of these values is tied to their religious foundation. The religious foundation of a value, which gives it meaning for the adherent, will shape its content. The value of life, in abstract terms, may be shared by all religious and moral traditions, but its implications in specific cases involving euthanasia or abortion, for example, will vary depending on its particular foundation. If religious reasons are excluded from political decision making because they are inaccessible, the presence of a secular argument or reason that happens to (partly) overlap with the adherent's religious reason for supporting a

---

86   Charles Taylor, *Dilemmas and Connections: Selected Essays* (Cambridge, MA: Belknap Press of Harvard University Press, 2011) at 328–29. See also Iain T Benson, "Notes Towards a (Re)Definition of the 'Secular'" (2000) 33 UBC L Rev 520; and Iain T Benson, *Living Together with Disagreement: Pluralism, the Secular and the Fair Treatment of Beliefs in Law Today* (Ballan, Australia: Connor Court Publishing, 2012).

87   See Rawls, above note 83.

particular policy will not correct the problem. If the individual's commitment to a widely shared value such as equality is based on her religion, her particular understanding of that value will be "inaccessible" to others, and this "inaccessibility" may make debate on specific issues difficult. But, as earlier noted, inaccessibility of this kind is not peculiar to religious belief systems. We may also find it difficult to understand larger or smaller components of the nonreligious perspectives—the comprehensive belief systems—of others.

The "inaccessibility" of religious beliefs and values to non-believers may be an issue in the case of revealed obligations that are highly specific (such as the ban on consuming pork) and for which there is no parallel in other belief systems, even in some loose or general form. As I will suggest in a moment, the courts have labelled beliefs of this kind as religious "practices," which the state is precluded from supporting. However, religious values that are general in character and resonate with widely held moral views cannot in any practical way be distinguished from secular values. Moral claims such as "love thy neighbour," "treat others as you would want to be treated," or "respect the equal value of all persons," whether secular or religious in form, are the premises from which individuals debate and develop more specific claims about right and duty. General principles that may be translatable across different "comprehensive" belief systems can provide the ground upon which interreligious debate or debate between religious and secular groups occurs. The extent of moral disagreement within the larger community is often overstated. Anne Phillips observes that disagreement within a particular religious tradition may be just as great as the disagreement between groups.[88] Moreover, as Anthony Appiah argues, we should be careful not to see our worlds as "hermetically sealed" or as "closed off from one another."[89] While our understanding of the views of other people (religious or otherwise) will often be approximate or partial, we have the capacity to give practical meaning to their values and concerns, and sometimes even to reach agreement. More than this, our attempts

---

88   Anne Phillips, *Multiculturalism without Culture* (Princeton, NJ: Princeton University Press, 2007) at 8: "[T]hose writing on multiculturalism (supporters as well as critics) have exaggerated not only the unity and solidity of cultures but the intractability of value conflict as well, and have often misrecognised highly contextual political dilemmas as if these reflected deep value disagreement."

89   K Anthony Appiah, *The Ethics of Identity* (Princeton, NJ: Princeton University Press, 2005) at 248. See also Jeremy Waldron, "Public Reason and 'Justification' in the Courtroom" (2007) 1 Journal of Law, Philosophy and Culture 107 at 112: "The difficulties of intercultural or religious-secular dialogue are often exaggerated when we talk about the incommensurability of cultural frameworks and the impossibility of conversation without a common conceptual scheme."

to understand the deep values of others may affect our own understanding of truth and right in subtle and sometimes significant ways.[90] A debate about the importance, or proper understanding, of basic values that does not entirely ignore or suppress their religious foundations may be manageable and even beneficial. The possibility of political dialogue depends not on our ability to separate "political morality" from its foundations but rather on our willingness to engage with others in a way that takes their concerns and interests seriously, seeks to find common ground, and recognizes that even at its most foundational level, belief is not fixed and impervious to change.

I. *CHAMBERLAIN V SURREY SCHOOL DISTRICT:* RELIGIOUS VALUES IN SCHOOL POLICY MAKING

In *Chamberlain v Surrey School District No 36*, the Supreme Court of Canada held that elected officials could draw on their religious values (or the religious values of their constituents) when making political decisions.[91] According to McLachlin CJ, "Because religion plays an important role in the life of many communities, . . . [the] views [of parents and communities] will often be motivated by religious concerns. Religion is an integral aspect of people's lives, and cannot be left at the boardroom door."[92] In *Chamberlain*, a local school board rejected a proposal to include three books depicting same-sex parent families on the list of approved teaching resources for the primary grades. The appellants challenged the board's decision on two grounds: first, that the board had acted outside its mandate under the British Columbia *School Act*, which provided that "[a]ll schools . . . must be conducted on strictly secular and non-sectarian principles,"[93] and second, that the decision violated the *Charter*. A majority of the Court, in a judgment written by McLachlin CJ, held that the school board had "acted outside the mandate of the *School Act* . . . and [its] own regulation for approval of supplementary material" when it had refused to include these three books on the list of

---

90   See Charles Taylor, *Philosophy and the Human Sciences: Philosophical Papers 2* (Cambridge, UK: Cambridge University Press, 1985) at 130. See also Berger, above note 85 at 52.

91   2002 SCC 86 [*Chamberlain*].

92   *Ibid* at para 19.

93   RSBC 1996, c 412, s 76(1).

approved teaching resources.[94] Having reached this conclusion, the majority did not have to consider whether the decision breached the *Charter*. Chief Justice McLachlin accepted that the secularism requirement in the *School Act* did not preclude the school board from taking religious values and beliefs into account when making decisions, and in particular when making decisions about curriculum. What it did require, however, was that the board "conduct its deliberations on all matters, including the approval of supplementary resources, in a manner that respects the views of all members of the school community."[95] The board could not "prefer the religious views of some people in its district to the views of other segments of the community" and it could not "appeal to views that deny the equal validity of the lawful lifestyles of some in the school community."[96] The secularism requirement "simply signals the need for educational decisions and policies, whatever their motivation, to respect the multiplicity of religious and moral views that are held by families in the school community."[97] Chief Justice McLachlin found that the board, in acting on the concerns of some parents about the morality of same-sex relationships, had failed to take seriously the right of same-sex parents, and the children of such relationships, to be equally respected within the public school system. The board in this case had "failed to proceed as required by the secular mandate of the *School Act* by letting the religious views of a certain part of the community trump the need to show equal respect for the values of other members of the community."[98]

Chief Justice McLachlin accepted that religious values may play a role in political decision making; yet at the same time she seemed to say that the state must remain neutral in matters of basic value. If the "secularism" requirement means that the schools should not favour one moral perspective over another in their teaching (that they should remain neutral on moral and religious issues), then religion (and indeed any value system) will have a role in board (and public) decision making only when it has no bite—only when it does not involve the repudiation of other values or viewpoints. Moreover, if the board's rejection of the three books for use in the primary grades amounts to the improper exclusion of gay and lesbian perspectives or lifestyles, would not the inclusion of these books, by the same token, amount to the exclusion or rejection of the religious views of those parents who regard homo-

---

94   Above note 91 at para 2.
95   *Ibid* at para 25.
96   *Ibid.*
97   *Ibid* at para 59.
98   *Ibid* at para 71.

sexuality as sinful? Can the schools affirm the equal value of same-sex relationships without, in effect, repudiating the religious belief that homosexuality is immoral or unnatural?

Chief Justice McLachlin, though, thought that the inclusion of these books as teaching materials did not amount to the affirmation of same-sex relationships and the repudiation of contrary views. What the *School Act* demanded, she said, was tolerance:

> [T]he demand for tolerance cannot be interpreted as the demand to approve another person's beliefs or practices. When we ask people to be tolerant of others, we don't ask them to abandon their personal convictions. We merely ask them to respect the rights, values and ways of being of those who may not share those convictions. The belief that others are entitled to equal respect depends, not on the belief that their values are right, but only on the belief that they have a claim to equal respect regardless of whether they are right.[99]

Tolerance requires only that we respect the right of each individual to make his own judgments and, in this case, his choice of intimate partners or family arrangements. Teaching tolerance does not require that public actors, such as the schools, affirm a particular value or viewpoint. More specifically, it does not require that the schools teach or affirm that same- and opposite-sex relationships are equally valuable. In the Chief Justice's view, the books would simply "expose" children to non-traditional family forms and encourage them to tolerate these forms. According to McLachlin CJ, the use of the three books in the kindergarten classes would encourage "discussion and understanding of all family groups."[100] Quoting La Forest J in *Ross v New Brunswick School District No 15*, she described the school as an "arena for the exchange of ideas" that "must, therefore, be premised upon principles of tolerance and impartiality so that all persons within the school environment feel equally free to participate."[101] The problem with this view, however, is that at the kindergarten level, there is no way to simply expose children to same-sex relationships as a social reality or to engage them in an open discussion about such relationships. Including these stories in the kindergarten curriculum will normalize same-sex relationships and, in effect, affirm their value. To claim otherwise is to fail to recognize the

---

99 *Ibid* at para 66.
100 *Ibid* at para 72.
101 *Ibid* at para 23.

authority of the school in the lives of students, particularly those in the primary grades.[102]

Chief Justice McLachlin also seemed to say that the reason for including these stories was to affirm the value of same-sex parent families, not to all children (some of whose parents are deeply opposed to same-sex relationships), but only to the children from such families. She stressed the importance of providing "a nurturing and validating learning experience for all children, regardless of the types of families they come from."[103] In her view, the school board should seek to affirm the personal circumstances of students from non-traditional families without imposing any views or values on other students in the school community. Yet it is not clear that affirmation can be segregated in this way, either practically or normatively. If the three books were used as teaching resources, then every student in the class would be exposed to them, regardless of his family situation or perspective. Chief Justice McLachlin recognized this but was not troubled by it:

> The number of different family models in the community means that some children will inevitably come from families of which certain parents disapprove. Giving these children an opportunity to discuss their family models may expose other children to some cognitive dissonance. But such dissonance is neither avoidable or noxious. Children encounter it every day in the public school system as members of a diverse student body. They see their classmates, and perhaps also their teachers, eating foods at lunch that they themselves are not permitted to eat, whether because of their parents religious strictures or because of other moral beliefs. They see their classmates wearing clothes with features or brand labels which their parents have forbidden them to wear. And they see their classmates engaging in behaviour on the playground that their parents have told them not to engage in. The cognitive dissonance that results from such encounters is simply part of living in a diverse society. It is also part of growing up. Through such experiences, children come to realize that not all their values are shared by others.[104]

Once again McLachlin CJ's answer to concerns about "cognitive dissonance" was that the books will do no more than "expose" students to

---

102 For a critical discussion of the case and the Chief Justice's attempt to adopt a neutral stance, see Richard Moon, "The Supreme Court of Canada's Attempt to Reconcile Freedom of Religion and Sexual Orientation Equality in the Public Schools" in David Rayside and Clyde Wilcox, eds, *Faith, Politics and Sexual Diversity in Canada and the United States* (Vancouver: UBC Press, 2011) 321.

103 Above note 91 at para 49.

104 *Ibid* at para 65.

other perspectives or ways of life. But the impact on a primary student of exposure to these books in the classroom is not the same as discovering that some of her classmates have same-sex parents. The books would be used by teachers, and, as the court has elsewhere recognized, teachers are authority figures and role models.[105] More importantly, affirmation is not an individualized process. It is not particularly affirming to a child from a same-sex parent family when a teacher says to his class that same-sex parent families are fine for those who happen to be in them, but may not be fine for anyone else, or if a teacher informs the class that while some in the community feel this is an acceptable or valuable form of family, others regard it as immoral and that both views are entitled to respect. If what children need is affirmation of the equal value of their family arrangement, then the school must do more than indicate that there are such families and that this may or may not be a good thing. We have increasingly come to recognize that our sense of self, of our value, is tied up with the recognition we receive from others. To be meaningful, the acceptance or affirmation of same-sex relationships must involve a public statement or indication that such relationships are normal and valuable.

Chief Justice McLachlin seemed to accept that the schools should affirm the equal value of same-sex parent families. Yet, at the same time, she seemed to believe that the schools should remain neutral on religious or moral matters—that the state should neither affirm nor deny the value or truth of a particular religious belief, including the belief that homosexuality is immoral. I suspect that the Court's reluctance to repudiate the religious belief that homosexuality is sinful rests in part on the view that religion is a deeply rooted part of the individual's identity that should be treated with equal respect. However much the Court may wish to avoid repudiating a widely held religious value, (religious) value neutrality is not always an option. If equality, including sexual-orientation equality, is an important public value, it should be affirmed in the schools and should underpin classroom learning, even in the face of religiously based opposition from some parents. Indeed, the failure of the public schools to affirm clearly the equal value of same-sex relationships when opposite-sex relationships are constantly represented and affirmed in books and lessons will be experienced as discrimination. We cannot include or exclude all values in or from the schools. If a school board or provincial government decides to advance or affirm a particular set of values, it must also reject other values—values that may be part of the religious commitment of some community members. Parents may have to live with the democratic consequence that their

---

105 *Trinity Western University v British Columbia College of Teachers*, 2001 SCC 31.

values are not included in the civic curriculum and perhaps even that their children are exposed to, or taught, views to which they are opposed. Of course, when affirming certain values, the schools should be sensitive to the dissonance younger students may experience when they are taught something very different at home, but this is not the same thing as remaining neutral on questions of value. If religious values may play a role in public decision making, they may be adopted or they may be repudiated. The commitment to sexual-orientation equality involves a public repudiation of the view held by some religious adherents that same-sex relationships are immoral.

J. RELIGIOUS VALUES AND RELIGIOUS PRACTICES

While the Canadian courts have said, albeit ambiguously, that religious values are not constitutionally excluded from political decision making (that religious belief may be part of the input of law making), they have, at the same time, held that the state must not support particular religious practices. But this distinction between values and practices is not a simple one. An action might be viewed as a religious practice if the reasons motivating it are religious. But if all religiously motivated actions were viewed in this way—as religious practices toward which the state must remain neutral—then religious values would be indirectly excluded from political decision making. Any state action that was based on religious values would be illegitimate. The question becomes, when is it acceptable for the state to take action based on religious reasons? Or, from the other angle, what kind of religious act—or religiously motivated act—is the state permitted to advance? The distinction that the courts seem to rely on, if only implicitly, is between, on the one hand, beliefs or actions that address civic or worldly matters and, on the other, beliefs or actions that concern the worship or honouring of God. This distinction turns on the content of the belief or action rather than its foundation. A religious belief should not play a role in political decision making if the action it calls for is spiritual in character (i.e., relates simply to spiritual concerns involving the worshipping or honouring of God). Such an action will be seen as a "private" or personal matter and labelled as a "practice."[106] However, if the belief or "value" relates to a

---

106 In this way, then, the ban on state support for religious practices may be viewed as an exclusion of certain kinds of religious values or reasons from political decision making.

civic matter (individual rights or collective welfare), then it may play a role in political decision making, and the action it calls for will be viewed as public rather than private or spiritual.

The claim that a religious belief or value may play a role in political decision making when there is a parallel secular argument (when the same or a similar position can be stated in nonreligious terms) points to this distinction between spiritual and civic. A parallel or analogous secular argument in support of a particular policy will generally (perhaps necessarily) be available when the religious value has a civic or public orientation. Or perhaps more accurately, when a religious value or argument (such as the eradication of poverty or a ban on drug use) has a secular analogue, it will be seen as addressing a public or civic concern—as seeking to advance the public interest or to prevent injury to others. When there is no parallel secular argument, we are likely to see the religious position as simply a matter of honouring God's will. In other words, a religiously motivated action will be viewed as a practice—as the worshipping or honouring of God—if nonadherents cannot understand it as relating to human welfare.[107] If the state were to support (or compel) Sunday Sabbath observance or a particular form of prayer or the wearing of hijab or if it were to oppose (or ban) the consumption of pork, it would be seen as supporting a spiritual practice contrary to section 2(a) of the *Charter*. These actions are viewed as exclusively spiritual, as acts of worship, because they cannot be understood by non-believers (by those who adhere to another world view) as advancing human good. If the ban on eating pork were based on health reasons then it could be understood and, of course, contested by non-believers. Even if these reasons were set out in scripture (and valued by

---

107 This distinction, though, can be made only from a nonreligious vantage point or from a religious perspective that distinguishes between worldly and otherworldly concerns, and so the distinction is not itself religiously neutral. No such distinction is made by those who believe that natural and other disasters are God's punishment for the nation's failure to do his will—such as the state's refusal to permit prayers in the schools. See also Lori G Beaman, "Defining Religion: The Promise and the Peril of Legal Interpretation" in Richard Moon, ed, *Law and Religious Pluralism in Canada* (Vancouver: UBC Press, 2008) 192 at 196: "[T]he very concept of religion is embedded in Western and Christian ideas about the possibility of separating everyday belief/action as an analytical and conceptual category." The genealogy of the "Great Separation" is discussed by Mark Lilla in *The Stillborn God: Religion, Politics, and the Modern West* (New York: Knopf, 2007) at 298–99: "The Great Separation did not presume or promote atheism; it simply taught an intellectual art of distinguishing questions regarding the basic structure of society from ultimate questions regarding God, the world, and human spiritual destiny . . . . Such a theological transformation is unimaginable in many religious traditions and difficult in all of them. . . ."

believers on that basis) they could be understood by non-believers as concerned with public welfare—and so as "values." But if the ban is regarded by believers as a requirement of their faith that must be obeyed because it is set out in scripture then it will be considered a religious practice. If the reasons for such a ban are enclosed within a particular spiritual belief system, they will not be understood by non-believers as concerned with public welfare. In the case of some (religiously based) state actions such as a ban on (or disfavouring of) same-sex relationships or a ban on public nudity, it may be more controversial whether the action relates to human welfare or is simply a matter of honouring God's will, because these bans may be supported by other belief systems or may be defended on grounds that are more generally accessible.

The practical issue that arises from this distinction between value and practice is whether a particular religious argument should be regarded as a legitimate contribution to political debate and addressed on its merits or whether it should be excluded from political consideration because it is nothing more than an attempt to enforce or advance a religious practice. Whether we regard religiously grounded opposition to same-sex relationships as addressing an issue of civic welfare (and part of public debate) or as simply a matter of honouring God (and excluded from political decision making) will depend on whether this opposition can be comprehended within other normative systems—as addressing public or individual welfare. While the proponents of a ban on same-sex relationships sometimes offer nonreligious reasons in support of their position, these reasons are generally so flawed that it is hard not to see them as anything but window dressing. When the advocate of a ban seems indifferent to the facts and is prepared to advance the policy in the absence of any real evidence (that the activity is harmful), it may be reasonable to assume that her true reason for supporting the ban is simply that it is God's will as manifested in scripture. Yet, we must also recognize that there is plenty of disagreement about what counts as harm to an individual or to society. Every moral system, "secular" or religious, is premised on a conception of human value and flourishing that will support certain forms of human relationship and oppose or disfavour others as worthless or degrading—as harmful.[108] In Canada the religious argument against same-sex relationships has not been ruled out *a priori* but has, instead, been addressed directly by public decision makers, who have rejected the argument and responded with legal measures

---

108 See Kent Greenawalt, "What Are Public Reasons?" (2007) 1 Journal of Law, Philosophy and Culture 79 at 91.

that ban sexual-orientation discrimination and affirm the equal value of same-sex relationships.

The question of whether a particular belief or value should be excluded from political decision making because of its religious character or should instead be addressed on its merits by public decision makers (and either accepted or rejected as public policy) has arisen in the United States in relation to the teaching of "intelligent design" or "creation science" in the public schools. The issue that has come before the courts is whether intelligent design is simply a religious doctrine with no real scientific basis that should therefore be excluded on constitutional grounds from the school curriculum or whether the merits of the scientific case for and against intelligent design should be left to the state legislature or school board to consider when deciding the content of the curriculum. Proponents of intelligent design argue that it has a scientific basis—that it relies on empirical evidence that exposes weaknesses in the theory of natural selection and supports the idea that creation was a nonrandom event or series of events. Opponents of intelligent design argue that it is not science. They claim that its proponents are uninterested in scientific method and evidence and are committed to this "theory" simply because the Bible says that God created the earth and its creatures. The US courts have sided with the argument that intelligent design is simply a religious doctrine and so ought not to be taught in the public schools.[109]

The courts recognize that religious values cannot be excluded from political decision making simply because they are part of a religious belief system. But, at the same time, they accept that the state should not support particular religious practices. The courts, then, must distinguish between religious values that may be supported by the state and religious practices toward which the state must remain neutral. It appears that the neutrality requirement will be applied only to the spiritual dimension of religion (practices). The state should remain neutral toward those elements of a religious belief system that address spiritual or otherworldly matters (such as the proper forms of worship) and can be confined to the sphere of private life. Religious values that address worldly concerns or civic issues, and are concerned with individual

---

109 See *Tammy Kitzmiller, et al v Dover Area School District, et al*, 400 F Supp 2d 707
     (MD Pa 2005). The issue has not been significant in Canada, although complaints
     have been made about publicly funded religious schools not teaching the provincial
     curriculum, which includes evolution. For a case in BC, see JH, "Atheist Group
     Files Complaint against Christian School" *Kamloops Daily News* (23 March 2010),
     online: www.kamloopsnews.ca/article/20100323/KAMLOOPS0101/303239984/-1/
     KAMLOOPS/atheist-group-files-complaint-against-christian-school.

rights or public welfare, cannot simply be excluded from political deci-sion making but must be debated on their merits—on their conception of human good or the public welfare. However, the line between the "civic" and "private" elements of a religious belief system will be the subject of contest. Where the line is drawn by the courts will reflect their views about the ordinary forms of religious worship, the nature of human welfare, and the proper scope of political action.

CHAPTER 3

THE RESTRICTION AND ACCOMMODATION OF RELIGIOUS PRACTICES

A. INTRODUCTION

Freedom of religion, understood as a liberty, precludes the state from restricting a religious practice on the grounds that it is erroneous—the wrong way to worship God. The state must have a public reason to restrict a religious practice, but any public reason may be sufficient. This was John Locke's position and also the position taken by the US Supreme Court in the case of *Employment Division, Department of Human Resources of Oregon v Smith*.[1] In Locke's opinion, just "[a]s the magistrate has no power to impose by his laws the use of any rites and ceremonies in any Church, so neither has he any power to forbid the use of such rites and ceremonies as are already received, approved, and practised by any Church."[2] The government's role, according to Locke, "is only to take care that the commonwealth receive no prejudice, and that there be no injury done to any man, either in life or estate."[3] The government may prohibit a practice such as animal slaughter provided the prohibition has a civic purpose and is not enforced exclusively against those who engage in animal slaughter for religious reasons, as a form of worship:

---

1   494 US 872 (1990) [*Oregon v Smith*].
2   John Locke, *A Letter Concerning Toleration* (1685; repr, New York: Irvington Publishers, 1979) at 197–98.
3   *Ibid* at 198.

Whatsoever is lawful in the Commonwealth cannot be prohibited by the magistrate in the Church. Whatsoever is permitted unto any of his subjects for their ordinary use, neither can nor ought to be forbidden by him to any sect of people for their religious uses. If any man may lawfully take bread or wine, either sitting or kneeling in his own house, the law ought not to abridge him of the same liberty in his religious worship; though in the Church the use of bread and wine be very different and be there applied to the mysteries of faith and rites of Divine worship. But those things that are prejudicial to the commonweal of a people in their ordinary use and are, therefore, forbidden by laws, those things ought not to be permitted to Churches in their sacred rites. Only the magistrate ought always to be very careful that he do not misuse his authority to the oppression of any Church, under pretence of public good.[4]

In *Oregon v Smith*, the US Supreme Court held that the free exercise clause of the First Amendment did not require the state to exempt individuals, who were engaged in a religious practice, from an otherwise valid law. Two Aboriginal men were dismissed from their employment with a drug rehabilitation program after it was learned that they had used peyote as part of a spiritual practice. Because the use of peyote was contrary to the state's criminal law, they were found to have been dismissed by their employer for cause and were therefore denied unemployment insurance benefits. They argued unsuccessfully that the legislative exclusion from unemployment insurance should not be applied to them, because the reason for their dismissal was that they had engaged in a religious practice.[5] Justice Scalia thought that to exempt them from the ordinary law

---

4   *Ibid* at 199. For an example of this, see *Church of the Lukumi Babalu Aye, Inc v Hialeah*, 508 US 520 at 553 (1993), in which the US Supreme Court held that a municipal ban on slaughtering "an animal in a public or private ritual or ceremony not for the primary purpose of food consumption" breached the free exercise clause of the First Amendment. The ban was put in place after the local council had learned that a group practising Santeria, which involves ritual animal slaughter, was planning to establish a church in the area.

5   The Court had to reconcile its conclusion in this case with earlier decisions in which it seemed to grant exemptions to religious groups from laws of general application, for example *Wisconsin v Yoder*, 406 US 205 (1972), in which the Court held that Amish children should be exempted from the requirement that they attend school until the age of sixteen. The Court in that case said at 220–21:

   A regulation neutral on its face may, in its application, nonetheless offend the constitutional requirement for governmental neutrality if it unduly burdens the free exercise of religion . . . . The Court must not ignore the danger that an exception from a general obligation of citizenship on religious grounds may run afoul of the Establishment Clause, but that danger cannot be allowed

would be "to make the professed doctrines of religious belief superior to the law of the land, and in effect to permit every citizen to become a law unto himself."[6] The US Congress responded to the *Oregon v Smith* decision, and its narrow reading of the free exercise clause, by enacting the *Religious Freedom Restoration Act of 1993*, which provides that the US government "shall not substantially burden a person's exercise of religion, even if the burden results from a rule of general applicability," unless "it demonstrates that application of the burden to the person (1) is in furtherance of a compelling governmental interest; and (2) is the least restrictive means of furthering that compelling governmental interest."[7]

The Canadian courts, at least formally, have adopted a different approach to the justification of limits on religious practice. According to the Canadian courts, the *Charter's* section 2(a) right to freedom of religion is breached any time the state restricts a religious practice in a nontrivial way.[8] Even when a law advances a legitimate public purpose, such as the prevention of drug use or cruelty to animals or violence in the schoolyard, the state must justify, under section 1 of the *Charter*, the law's nontrivial interference with a religious practice.[9] In *Alberta v Hutterian Brethren of Wilson Colony*, McLachlin CJ, writing for a majority of the Supreme Court of Canada, said that a law that restricts a religious practice will be upheld only if it satisfies the different elements of

---

to prevent any exception no matter how vital it may be to the protection of values promoted by the right of free exercise.

See also *Sherbert v Verner*, 374 US 398 (1963), the facts of which were similar to those in *Oregon v Smith*. Mrs Sherbert was dismissed from her sales job because she was unable for religious reasons to work on Saturdays. The Court held that the government could not ordinarily deny unemployment insurance to an individual who was dismissed from her employment because of a conflict between her religious practice and the formal requirements of the job.

6   *Reynolds v United States*, 98 US 145 at 167 (1879) quoted by Scalia J in above note 1 at 879.

7   Pub L No 103–141, 107 Stat 1488, s 3(a) & (b) (1993). A number of US states have enacted similar laws.

8   *Canadian Charter of Rights and Freedoms*, Part 1 of the *Constitution Act, 1982*, being Schedule B to the *Canada Act 1982* (UK), 1982, c 11 [*Charter*].

9   For a valuable and influential discussion of the issue, see José Woehrling, "L'obligation d'accommodement raisonnable et l'adaptation de la société à la diversité religieuse" (1998) 43 McGill LJ 325. For a review of the caselaw dealing with the obligation of private-sector employers to accommodate religious practices, see Ontario Human Rights Commission, "Creed Case Law Review" *Ontario Human Rights Commission* (May 2012), online: www.ohrc.on.ca/en/creed-case-law-review.

the test in *R v Oakes*, including the proportionality requirements.[10] The state must sometimes compromise its policies, at least to some degree, to make space for such a practice.

Yet, despite the Supreme Court of Canada's formal declaration that the state must justify any nontrivial restriction of a religious practice (or reasonably accommodate the practice), the Court has given this requirement little substance. The Court appears willing to uphold a legal restriction if it has a legitimate objective (i.e., an objective other than the suppression of an erroneous religious practice) that would be noticeably compromised if an exception were made. In other words, even though the courts have structured their approach to section 2(a) so that it has the form of an equality right (that draws on human rights code and *Charter* equality jurisprudence), they have adopted in practice a very weak standard of justification under section 1 so that the right protects only a limited form of liberty—a standard not very different perhaps from that advocated by Locke or adopted by the US Supreme Court in *Oregon v Smith*.[11] The courts' weak standard of justification for limits (their reluctance to exempt a religious practice from ordinary law) reflects their uncertainty about whether religious practices are different from other practices in a way that justifies their insulation from otherwise legitimate political action.

The Canadian courts have said that freedom of religion protects practices or activities that have for the individual "a nexus with religion" or "connect" her "with the divine" or stem from her spiritual faith.[12] These practices do not have to be part of an established belief system. Nor is it necessary that the individual or group understand them to be mandatory. A practice will fall within the scope of section 2(a) if it is

---

10 *Alberta v Hutterian Brethren of Wilson Colony*, 2009 SCC 37 [*Wilson Colony*]; *R v Oakes*, [1986] 1 SCR 103 [*Oakes*].

11 The differences between the US and Canadian approaches may simply reflect structural differences between the two bills of rights—specifically the inclusion of a separate limitations provision in the Canadian document. As described by Carolyn Evans, *Freedom of Religion under the European Convention on Human Rights* (Oxford: Oxford University Press, 2001) at 134, the approach of the European Court of Human Rights to art 9 may be similar:

> While the Commission and the Court are prepared to scrutinize State action with some care in cases where there has been overt and intentional discrimination against members of a religious group, they have generally given States a wide margin of appreciation in determining whether or not a restriction on the manifestation of religion or belief is necessary. In most cases it seems to be sufficient in practice for the State to show that it has acted in good faith in order for it to be able to justify limitations on religion or belief under Article 9(2).

12 *Syndicat Northcrest v Amselem*, [2004] 2 SCR 557 at para 46 [*Amselem*].

spiritually significant to the individual. Section 2(a) protects forms of worship or observance, including dress and diet requirements. It protects spiritual ways of life, such as living in an agrarian collective or living "separate and apart" from mainstream society. It protects proselytization activities—the teaching or promoting of one's faith to others.[13] It protects also the collective dimension of religious practice—the joining with others in worship or in advancing shared religious purposes.

According to the Canadian courts, "[t]he freedom to hold beliefs is broader than the freedom to act on them."[14] This seems to be not so much an assertion as an observation that beliefs are less likely than practices to come into conflict with government actions and so, as a practical matter, are less likely to be limited by such actions. Indeed, it is not entirely clear what it means to protect a belief that is not manifested in a practice. A practice involves outward behaviour that may be prevented or impeded in some way by government action. But when does government action interfere with, or restrict, a belief? Attempts by the state to indoctrinate individuals into a particular faith or belief system might be seen as an interference with their (existing) beliefs, although inculcation of religion appears already to be caught by the ban on state support for religion. The state might also be seen as interfering with belief when it requires an individual to participate in an activity that he regards as immoral—as contrary to his spiritual commitments—for example, when it requires a pacifist to serve in the military.[15] The issue becomes more difficult, though, when the state does not require the individual to engage in a practice that is contrary to his religious beliefs but instead requires him to do what, at least in his view, amounts to supporting or condoning an activity that he views as immoral, for example, when it enacts an antidiscrimination law that prohibits a market actor from

---

13   The proselytization practices of the Jehovah's Witness community were the subject of several of the Supreme Court of Canada's pre-*Charter* freedom of religion decisions. See, for example, *Saumur v City of Quebec*, [1953] 2 SCR 299, which is discussed in Chapter 1. The European Court of Human Rights recognized a right to engage in proselytization in *Kokkinakis v Greece*, Application no 14307/88, Eur Ct HR (Chamber), 23 May 1993. In *Larissis and others v Greece*, Application nos 140/1996/759/958-960, Eur Ct HR, 24 February 1998, this right was found not to protect military officers seeking to convert those under their command.

14   *Trinity Western University v British Columbia College of Teachers*, 2001 SCC 31 at para 36 [*TWU*].

15   See Chapter 7 for a discussion of conscientious objection to military service. The term "freedom of conscience" has sometimes been applied to the right of the individual not to be compelled to act in a way that is contrary to her religious beliefs (although, as discussed in Chapter 7, the term is now most often used to refer to the protection of nonreligious moral positions).

denying services to a gay and lesbian group. It cannot be enough that the religious belief of an individual or group is rejected or disfavoured by the state in its public policy, provided the individual or group is not prevented from practising its religion. The question then is, what form or degree of compelled support or involvement will count as an interference with religious belief or freedom of "religious conscience," subject of course to limits under section 1?

B. *R v EDWARDS BOOKS AND ART LTD*

The Supreme Court of Canada has decided a number of cases involving state restriction of a religious practice, beginning with *R v Edwards Books and Art Ltd.*[16] In that case, several retailers challenged the constitutionality of an Ontario law that prohibited stores from operating on Sunday unless they were under a certain size and were closed on Saturday. A majority of the Court, in a judgment written by Dickson CJ, accepted that the purpose of the law was not to enforce Sunday as the Sabbath (a religious practice) but was instead to create a common pause day, enabling retail workers to be with their families at least one day during the week. However, Dickson CJ held that even though the law did not compel anyone to engage in a religious practice, it restricted *indirectly* the religious practice of those who regarded Saturday as the Sabbath and so breached section 2(a). He recognized that if a Jewish or Seventh-day Adventist retailer was required by law to remain closed on Sunday, she would find it very costly, perhaps commercially unviable, to follow her religion and remain closed on Saturday as well.

The claim that the Sunday closing law *indirectly* restricted the religious practice of Saturday Sabbatarians raised two issues for the Court. The first concerned the type or degree of burden on religious practice that would breach section 2(a). If a law does not ban a religious practice outright but

---

16   [1986] 2 SCR 713 [*Edwards Books*]. A number of other Supreme Court of Canada "accommodation" decisions are examined in later chapters, including *RB v Children's Aid Society of Metropolitan Toronto*, [1995] 1 SCR 315, in which the state was justified in overriding the parents' right to make decisions about the medical treatment of their infant child; *Young v Young*, [1993] 4 SCR 3, in which it was determined that the "best interests of the child" test in custody or access decisions did not breach s 2(a) or was a justified restriction under s 1; and *AC v Manitoba (Director of Child and Family Services)*, 2009 SCC 30, in which it was held that the "best interests of the child" test in cases concerning medical treatment of an older minor did not breach the *Charter*, particularly if the assessment of the minor's best interests took into account her religious views.

simply makes engagement in the practice more difficult, its interference with (or burden on) the practice might be either minor or substantial. As a practical matter, not every burden on religious practice can be treated as a violation of section 2(a) that the government must justify under section 1. How significant, then, must the burden or impediment be before a court will decide that it breaches section 2(a)? Chief Justice Dickson accepted that "trivial or insubstantial" burdens on religious practice would not breach section 2(a): "Section 2(a) does not require the legislature to eliminate every minuscule state-imposed cost associated with the practice of religion. Otherwise the *Charter* would offer protection from innocuous secular legislation such as a taxation act that imposed a modest sales tax extending to all products, including those used in the course of religious worship."[17] A sales tax on Bibles or other items used in religious worship may have an impact on a religious practice, making it more costly, but not to such an extent that the tax should be seen as a restriction on freedom of religion that the government must justify. However, in some cases it may be difficult to decide whether an interference is trivial or substantial.[18]

The second, and more fundamental, issue concerned the state's responsibility for the "impact" on a religious practice of a law that advances an otherwise legitimate public purpose. When should the state be seen as responsible for the "burden on" a particular religious practice, and when should the disadvantage be seen simply as a "cost of" the practice, for which the state is not responsible? The provincial government had argued that any harm to the business interests of Saturday Sabbatarians was the consequence of their religious practice rather than the law. Justice Beetz, in his dissenting judgment, agreed with the government. In his view, religious commitment sometimes involves costs or burdens for which the state should not be held responsible. He thought that while section 2(a) prohibits the state from restricting religious practices (from imposing burdens or penalties on particular practices), it does not require the state to facilitate or support such practices. And, in his view, state support for religious practice was what the retailers in this case were seeking. He observed that if the government had not established a common pause day (Sunday or otherwise) and had permitted stores to remain open every day of the week, then anyone who wanted to keep either Saturday or Sunday as the Sabbath would have

---

17   *Edwards Books*, above note 16 at para 97.

18   This question (whether an interference with a religious practice is trivial) is connected to the issue raised in the s 1 analysis in later judgments such as *Wilson Colony*, above note 10, of whether the individual retains some choice or ability to practise his religion despite the restrictive state action.

been at a competitive disadvantage. For religious reasons they would have had to close on Saturday or Sunday, one day of the week, while other retailers could have remained open for the whole of the week. For Beetz J, the fact that observant Jews (and others) would be at a relative disadvantage even if there were no Sunday closing law made clear that the disadvantage or burden at issue arose from their religious commitment and not from the law, which advanced a legitimate public policy.

Chief Justice Dickson acknowledged "that the state is normally under no duty under s. 2(a) to take affirmative action to eliminate the natural costs of religious practices."[19] However, he thought that in this particular case the "burden on" religious practice was the consequence of the Sunday closing law. The Act in question had the effect of creating a "purely statutory disadvantage" in that it required the Saturday observer to be closed for "an extra day relative to the Sunday observer": "Just as the Act makes it less costly for Sunday observers to practise their religious beliefs, it thereby makes it more expensive for some Jewish and Seventh-day Adventist retailers to practise theirs."[20] The Chief Justice noted that the Sunday closing requirement did not simply impose a burden on the religious practice of those who would keep Saturday as the Sabbath; it also gave Christians, who honour Sunday as the Sabbath, an advantage over Saturday Sabbatarians. While Dickson CJ was unwilling to see the law as compelling a religious practice (or even as having a religious purpose), the Christian roots of the law and its favouring of Christian practice (its unequal impact on different religious groups) seemed to play a role in his determination that the law (indirectly) restricted the religious liberty of Saturday Sabbatarians. In the Chief Justice's view, the state should endeavour to advance its civic objective in a way that does not disadvantage one group of believers relative to another. We can see in the Chief Justice's reasoning a link between the two dimensions of religious freedom. State support or preference for a particular religious practice may also be seen as disadvantaging the practices of one religious group relative to another (or as excluding the members of one group from a benefit). When the relative disadvantage is significant, it may be viewed as a limitation or restriction on the practice of the nonfavoured religious group. The Court in *Edwards Books* found that the purpose of the Sunday closing law did not compel or promote a religious practice, even though the choice of Sunday reflected the dominant religious practice in the community. The Court held instead that the law restricted religious freedom because it

19   Above note 16 at para 111.
20   *Ibid.*

had the *effect* of disadvantaging the members of one religious group relative to another.

However, Dickson CJ, for the majority of the Court in *Edwards Books*, upheld the restriction under section 1, as reasonable and demonstrably justified. He accepted that the law had a substantial and compelling purpose and impaired the freedom no more than was necessary, since it permitted smaller retail operations to open on Sunday if they were closed on Saturday. The retailers had argued that the exception in the law (that enabled smaller operations to open on Sunday) should have included all stores, regardless of size, that were operated by Saturday Sabbatarians. In holding that the exception was not unduly narrow, the Chief Justice indicated that the state should be given considerable latitude in deciding both the necessity and the scope of an exception. He noted that a larger exception would detract from the effectiveness of the law's policy, the creation of a common pause day.[21] While Dickson CJ was prepared to find that the law breached section 2(a) (even though it advanced a secular civic purpose), he found that the law's purpose, the creation of a common pause day, was sufficient to justify the limit. At the first stage of his analysis, he seemed to regard freedom of religion as an equality right while at the second stage (section 1), he treated it as simply a liberty to practise one's religion that is subject to limits in the public interest.

Justice Wilson, dissenting in *Edwards Books*, found that the restriction was not justified under section 1, because the partial exemption was unprincipled:

> [T]he legislature must decide whether to subordinate freedom of religion to the objective of a common pause day, one scheme of justice, or subordinate the common pause day to freedom of religion, the competing scheme of justice, and, having decided which scheme of justice to adopt, it must then apply it in all cases . . . . [The scheme] does not affirm a principle which is applicable to all. It reflects rather a failure on the part of the legislature to make up its mind which scheme of justice to adopt.[22]

Justice Wilson's dissent raised an issue that resurfaces in many of the Court's later "accommodation" decisions: the tension between the Court's commitment to resolve *Charter* issues on a principled basis and the un-

---

21   Chief Justice Dickson was not prepared to enlarge the legislative accommodation, nor can we be certain that he would have ordered the legislature to establish a narrow exemption if the legislature had not already done so.

22   Above note 16 at para 203.

avoidably pragmatic character of religious accommodation, which I will explore later in this chapter.[23]

C. *R v JONES*

The appellant in *R v Jones* was an Alberta pastor who educated his own and other children in the basement of his church.[24] The Alberta *School Act* permitted home-schooling and private religious schools, but the Act required parents who wished to withdraw their children from the public system and educate them at home to apply for permission from the Department of Education.[25] Mr Jones refused to make such an application arguing that he would be acting against his religious beliefs if he were to ask secular authorities for permission to educate his children according to "God's will."[26] He believed that when making decisions about the education of his children, he was answerable only to God.

A majority of the Supreme Court of Canada held that the requirement that Mr Jones apply to the Department of Education for permission to home-school his children (which was separate from any educational or curricular standards established by the *School Act*) either did not interfere with his religious freedom or was a trivial interference and so did not amount to a breach of section 2(a). According to Wilson J, "[i]t does not, in my view, offend the applicant's freedom of religion that he is required under the statute to recognize a secular role for the school authorities."[27] She went on to say that even if the legislation did affect Mr Jones's beliefs, "not every effect of legislation on religious beliefs or practices" breaches section 2(a).[28] But was this only a trivial burden on his religious belief or practice? There are two ways in which the state's

---

23   Generally speaking, s 1 has played a small role in s 15 cases; if a law is found to breach s 15, it is unlikely to be justified under s 1. In s 2(a) cases, the opposite seems to occur. The courts are quick to find a breach of s 2(a) but more often than not will then find that the breach is justified under s 1. The courts' reliance on s 1 in freedom of religion cases (and the contrast with s 15 cases) may reflect the courts' ambivalence about religion—which they see as an identity at the s 2(a) stage and as a choice or judgment at the s 1 stage. As noted in Chapter 1, a similar ambivalence about common law relationships—or cohabiting partners—may explain the use of s 1 in the recent equality rights case of *Quebec (AG) v A*, 2013 SCC 5.

24   [1986] 2 SCR 284.

25   RSA 1980, c S-3, s 143(1)(a).

26   Above note 24 at para 3.

27   *Ibid* at para 63.

28   *Ibid* at para 65.

interference with an individual's religious belief or practice may be described as trivial. First, a state measure may be seen as a trivial interference when it limits the individual's religious practice only partly or indirectly—when, as noted in *Edwards Books*, it amounts to only a minor impediment. However, if Mr Jones believes that he is not answerable to state authorities, then the *School Act* requirement is directly contrary to his religious beliefs and does not have simply an incidental effect on his belief or practice. Second, an interference may be seen as trivial because it restricts a belief or practice that is not a central or important part of the individual's religious belief system. But, as the Supreme Court of Canada has acknowledged on numerous occasions, this is not the sort of judgment a court can or should make when considering claims under section 2(a).[29] While a court may sometimes find it necessary to determine the sincerity of an individual's spiritual beliefs, it should generally refrain from making any judgment about the importance or centrality of a belief or practice to a particular religious belief system. Of course, as I will argue later, it is not clear how a court is to balance competing civic and religious interests if it is unable to attach particular weight to the religious interest at the limitations stage of the analysis.[30]

The problem with Mr Jones's claim was not that the state had interfered with his religious practice in only a trivial way or that the affected religious belief or practice was a trivial part of his belief system. The problem, instead, was that his claim amounted to a complete rejection of state authority. Mr Jones was not objecting to a state requirement that he teach his children things inconsistent with his religious beliefs, such as sex education or evolution. He was objecting to the very idea of state authority—to the state's claim to oversee his actions, or at least those that relate to the education of his children. Mr Jones believed that he was answerable to God and to no one else. The mere assertion of authority by the state over Mr Jones was contrary to his religious belief in the supremacy of God. Not surprisingly, the Court was unwilling to treat the rejection of state authority, regardless of how that authority is exercised, as a matter of religious freedom under section 2(a). When the state enacts a law that interferes with the religious practice of some members of the general community, it may be required under section 2(a) to accommodate that practice. But it is quite another thing for an

---

29   See, for example, the judgment of La Forest J, *ibid* at para 20.

30   In the more recent case of *R v NS*, 2012 SCC 72 [*NS*], which is examined later in this chapter, the Supreme Court of Canada seemed to say that the significance of the practice should be taken into account when the court is balancing competing interests. Yet, in that case, the Court appeared to give the practice little or no weight and to give clear priority to the competing interest in a fair trial.

individual to argue that any exercise of state power interferes with her religious freedom. While Mr Jones may have a right to home-school his children, he does not have the right to do so free of any state oversight. This may be what Wilson J was getting at when she held (initially) that the law did not breach section 2(a), although formally her position was that the law did not restrict Mr Jones's religious belief or practice and not, as I have suggested, that his belief or practice fell outside the scope of section 2(a) protection.[31]

The plausibility of Mr Jones's argument rests on the widely held assumption that the actions of the secular state are based exclusively on nonreligious values or concerns. In Mr Jones's view, the nonreligious or secular state was interfering with a religious or spiritual matter—the education of his children. But if government action rests on the religious and nonreligious values of its citizens (if the commitment to public secularism does not require the exclusion of all religious values and concerns from political decision making), then Mr Jones is asserting the right to be free from any value-based oversight of his actions, an extreme form of libertarianism. He is not simply arguing for the right to live according to spiritual rather than secular (nonreligious) values. He is instead claiming a right to live according to his understanding of fundamental (spiritual) values rather than those determined by the democratic community. A democratic government, though, must sometimes take collective action based on judgments about what is right and just, adopting the views or values of some and rejecting those of others. Remembering that laws may be grounded on religious or secular values could also help us to resolve or reduce the perceived tension between the two assertions in the preamble of the *Constitution Act, 1982* that our political community is subject to God and to the rule of law.[32] The reference to God may be a reminder that law must be grounded in deeper values that for many people are religious or that fundamental rights are not simply granted to citizens by the state but have a deeper foundation.

---

31   There is a parallel between Mr Jones's claim and the parents' claim in the later *SL v Commission scolaire des Chênes*, 2012 SCC 7 [*SL*]. In both cases, the claimants described their belief or practice in very broad terms—not just as a particular activity, which they claimed was being interfered with by the state, but as a view, or belief, about their relationship to society and to the state, which challenged the prevailing assumptions of democratic politics.

32   Schedule B to the *Canada Act 1982* (UK), 1982, c 11.

D. *TRINITY WESTERN UNIVERSITY v BRITISH COLUMBIA COLLEGE OF TEACHERS*

In *Trinity Western University v British Columbia College of Teachers*, the issue was whether the British Columbia College of Teachers [BCCT] acted outside its powers when it refused to accredit the teacher training program of a private evangelical Christian university because the program taught or affirmed the view that homosexuality was sinful.[33] In deciding not to accredit the Trinity Western University [TWU] program, the BCCT referred specifically to the contract of "Responsibilities of Membership in the Community of Trinity Western University," which teachers and students were expected to sign. Of particular concern to the BCCT was the obligation, assumed by teachers and students, to "refrain from practices that are biblically condemned" such as "homosexual behaviour."[34] According to the BCCT, an institution that wishes to train teachers for the public school system must "provide an institutional setting that appropriately prepares future teachers for the public school environment, and in particular for the diversity of public school students."[35]

The majority of the Supreme Court of Canada, in a judgment written by Iacobucci and Bastarache JJ, held that the decision of the BCCT to deny accreditation to TWU's teaching program should be overturned. The majority found that while the BCCT acted properly in considering whether the TWU program might contribute to discrimination against gays and lesbians in the public schools, the college should also have taken account of the religious freedom rights of TWU faculty, students, and graduates. "The issue at the heart of this appeal," said the majority, "is how to reconcile the religious freedoms of individuals wishing to attend TWU with the equality concerns of students in B.C.'s public school system. . . ."[36] The majority observed that the denial of accreditation "places a burden on members of a particular religious group . . . pre-

---

33   Above note 14.

34   *Ibid* at para 4. While the contract prohibited sex outside marriage for heterosexuals, it prohibited same-sex physical relations in any context.

35   *Ibid* at para 11. A distinct issue is whether TWU's policy unfairly discriminated against gays and lesbians as students in the program or as applicants to the program. This appears to be the issue in the recent debate concerning the accreditation of a law program at TWU, particularly since the number of students admitted into Canadian law schools is still very limited. The extent to which religious organizations are or should be exempted from antidiscrimination laws is examined in the next chapter.

36   *Ibid* at para 28.

venting them from expressing freely their religious beliefs and associating to put them into practice."[37] The BCCT decision means that TWU must abandon its religiously based "community standards" if it is to run a program that trains teachers for the public school system. Graduates of TWU "are likewise affected because the affirmation of their religious beliefs and attendance at TWU will not lead to certification as public school teachers. . . ."[38]

If a teacher engages in discriminatory conduct, she "can be subject to disciplinary proceedings before the BCCT"; but, said the majority, the right of gays and lesbians to be free from discrimination is not violated simply because a teacher holds discriminatory views.[39] According to the majority, "the proper place to draw the line in cases like the one at bar is generally between belief and conduct. The freedom to hold beliefs is broader than the freedom to act on them."[40]A teacher may believe that homosexuality is sinful or wrongful, and even that gays and lesbians are less worthy or deserving than others, but as long as she does not act on those views, denying benefits to, or imposing burdens on, particular individuals because of their sexual orientation, she will not be found to have breached their right to equality. The majority found no evidence that any TWU graduate had acted in a discriminatory way in the classroom. And so the limitation on the religious freedom of the staff and graduates of TWU (the denial of accreditation) was imposed in the absence of any evidence that the program had a detrimental impact on the school system.[41] The majority concluded that in the absence of any

---

37   *Ibid* at para 32.

38   *Ibid*.

39   *Ibid* at para 37.

40   *Ibid* at para 36. The majority judgment seemed to say that had there been evidence of clear and direct acts of discrimination on the part of TWU graduates, the BCCT would have been justified in refusing to accredit the TWU teacher training program. Yet, it is not clear why this should be so. Once the court distinguished between antigay/antilesbian belief and action, and accepted that a teacher may hold such beliefs provided he does not act on them, why was it relevant whether any TWU graduates had engaged in acts of discrimination? If belief and action are separable in this way (public action as wrongful and personal belief as not), then TWU, even though it supported antigay and antilesbian views, should not be held responsible for any discriminatory actions taken by its graduates. Similarly, the improper actions of some graduates should not affect the accreditation of other graduates who may believe that homosexuality is immoral but refrain from engaging in acts of discrimination. The inconsistency in the majority's reasoning may reflect a deeper uncertainty about the distinction between belief and action in the school context.

41   The majority noted that the TWU community standards simply prescribed the conduct of members while attending TWU and so gave no reason to anticipate

"concrete evidence that training teachers at TWU fosters discrimination in the public schools of B.C.," the BCCT had no grounds to deny accreditation to TWU and interfere with the religious freedom of TWU instructors and students to hold certain beliefs.[42]

While the distinction between belief and action is central in human rights codes (which prohibit acts of discrimination in the market but do not otherwise regulate an individual's beliefs or the decisions he makes concerning "private" matters), it may not be applicable to the role of a teacher in a public school. An important part of a teacher's role is to teach her students basic values, including tolerance for different religious belief systems and respect for the equal worth of all people. As the majority in *TWU* observed, "Schools are meant to develop civic virtue and responsible citizenship, to educate in an environment free of bias, prejudice and intolerance."[43] Teachers, though, do not simply instruct students in these values. They are role models and counsellors. If sexual-orientation equality is to be affirmed in the public schools, teachers must do more than simply refrain from direct acts of discrimination against gay and lesbian students. A teacher, when confronted with bigoted words from students about gays and lesbians, should contradict those words or when approached by a student who is struggling with his sexual identity should provide support and reassurance or direct him to an individual or group that can offer support.[44] Because the public values of the school curriculum (broadly understood) are taught by example and because they must be affirmed in different ways, it may be that a teacher who is not personally committed to these values cannot perform his role effectively.

This is not to say that individual teachers should be closely examined on their views about sexual-orientation equality (or racial or gender equality). A serious probe into the individual's thoughts or attitudes about sexual orientation might involve too great an invasion into her personal sphere. Nor should we preclude an individual from teach-

---

intolerant behaviour by TWU-trained teachers in the public schools. The Court also said that even if some or all of the graduates of TWU believe that homosexuality is sinful, they are as Christians bound to treat others, even sinners, with love and respect. The university was regarded as a private religious institution performing a religious mission, even though it was seeking to train teachers for the public school system.

42   Above note 14 at para 36.

43   *Ibid* at para 13. Also, a teacher in the public system must be able "to support all children regardless of race, colour, religion or sexual orientation with a respectful and nonjudgmental relationship . . ." (*ibid* at para 75).

44   This appears to have been the position of L'Heureux-Dubé J in her dissenting judgment in *TWU*.

ing in the public schools simply because we suspect he may be racist or homophobic — because, for example, he belongs to a particular church or attended a particular religious school.[45] But this is not the same as saying that it is all right to employ an antigay or antilesbian teacher provided she refrains from explicit acts of discrimination in the classroom. A teacher should be excluded from the schools if he has indicated in his public statements or actions that he regards homosexuality as sinful or objectionable, even though there is no evidence that he has directly discriminated against gays and lesbians in the classroom. He should be excluded because discrimination is sometimes subtle and difficult to prove but also because a teacher should do more than simply tolerate gays and lesbians.

In *Ross v New Brunswick School District No 15*, the Supreme Court of Canada held that an individual who holds racist views as evidenced by her words or actions outside the classroom may be disqualified from serving as a classroom teacher in the public schools.[46] Justice La Forest, for the Court, upheld the decision of an adjudicator, appointed under the New Brunswick *Human Rights Act*, that ordered the school board to remove from the classroom a teacher who had expressed in a public setting racist views, which he claimed were religiously based. In *Ross*, there was no evidence that the teacher had treated any minority students in his class unfairly, or differently from other students, or had deviated from the curriculum and taught racist views. However, because Mr Ross had expressed racist opinions at public meetings and in the local media, students in his school (and the general community) had come to know of his views. The Court found that Mr Ross's public racist statements had "poisoned" the learning environment in the school.[47] The Court recognized that a teacher is a role model, an authority figure, and a conduit for public values. Public knowledge of Mr Ross's racist views mattered because his support for such views might have legitimized them in the minds of some students and undermined the school's affirmation of racial equality. If all that is expected of a teacher is that she refrain from teaching racist views, then it might be possible to separate what she says and does in the classroom from what she says and does outside, on her own time. There are very few jobs from which an individual would be dismissed because he (publicly) expressed racist views after work hours

---

45 Moreover, no person is free entirely of the taint of prejudice, and so there is no simple or easy test for determining whether someone is or is not homophobic (or racist or sexist).

46 [1996] 1 SCR 825 [*Ross*]. See also *Kempling v BCCT*, 2005 BCCA 327, in which the teacher had signalled his intent to act on his antigay beliefs in the school.

47 *Ibid* at paras 40 & 41.

(unless contrary to the *Criminal Code*). Moreover, there are views that a teacher is not permitted to express inside the classroom but is free to express outside. For example, a teacher should not expressly support the Liberal Party, or the Communist Party, inside the classroom but is permitted to do so outside. We expect the teacher in the classroom to remain neutral on issues of partisan politics. But in the case of racial equality, we expect more than formal neutrality in the classroom. We expect the teacher to positively support the value of equality. A teacher who publicly affirms racist views cannot perform this role. It would seem even more obvious that a teacher training program that affirms such views does not adequately prepare students to teach in the public school system.

The issue in the *TWU* case was not whether a particular graduate and prospective teacher might be antigay or antilesbian because she attended an educational institute that affirmed antigay or antilesbian views. It was, instead, whether a teacher training program that affirmed values that are incompatible with those of the civic curriculum should be denied accreditation because it will not adequately prepare its students to teach in the public school system—a system in which gays and lesbians should be treated with equal respect and not simply tolerated. Had the BCCT denied accreditation to a teacher training program that had a racist element in its curriculum, it seems unlikely that the BCCT's decision would have been overturned by the Court, even though not every graduate of the program would carry the lesson of racism with him. A program that taught or affirmed values so fundamentally at odds with the basic civic values of the public school system would not be accredited. Yet TWU sought accreditation for a program that supported values the BCCT thought were incompatible with the civic mission of the public schools—based on the public commitment to sexual-orientation equality expressed in both provincial and federal human rights codes. The existence of TWU, and more specifically its teacher training program, rests on a belief that the values of those who teach are important in the education process. TWU recognizes that its students will become better Christians, or Christian school teachers, if they are taught in an environment that is fully Christian in its values and practices. This is why TWU requires that all instructors adhere to the code of conduct, which, among other things, forbids "homosexual behaviour." Even if antigay views are not an explicit part of the teacher training program, they form part of the ethos of TWU. Moreover, TWU has applied for accreditation so that it can train teachers who will support or model evangelical Christian virtues in the public school system.

The Court in *TWU* seemed unwilling to confront the antigay or antilesbian content of the TWU program. The most obvious explanation for this is that the Court wanted to avoid repudiating, directly, the religious view that homosexuality is sinful or, at least, to avoid excluding from the schools teachers who believe that homosexuality is sinful. In the Court's view, the public schools are a "secular" or common space that must be open to individuals from diverse religious communities or belief systems. The requirement that public schools be inclusive and respect diversity in the community may be understood to mean that they must be "agnostic" or neutral on questions of religious truth or on issues that are the subject of religious or moral disagreement in the community. Or it may mean that the schools must tolerate all moral and religious values or perspectives—that they must not exclude or marginalize any particular view. Yet the difficulty with this position is that a school is not simply a public forum. Students should be educated in an environment where everyone is treated with equal respect, regardless of race, gender, or sexual orientation. The public schools cannot include or tolerate those views that oppose diversity and deny respect to certain individuals or groups on racial or other grounds. The schools have a civic purpose that is incompatible with certain religious and moral perspectives. If the public schools are to prepare students for life in a culturally and religiously diverse society, and a democratic political community, they must foster civic virtues such as religious tolerance, racial equality, and democratic engagement. While the schools should endeavour to respect deeply held religious commitments, they cannot be neutral toward, or even tolerate, all values. The affirmation of any value, or set of values, will involve the exclusion or rejection of other values, perspectives, or commitments in the community, including the deeply held religious beliefs of some teachers, parents, and students.

Because the public school system is meant to encompass all members of the community, whatever their religious beliefs, the Court in *TWU* was unwilling to accept that the adherents of widely held religious views could not serve as teachers or that a teacher training program affirming such views did not adequately prepare teachers to work in the public school system. Instead, the Court struck an awkward balance: the individuals are included (and may serve as teachers), but their beliefs are not (and must not be manifested in the classroom). The individual must leave her religious beliefs about homosexuality at the entry to the school and must act in accordance with the civic curriculum's values of tolerance and respect. She must separate her private beliefs from her public actions and conform to, and even teach, civic values that are at odds with her personal religious beliefs. This approach fits with the contemporary understanding of public secularism as the exclusion of religion from public life, or the "privatization" of religious commitment.

Yet, if an individual's religious beliefs should be respected because they are deeply rooted, is it realistic to expect him to put them aside when he serves as a teacher? The Court in *TWU* accepted that religious beliefs are a central part of the individual's identity and should therefore be respected and even accommodated; yet, at the same time, the Court also accepted that the individual can and should separate herself from her religious beliefs when participating in public life—or at least should do so if her beliefs are inconsistent with public values. As noted in Chapter 2, in the *Chamberlain v Surrey School District No 36* case, McLachlin CJ observed that because "[r]eligion is an integral part of people's lives," it is unrealistic to ask the members of a school board to leave their religious values and concerns "at the boardroom door" and take no account of them when making decisions.[48]

Even if the general community must tolerate the expression of a wide range of views, including some that are sexist or racist or antigay, it does not follow that the schools should remain neutral on these issues or that all individuals, regardless of their religious beliefs, can effectively perform the role of teacher. The Court downplayed the teacher's role and described sexual-orientation equality in narrow terms to avoid the conclusion that a particular religious teaching program does not adequately prepare its graduates to serve as teachers in the public school system. The Court did this, I suppose, because it thought that the state fails to treat religious believers with equal respect when it repudiates their beliefs.

E. *SYNDICAT NORTHCREST V AMSELEM*

In *Syndicat Northcrest v Amselem*, the Supreme Court of Canada held that a condominium association's refusal to permit Orthodox Jewish unit owners to construct succahs on their balconies, as part of the Jewish festival of Sukkot, breached their freedom of religion under the Quebec *Charter of Human Rights and Freedoms*.[49] Because a nonstate actor imposed the restriction on religious practice, the *Canadian Charter of*

---

48   2002 SCC 86 at para 19.

49   *Amselem*, above note 12; CQLR c C-12 [Quebec *Charter*]. The condominium bylaws, to which all unit owners formally agreed before purchasing or occupying their particular unit, prohibited decorations, alterations, and constructions on their balconies. However, the bylaws also provided that an individual owner might apply to the condominium association for an exemption from this general prohibition. For a discussion of the case, see Richard Moon, "Religious Commitment and Identity: *Syndicat Northcrest v. Amselem*" (2005) 29 Sup Ct L Rev 201

Rights and Freedoms was not applicable. However, the majority judgment of Iacobucci J was clear that "the principles . . . applicable in cases where an individual alleges that his or her freedom of religion is infringed under the Quebec *Charter*" are also applicable to a claim under section 2(a) of the Canadian *Charter*.[50]

In holding that the condominium association had violated the appellants' freedom of religion, Iacobucci J made two significant determinations concerning the scope of the freedom. First, he held that a spiritual practice or belief will fall within the protection of section 2(a) even though it is idiosyncratic and not part of an established or widely held religious belief system. Second, a practice will be protected under section 2(a) even though it is not regarded as obligatory by the individual claimant. Freedom of religion protects practices that have spiritual significance for the individual, subjectively connecting her to the divine.[51] So even though not all of the appellants in this case regarded the practice of erecting a succah on their property as a religious obligation, the practice was protected because it had for them spiritual significance. The two rabbis who gave evidence at the *Amselem* trial gave different answers to the question of whether residing in a personal succah was a religious obligation. The Court, though, had no wish to adjudicate a dispute about religious doctrine. According to Iacobucci J, the Court should consider the sincerity of an individual's belief but not its validity—neither its objective truth nor the extent of its acceptance within the particular religious group. It was not for the courts, said Iacobucci J, to decide what is required by a particular belief system or which interpretation of that system is correct. Religion, he said, is a matter of "personal choice and individual autonomy and freedom."[52] This individualistic conception of religion seemed to involve more than a recognition that religious beliefs are contestable, that (from a public perspective) there is no single authentic version of Judaism, and that religious belief systems or traditions may be interpreted by individual adherents in a personal way.

There was no doubt in this case that the claimants had a sincere belief in the spiritual significance of the succah. Erecting and "residing in" a succah (on one's property) is an established practice in Judaism, even

---

and Robert E Charney, "How Can There Be Any Sin in Sincere? State Inquiries into Sincerity of Religious Belief" (2010) 51 Sup Ct L Rev (2d) 47.

50 *Amselem*, above note 12 at para 37. As will become apparent in the discussion that follows, I am not sure that the Court was correct in equating private and public sector restrictions on religious practice.

51 *Ibid* at para 46.

52 *Ibid* at para 40. He added that "[r]eligious belief is intensely personal and can easily vary from one individual to another" (*ibid* at para 54).

if there are different views about whether this is obligatory. Moreover, there is no obvious nonspiritual benefit to "residing in" a succah and so little reason to doubt the claimants' sincerity. However, Iacobucci J recognized that there will be cases in which the sincerity of the individual's claim is in dispute, and so he offered some general comments about the determination of sincerity in such cases. In assessing sincerity, said Iacobucci J, the role of the courts is "only to ensure that a presently asserted religious belief is in good faith, neither fictitious nor capricious . . . ."[53] According to Iacobucci J, the court may consider past practice but must be careful not to rely too much on such practice, since individuals often revise their beliefs or sometimes fail to live up to their religious ideals. The court may hear expert evidence about religious practices but should not put any weight on the absence of such evidence, since section 2(a) protects beliefs and practices that are not part of an established or shared belief system. In the words of Iacobucci J:

> Assessment of sincerity is a question of fact that can be based on several non-exhaustive criteria, including the credibility of a claimant's testimony . . . as well as an analysis of whether the alleged belief is consistent with his or her other current religious practices. It is important to underscore, however, that it is inappropriate for courts rigorously to study and focus on the past practices of claimants in order to determine whether their current beliefs are sincerely held. Over the course of a lifetime, individuals change and so can their beliefs. Religious beliefs, by their very nature, are fluid and rarely static. A person's connection to or relationship with the divine or with the subject or object of his or her spiritual faith, or his or her perceptions of religious obligation emanating from such a relationship, may well change and evolve over time. Because of the vacillating nature of religious belief, a court's inquiry into sincerity, if anything, should focus not on past practice or past belief but on a person's belief at the time of the alleged interference with his or her religious freedom.[54]

---

53   *Ibid* at para 52.

54   *Ibid* at para 53. Justice Iacobucci continued (*ibid* at para 54):

> A claimant may choose to adduce expert evidence to demonstrate that his or her belief is consistent with the practices and beliefs of other adherents of the faith. While such evidence may be relevant to a demonstration of sincerity, it is not necessary. Since the focus of the inquiry is not on what others view the claimant's religious obligations as being, but rather what the claimant views these personal religious "obligations" to be, it is inappropriate to require expert opinions to show sincerity of belief. An "expert" or an authority on religious law is not the surrogate for an individual's affirmation of what his or her religious beliefs are.

In some cases, past practice and religious tradition may determine the issue. But in cases where an individual claims both that her spiritual belief is personal to her (not part of an established belief system) and that it has only recently been adopted, the court must judge her sincerity simply on the basis of her claim. If the claimed practice has no obvious nonspiritual benefits for the claimant, then the court may accept that the belief is sincere. However, in other cases, the court may hesitate to find that the asserted spiritual belief is sincere. Consider, for example, the case of *MAB, WAT and J-AYT v Canada*, in which the Human Rights Committee dismissed a claim made against Canada under the *International Covenant on Civil and Political Rights*.[55] In that case, a group of individuals claimed to be members of a religious association or church that regarded marijuana as spiritually significant—as a "sacrament." The committee expressed the view that this practice did not fall within the scope of freedom of religion under the *ICCPR*: "[A] belief consisting primarily or exclusively in the worship and distribution of a narcotic drug cannot conceivably be brought within the scope of article 18 of the Covenant . . . ."[56] The committee did not directly comment on the sincerity of the complainants' beliefs, although one suspects that the committee doubted their sincerity but was reluctant to make such a factual determination. I would note here that the adoption of a subjective test for belief presents challenges for the courts, not just in determining whether the claimant's "beliefs" are sincere, but also in determining the content of his beliefs. A court must rely on the claimant's account of his beliefs and practices, but its ability to grasp the precise content or nuance of the beliefs may be limited.[57]

Justice Iacobucci in *Amselem* held that preventing the appellants from erecting succahs on their balconies amounted to a nontrivial interference with their religious practice and that this interference was not justified under the limitations provision of the Quebec *Charter*. In response to the safety concerns raised by the condominium association, Iacobucci J observed that the appellants had agreed to set up their succahs in a way that would not obstruct the fire escape routes. He regarded

---

55 *MAB, WAT and J-AYT v Canada*, Communication No 570/1993, UN Doc CCPR/ C/50/D/570/1993 (1994) [*MAB*]; *International Covenant on Civil and Political Rights*, GA Res 2200A(XXI), 21 UNGAOR Supp (No 16) at 52, UN Doc A/6316 (1966) (entered into force 23 March 1976) [*ICCPR*], online: http://www.ohchr. org/en/professionalinterest/pages/ccpr.aspx.

56 *MAB, ibid* at para 4.2.

57 See, for example, the *SL* case, above note 31, discussed below, in which the Supreme Court of Canada decided that the claimants were mistaken in thinking that the law interfered with their religious beliefs or practices.

the association's interest in the aesthetic appearance of the building as a minor concern, noting that only a small number of succahs would be erected for nine days in the year. Moreover, the association could require that the succahs be constructed so as to blend in, as much as possible, with the general appearance of the building. Justice Iacobucci concluded that "the alleged intrusions or deleterious effects on the respondent's rights or interests under the circumstances are, at best, minimal and thus cannot be reasonably considered as imposing valid limits on the exercise of the appellants' religious freedom."[58]

Even though the limitation in *Amselem* was struck down, Iacobucci J's focus on individual belief rather than community practice, when defining the scope of religious freedom, may have contributed to a weak standard of justification and accommodation at the limitations stage in subsequent decisions.[59] This is so for three reasons. First, the focus on individual belief raises the question of why religious or spiritual beliefs should be treated differently from nonreligious beliefs. All deeply held beliefs, religious and nonreligious, would appear to have the same claim to protection from state interference. Second, if the test for determining whether a practice is protected under section 2(a) is subjective (does the individual have a sincere belief in its spiritual significance), then it is not clear what weight should be given to the practice in the court's balancing of competing religious and public interests or even why the state should be expected to compromise its public policy for a subjectively valued practice. The requirement of neutrality (that the state neither support a particular religious practice nor restrict such a practice without a compelling public reason) must rest to some extent on equality concerns—that identity groups not be socially excluded or politically marginalized. Third, the subjective test means that the scope of section 2(a) is uncertain or unstable. Any law may potentially breach section 2(a). And the number of individuals seeking exemption from a particular law is potentially unlimited. A decision to grant an exemption to a small number of individuals may not have a significant impact on a law's effectiveness; however, if more individuals seek exemption—and there is always the (theoretical) possibility that more may do so—then a law's purpose may be entirely undermined. Given the potential breadth of section 2(a), the courts may be reluctant to require the state to grant an exemption for a religious practice. Lawmakers can

---

58   Above note 12 at para 84.

59   For a discussion of the problems raised by the Court's broad reading of the scope of s 2(a), see Louis-Philippe Lampron, "Pour que la tempête ne s'étende jamais hors du verre d'eau: Réflexions sur la protection des convictions religieuses au Canada" (2010) 55 McGill LJ 743.

take account of established religious practices when formulating law, and they can assess the practicalities of reshaping the law or creating an exemption to its application for an established religious group. But, as McLachlin CJ recognized in the *Wilson Colony* case, the legislature, when enacting a law, cannot be expected to anticipate every possible claim to exemption.[60]

The dissenting judgment of Bastarache J in *Amselem* adopted a much narrower approach to the scope of freedom of religion. He acknowledged the personal and private nature of religious belief but emphasized that "religion is a system of beliefs and practices based on certain religious precepts."[61] In his view, an individual who claims that her beliefs or practices fall within the protection of section 3 of the Quebec *Charter* (section 2(a) of the Canadian *Charter*) must show a "nexus" between her personal beliefs and the precepts of her religion.[62]

Justice Binnie in his dissent thought that when the appellants agreed to the bylaws at the time they purchased their units, the other unit owners were entitled to conclude that the practice of the appellants' religion was compatible with the bylaws. "There is a vast difference," said Binnie J, "between using freedom of religion as a shield against interference with religious freedoms by the State and as a sword against co-contractors in a private building."[63] In holding them to their agreement, Binnie J noted that the appellants were in the best position to determine, before purchasing units in the building, what their religion required. They could have chosen to purchase units in another building if they were unhappy with the terms of the agreement. If religious commitment is, as the majority judgment described it, personal and individual, then Binnie J's response might be the right one. A particular religious practice has no intrinsic value, at least from a perspective external to the belief system. An individual's religious belief is valuable because she has chosen it or made a personal commitment to it. As Binnie J recognized, who better to determine the content of an individual's personal religious commitment than the individual himself? When an individual undertakes not to perform a particular act or practice, others might reasonably assume that she is not, or at least not deeply, committed to the particular practice. Since religion is a personal matter, others can rely only on the individual's statements about what is important to her—about what she thinks she can and cannot do without. More fundamentally, if religious practice is personal and protected as a matter of autonomy or liberty,

---

60   Above note 10 at para 69.
61   Above note 12 at para 135.
62   *Ibid.*
63   *Ibid* at para 185.

then an individual should be free to decide that he does not want or
need to take certain actions, or he should be free to bind himself con-
tractually not to take particular actions. Provided it is given voluntarily,
his undertaking not to act on a particular belief or judgment is also an
expression of his autonomous judgment. However, the issue of waiver
or consent may be less straightforward if religious belief or practice is
regarded as a matter of cultural identity that must be accommodated or
treated with equal respect by both public and private actors. Justice Binnie seemed to assume that the condominium association could refuse to
sell a unit to anyone who for religious reasons objected to the bylaws. In
his view, prospective purchasers who were unwilling or unable to agree
to the bylaws could choose to purchase a unit in another building. But
if the condominium association is obligated to accommodate minority
religious practices, then it cannot condition the sale of one of its units
on the purchaser's agreement not to practise her religion, or more particularly not to erect a succah on the unit's balcony.

F. *REFERENCE RE SAME-SEX MARRIAGE*

In *Reference re Same-Sex Marriage*, the federal government asked the
Supreme Court of Canada for its opinion on three issues, the second
of which was whether the redefinition of marriage to include same-sex
relationships was consistent with the *Charter*.[64] It was argued before the
Court that the recognition of same-sex marriages would breach both the
section 2(a) and the section 15 rights of those who regarded same-sex
marriage as morally objectionable. The proposed law, the opponents
said, "will have the effect of imposing a dominant social ethos and will
thus limit the freedom to hold religious beliefs to the contrary."[65] The
claim seemed to be that the recognition of same-sex marriages would
undermine traditional marriage or erode its value and meaning. The
opponents further argued that it would have "the effect of forcing religious officials to perform same-sex marriages."[66] To each of these arguments, the Court gave a simple and direct response. In the Court's view,
"[t]he mere recognition of the equality rights of one group cannot, in itself, constitute a violation of the rights of another."[67] In response to the

---

64   2004 SCC 79 [*re Same-Sex*].
65   *Ibid* at para 47.
66   *Ibid*.
67   *Ibid* at para 46. The Court continued, "[t]he promotion of *Charter* rights and
     values enriches our society as a whole and the furtherance of those rights cannot
     undermine the very principles the *Charter* was meant to foster" (*ibid*).

second argument, the Court expressed the view that if the state ever did enact a law requiring religious officials to perform same-sex marriages, it would be in breach of the *Charter*. In the Court's opinion, "state compulsion on religious officials to perform same-sex marriages contrary to their religious beliefs would violate the guarantee of freedom of religion under s. 2(*a*) of the *Charter*," and "absent exceptional circumstances which we cannot at present foresee, such a violation could not be justified under s. 1 . . . ."[68]

The Court found that the state's act of enlarging the definition of civil marriage to include same-sex marriage did not restrict the religious beliefs or practices of those in the community who believe on religious grounds that marriage should only be between a man and a woman. In most of the restriction and accommodation cases, there is a conflict of some kind between an individual's (or group's) religious practices and state law. The law makes it impossible or more difficult for the individual to engage in a particular religious practice. The issue for the court in these cases is whether an exception can be made to the law without significantly compromising the law's purpose (or, as the courts sometimes frame it, whether the restriction is justified in the public interest). But the legal change at issue in *re Same-Sex* did not require the individual to enter a marriage or live in a relationship that is contrary to his religious beliefs. The consequence of the change was simply that the individual must now live in a society that permits others to engage in an activity that she regards as immoral—or that supports a moral view inconsistent with her own. The Court found that the individual's ability to practise his faith is not restricted merely because public policy is at odds with his beliefs.

Even if the redefinition of civil marriage does not force anyone to engage in or refrain from any form of (religious) practice, it involves a public rejection of the deeply held religious beliefs of some members of the community. For the religious adherent, the sinfulness of homosexuality is not just an abstract idea, with no relevance to community life. The state's commitment to sexual-orientation equality, even though framed in secular or civic terms, must be understood as a rejection of the belief that homosexuality is wrongful. But, of course, the state cannot remain neutral on important issues of value. While the state may avoid passing direct judgment on the truth of a particular religious belief (as religious truth), it cannot avoid doing so indirectly, when determining public policy. When the legislature decides that a particular activity should be either supported or restricted, it does not frame its

---

68   *Ibid* at para 58.

judgment in terms of what God has or has not commanded. But unless we hold on to some artificial distinction between public and religious morality, the legislature's judgment must be seen as a repudiation of a religious belief that is held by some in the community. The state must sometimes support the values of some over those of others. In a democracy we cannot expect public action to conform to our world view. If the Court had agreed with those who claimed that the redefinition of marriage breached their rights, what would the remedy have been—to retain a narrow definition of civil marriage, which discriminated against gays and lesbians and was at odds with the moral views of others in the community?

As we will see in some of the cases that follow, the issue of conflict between religious belief and public policy becomes more complicated when an individual who, for example, believes that homosexuality is sinful is required by law to act in a way that (in her view) supports or condones this "behaviour." The Court in the re Same-Sex case accepted that a religious official could not be required to perform a marriage that was inconsistent with his religious beliefs. However, in *Re Marriage Commissioners Appointed Under The Marriage Act*,[69] *Brockie v Ontario (Human Rights Commission)*,[70] and *Smith v Knights of Columbus*,[71] which are discussed later in this chapter, the courts were less certain about whether the particular action required by antidiscrimination laws in each of these cases (to perform a same-sex civil marriage, to do printing work for a gay organization, and to rent a hall to a same-sex couple for their wedding reception) amounted to an interference with the actor's religious freedom. In none of these cases was a religious individual prevented from practising her faith. Nor was she required to engage directly in activity she regarded as immoral—to go to war, for example. The individual was, however, required to do more than simply live in a society that rejected his moral views. In each case the individual was required to take action that he believed supported or condoned the immoral behaviour of others. The question then is what kind or degree of involvement or association with same-sex relationships or homosexuality, when required by the state, should be viewed as compromising the individual's religious belief that homosexuality is immoral.

The issue in these cases is complicated by the fact that religious beliefs are truth claims that sometimes concern the rights and interests of others in the community—and that democratic lawmakers may

---

69   2011 SKCA 3 [*Marriage Commissioners*].
70   [2002] OJ No 2375 [*Brockie*].
71   2005 BCHRT 544 [*Knights of Columbus*].

have rejected as wrong and contrary to public justice. If the state has decided that discrimination on the ground of sexual orientation should be prohibited (that gays and lesbians should be treated as full members of the community), it is not clear why those who hold to a different view and believe that gays and lesbians should not be treated equally, because they are sinners, ought to be exempted from the law and permitted to engage in discrimination. Or, to make the point in a different way, if religious values can play a role in politics (and sometimes shape public policy), then they should also be subject to politics and to the possibility of rejection by democratic decision makers. The issue is also complicated by the courts' subjective or individualistic understanding of religious belief and practice—in which any sincerely held belief or practice falls within the scope of section 2(a). An individual may claim that she sincerely believes, not just that it is wrong to engage in homosexuality, but that it is wrong to support or condone it, or even to allow it to occur in her community. It is not clear when the courts will decide that such a "belief" (rather than practice) falls within the scope of section 2(a) protection (so that its restriction must be justified under section 1) or when, instead, they will view it as simply a belief about the way others in the community should behave that is not protected under section 2(a). In the antidiscrimination cases, the line the courts seem willing to draw is between, on the one side, requiring a market actor to provide goods and services to gay and lesbian customers and, on the other side, excusing him from actively and directly supporting the behaviour he regards as sinful. But it turns out that even this may not be a workable line, given the problems involved in distinguishing identity and behaviour in the context of sexual orientation.

G. *MULTANI v COMMISSION SCOLAIRE MARGUERITE-BOURGEOYS*

In *Multani v Commission scolaire Marguerite-Bourgeoys*, the Supreme Court of Canada held that the decision by a public school authority to prohibit a Sikh student from wearing a kirpan to school breached section 2(a) and was not justified under section 1.[72] The school did not dispute that the student had a sincere belief in the spiritual significance of

---

72   2006 SCC 6 [*Multani*]. The council of school commissioners interpreted the ban on weapons in its code of conduct as excluding the kirpan. For a discussion of the case, see Mahmud Jamal, "Freedom of Religion in the Supreme Court: Some Lessons from *Multani*" (2007) 21 NJCL 291.

the kirpan and, indeed, that he considered himself bound to wear it at all times. The position of the school was that the kirpan was a weapon and so was caught by the school's general ban on weapons. According to the majority judgment of Charron J, the school had a duty to make reasonable accommodation for the religious practices of minorities and so could ban the kirpan only if it represented a threat to school safety. Justice Charron noted that the school's policy was to ensure reasonable safety, since it was unrealistic to imagine that the school could ban all safety risks. Pens, scissors, and bats were all permitted despite their potential use as weapons. She found that the safety of the school would not be compromised in any real way if the student was permitted to wear the kirpan subject to certain conditions. Justice Charron observed that for Sikhs the kirpan was a religious symbol rather than a weapon: "[W]hile the kirpan undeniably has characteristics of a bladed weapon capable of wounding or killing a person . . . for orthodox Sikhs [it] is above all a religious symbol."[73] She rejected the school authority's claim that "kirpans are inherently dangerous" and noted that there were no recorded incidents in Canada of a Sikh student drawing his kirpan in a public school.[74] She further observed that in contrast to an airplane or a court house, where a ban on the kirpan might be justified, the school had an ongoing relationship with its students and so could monitor their actions and assess the risk of violent behaviour.[75] Finally, Charron J thought that if the kirpan was sewn into the student's clothes (something his family and the school administration had previously agreed to), there would be little risk of it falling out or being taken by anyone else and used as a weapon. After determining that the kirpan was a weapon in form only and presented no real risk to school safety, the Court held that it should be exempted from the weapons ban.

H. *ALBERTA v HUTTERIAN BRETHREN OF WILSON COUNTY*

The case of *Alberta v Hutterian Brethren of Wilson County* involved a challenge to the regulations in Alberta dealing with driver's licences,

---

73   *Multani, ibid* at para 37. The kirpan could of course be both a weapon and a religious symbol in the sense that its symbolic role is tied to its history or character as a weapon. The issue, though, is whether it is being carried as a weapon.

74   *Ibid* at 67.

75   See *Hothi v R*, [1986] 3 WWR 671 (Man CA) (kirpans banned in the courts); and *Nijjar v Canada 3000 Airlines Ltd* (2000), 36 CHRR D/76 (HRT) (kirpans banned in airplanes).

which had been amended in 2003 to require that all licence holders be photographed.[76] The licence holder's photo would appear on her licence and be included in a facial recognition data bank maintained by the province.[77] Before this change, the regulations had permitted the Registrar of Motor Vehicles to grant an exemption to an individual who for religious reasons objected to having his photo taken. Members of the Hutterian Brethren of Wilson Colony, who believed that the second commandment prohibited the making of photographic images, had been exempted from the photo requirement under the old regulations but were required under the new law to be photographed before a licence would be issued.[78] The colony members argued that the photo requirement breached their section 2(a) and section 15 *Charter* rights and could not be justified under section 1. They claimed that no one from the colony would be able to obtain a driver's licence and that this would affect the colony's ability to purchase goods and sell produce, activities that were necessary to the maintenance of their agrarian and communal way of life.

The majority judgment of McLachlin CJ accepted (reluctantly) that the photo requirement breached the section 2(a) rights of the Wilson Colony members but found that the breach was justified under section 1. Chief Justice McLachlin insisted that "reasonable accommodation analysis" is not appropriate when the court is considering whether a *law* that restricts a religious practice is justified under section 1.[79] According to McLachlin CJ, "A law's constitutionality under s. 1 of the *Charter* is determined, not by whether it is responsive to the unique needs of every individual claimant, but rather by whether its infringement of *Charter* rights is directed at an important objective and is proportionate in its

---

76   *Wilson Colony*, above note 10. For a discussion of the case, see Benjamin L Berger, "Section 1, Constitutional Reasoning and Cultural Difference: Assessing the Impacts of *Alberta v. Hutterian Brethren of Wilson Colony*" (2010) 51 Sup Ct L Rev (2d) 25; Richard Moon, "Accommodation without Compromise: Comment on *Alberta v. Hutterian Brethren of Wilson Colony*" (2010) 51 Sup Ct L Rev (2d) 95; and Sara Weinrib, "An Exemption for Sincere Believers: The Challenge of *Alberta v. Hutterian Brethren of Wilson Colony*" (2011) 56 McGill LJ 719.

77   Driver's licences in Alberta are governed by the *Traffic Safety Act*, RSA 2000, c T-6, and the regulations made pursuant to the Act.

78   The members of the colony considered photographs to be "likenesses" within the meaning of the second commandment (Exod 20:4): see *Wilson Colony*, above note 10 at para 29.

79   The Chief Justice, though, suggested that this might be an appropriate approach in the case of an individualized decision or restriction, as occurred in *Multani*, above note 72.

overall impact."[80] She found that the purpose behind the photo requirement (reducing the risk of identity theft by ensuring the integrity of the
driver's licence system) is pressing and substantial. Chief Justice Mc-
Lachlin accepted that the inclusion of driver's licence photos in a digital
data bank will "ensure that each licence in the system is connected to
a single individual, and that no individual has more than one licence,"
which in turn will help to prevent the fraudulent acquisition of driver's
licences.[81] She also accepted that requiring *all* licence holders in the
province to have their photo included in a digital data bank "will ac-
complish these security-related objectives more effectively than would
an exemption for an as *yet undetermined number* of religious objectors."[82]

Despite her formal rejection of reasonable accommodation analysis, McLachlin CJ did ask at the final step of the *Oakes* test whether an
exception to the law should be made for the members of the colony;
however, she rejected the claim because it would compromise the law's
purpose — which of course any exception must do, unless it is not truly
an exception. In her view, an exemption from the requirement would
detract from the system's effectiveness in preventing identity theft. At
the same time, she noted that the photo requirement does not compel the colony members to have their photos taken and that the colony
members could hire others to do their necessary driving, although she
acknowledged that relying on outsiders might detract from the community's "traditional self-sufficiency."[83] In her view the costs of the regulation "do not rise to the level of seriously affecting the claimants' right
to pursue their religion" and "do not negate the choice that lies at the
heart of freedom of religion."[84] She concluded that the benefit of the law
outweighs its negative impact on religious practice.

The Chief Justice distinguished the claim in this case from that in
Multani, "where the incidental and unintended effect of the law [was]
to deprive the adherent of a meaningful choice as to the religious
practice."[85] In *Multani*, "the adherent is left with a stark choice between
violating his or her religious belief and disobeying the law."[86] Yet, the

---

80   *Wilson Colony*, above note 10 at para 69.
81   *Ibid* at para 42.
82   *Ibid* at para 80 [emphasis added]. She also ruled out this "accommodation" as an
     option when she said that the claimants for exemption are potentially unlimited
     and that a court cannot know in advance how many individuals might have a
     sincere religious objection to having their photo taken.
83   *Ibid* at para 97.
84   *Ibid* at para 99.
85   *Ibid* at para 96.
86   *Ibid* at para 94.

question not clearly answered by McLachlin CJ is when is a constraint so significant that it removes the individual's choice to practise his religion? She cited *Multani* as an example of a substantial constraint; but perhaps it could be argued that there was an alternative available to the parents in that case, which was to send their child to a private school – the alternative they chose. Is the cost of private schooling so great that the individual's "choice" is removed while the cost of hiring private transportation is not (without even taking account of any loss to the colony's self-sufficiency)? According to McLachlin CJ, the "choice" to practise their religion (to not have their photos taken) remains open to the colony members. I suspect that the Chief Justice's judgment that the colony members' "choice" to practise their faith is not significantly curtailed by the photo requirement (and her description of driving as a privilege) is based in part on her conception of religion as a choice, for which the individual is responsible and for which he may be expected to bear certain costs. Even if the state has some duty to accommodate an individual's religious practices (because religion is an identity), the individual may also be expected to make certain compromises for her faith (because it is also a choice)—if not compromises to her religious practices, then at least to her nonreligious activities such as driving or engaging in certain kinds of work.[87]

In repudiating "reasonable accommodation" analysis in the *Wilson Colony* case, the Chief Justice made what is sometimes referred to in law as a "floodgates" argument: if the courts recognize a particular claim, they may be opening the floodgates to an overwhelming number of claims and may, as a consequence, undermine the effectiveness or predictability of the law. She expressed concern that accommodating every religious claim "could seriously undermine the universality of many regulatory programs . . . ."[88] This concern appeared to play a significant role in her decision not to exempt the members of the Wilson Colony from the driver's licence photo requirement. There were very few claimants in this case, as Abella J noted in her dissenting judgment. Had they

---

87   The British courts as well as the European Court of Human Rights have held that an individual may not have a right to accommodation when his religious obligations are incompatible with the ordinary requirements of a particular job. The individual, instead, should look for other work that is compatible with his religious practice. See, for example, *Stedman v UK*, (1997) 23 EHRR CD 168, in which an employer required an existing employee to work on Sundays. See also *R (On the application of Begum) v Headteacher and Governors of Denbigh High School*, [2006] UKHL 15 [*Denbigh*], in which a student's religious dress did not conform with her school's particular dress code. The *Denbigh* case is discussed below.

88   *Wilson Colony*, above note 10 at para 36.

been granted an exemption, the impact on government policy would have been minor. Chief Justice McLachlin, though, seemed concerned about the possibility of more claimants coming forward later. It is unreasonable, said the Chief Justice, to expect the state (when it is seeking to advance the public interest through law) to respond to, or anticipate, every possible claim for exemption on religious grounds. But on this reasoning no exemption could ever be given, because it might significantly undermine the law's purpose—if additional claimants were to come forward at some future time. Or, as in *Multani*, an exception could be made only if it was not truly an exception in the sense that its recognition (regardless of how many people sought "exemption") would not undermine the law's purpose. The difficulty in a case like *Wilson Colony* is that the accommodation issue—the question of whether an exception should be made to an otherwise legitimate law—requires the Court to make a pragmatic judgment about whether and to what extent the law's purpose should be compromised to make space for a religious practice. But this sort of pragmatic judgment does not fit with the Court's self-understanding as a principled decision maker, engaged in defining the scope of individual rights and determining the appropriate balance between competing rights. In seeking to follow a consistent and principled approach to religious freedom claims, the Chief Justice was led to reject reasonable accommodation analysis and to rule out the creation of an exception to the law.

The Chief Justice disposed of the section 15 claim very quickly:

> Assuming the respondents could show that the regulation creates a distinction on the enumerated ground of religion, it arises not from any demeaning stereotype but from a neutral and rationally defensible policy choice . . . . The Colony members' claim is to the unfettered practice of their religion, not to be free from religious discrimination. The substance of the respondents' s. 15(1) claim has already been dealt with under s. 2(*a*).[89]

Yet in other section 15 cases dealing with other forms of discrimination, the courts have said that a law that has a disadvantaging impact on the members of a historically disadvantaged group will be found to breach the section.[90] The courts have found a breach of section 15 in other cases, even when, as in *Wilson Colony*, the "distinction . . . arises . . . from a neutral and rationally defensible policy choice."[91] And so while

---

89 *Ibid* at para 108.
90 See, for example, *Withler v Canada (AG)*, 2011 SCC 12.
91 *Wilson Colony*, above note 10 at para 108.

the Court in some cases has interpreted section 2(a) as a form of equality right, in *Wilson Colony* it has interpreted section 15 (or at least the ban on religious discrimination) as a form of liberty right.

I. *SL V COMMISSION SCOLAIRE DES CHÊNES*

In *SL v Commission scolaire des Chênes*, the Supreme Court of Canada rejected a claim by a group of Roman Catholic parents that their children be exempted from a compulsory Ethics and Religious Culture [ERC] course in the Quebec public school system.[92] The majority judgment of Deschamps J described the parents' objection to the course in this way:

> The principal argument that emerges from the reasons given by the appellants in their requests for an exemption is that the obligation they believe they have, namely to pass on their faith to their children, has been interfered with . . . . The common theme that runs through the appellants' objections is that the ERC Program is not in fact neutral. According to the appellants, students following the ERC course would be exposed to a form of relativism, which would interfere with the appellants' ability to pass their faith on to their children.[93]

Justice Deschamps, however, found no basis for thinking that the course (which had not yet been implemented) was religiously partisan or that it advanced a relativistic view of religion. In her view, the course simply "exposed" children to a "comprehensive presentation of various religions."[94] It did not seek to indoctrinate the children into a particular faith or world view and so did not infringe the parents' freedom of religion. Justice Deschamps emphasized that to establish a breach of section 2(a), a claimant must show not only that he sincerely believes in the spiritual significance of a particular practice (a subjective test) but also that this practice has been infringed by government action (an objective test). In this case, Deschamps J found that the mandatory course did not (objectively) interfere with the parents' ability to instruct their children in Roman Catholicism, understood as the one true faith.[95] In

---

92 Above note 31. The course was introduced following the reorganization of the state-funded schools in Quebec from a religion-based system to a language-based system.

93 *Ibid* at para 29.

94 *Ibid* at para 36.

95 A similar conclusion was reached in *Mozert v Hawkins County Board of Education*, 827 F 2d 1058 (1987), a decision of the US Court of Appeals for the Sixth Circuit. In that case, the parents of children enrolled in the Tennessee public school sys-

their concurring judgment, LeBel and Fish JJ noted that at the time the complaint was made, the course had not yet been implemented in the schools. They found no breach of section 2(a) but left open the possibility that the course, once in place, might be shown to advance a relativistic view of religion, contrary to the parents' beliefs.

The majority in SL thought that the parents were mistaken in their belief (or at least brought no evidence to show) that the religion course taught a relativistic view of religion — that the course presented all religions as equally valid (or invalid). However, the parents' objection to the course may have been more basic than this. Their objection may have been that their children would be taught about different belief systems without being told that one of these systems, Roman Catholicism, was right and the others were wrong. Or the parents may also have doubted that a distinction could be drawn in classroom teaching between exposure and affirmation, and thought that religious education (or education about religion) should be left to parents. If this is what the parents thought, then the provincial course requirement could be seen as interfering with their religious beliefs and, more particularly, with their right to decide the religious education of their children. The problem with such a claim, though, is that it is fundamentally at odds with the public commitment to religious freedom (and to the development of a tolerant or respectful political community) and the conception of religious adherence that underlies that commitment. The majority said as much at the end of their judgment: "The suggestion that exposing children to a variety of religious facts in itself infringes their religious freedom or that of their parents amounts to a rejection of the multicultural reality of Canadian society and ignores the Quebec government's obligations with regard to public education."[96] Applying the two-part section 2(a) test, according to which a claimant must show not only that she has a sincere belief in the spiritual significance of a particular practice but also that the law restricts that practice in a nontrivial way, the Court defined the scope of the parents' practice narrowly and found

tem argued that their children should be exempted from reading a series of books that depicted views and practices (such as gender equality and magic) that were contrary to their religious beliefs. The court held that the compulsory course did not breach the parents' free exercise rights. The course simply "exposed" children to other views. It did not affirm views that were inconsistent with the parents' religious beliefs, and it did not require the children to participate in practices that were contrary to the parents' beliefs. In *Quebec (AG) v Loyola High School*, 2012 QCCA 2139, the Quebec Court of Appeal held that the government could also require a private Roman Catholic high school to teach the ERC course.

96 Above note 31 at para 40.

no conflict between the religious practice and the government's policy. In this way, the Court avoided addressing the more basic question of whether the parents' belief that their children should not be exposed to, or taught about, "erroneous" belief systems fell within the scope of section 2(a).[97]

J.   *R v NS*

In *R v NS*, the Supreme Court of Canada considered whether a witness in a criminal trial or hearing had a right under section 2(a) to wear a niqab when giving evidence.[98] The majority judgment of McLachlin CJ began with the observation that two sets of *Charter* rights were "potentially engaged" in the case: the witness's freedom of religion and the accused's right to a fair trial. In a case such as this, said the Chief Justice, a court must determine the "just and proportionate balance" between these two rights.[99] The issue, in her view, could not be resolved by a fixed rule that was applicable in all cases — either that the witness will always be required to remove her niqab when giving evidence or that she will never be required to do so — but must instead be resolved on a case-by-case basis.[100]

The Chief Justice set out the general approach for a trial judge to follow when deciding whether the witness should be permitted to testify wearing a niqab. The trial judge (and, in this particular case, the preliminary inquiry judge) should take account of the particular circumstances of the case before him and ask the following questions. First, does the witness have a sincere religious belief that would be compromised if she were required to testify without the niqab? Second, "[w]ould

---

97 A similar view of the case is taken by Faisal Bhabha in "From *Saumur* to L.(S.): Tracing the Theory and Concept of Religious Freedom under Canadian Law" (2012) 58 Supreme Court LR 109; Richard Moon, "Freedom of Conscience and Religion" in Stéphane Beaulac and Errol Mendes, eds, *Canadian Charter of Rights and Freedoms*, 5th ed (Markham, ON: LexisNexis, 2013) 375; and Benjamin L Berger, "Religious Diversity, Education, and the 'Crisis' in State Neutrality" CJLS [forthcoming].

98 Above note 30. The ruling under appeal concerned the right of a witness to wear a niqab in a preliminary inquiry.

99 *Ibid* at para 31.

100 See *ibid*: "Rather, the answer lies in a just and proportionate balance between freedom of religion on the one hand, and trial fairness on the other, based on the particular case before the Court." Justice Abella, in her dissenting judgment in *NS*, thought that the Court should adopt a rule permitting the witness to wear a niqab when testifying.

permitting the witness to wear the niqab while testifying create a serious risk to trial fairness?"[101] The answer to this second question, said the Chief Justice, will depend on the nature of the witness's evidence. If, for example, the witness's evidence is uncontested so that credibility is not at issue, then wearing a niqab while testifying will not affect the fairness of the trial.[102] Third, if both rights are "engaged" in the particular case, the judge should consider whether there is a way in which both can be "accommodated" so as to avoid any conflict or trade-off between them.[103] In other words, is there a way in which the witness may be permitted to give evidence while wearing a niqab without putting the fairness of the trial at risk?[104] Finally, if accommodation is not possible, the issue becomes, whether "the salutary effects of requiring the witness to remove the niqab outweigh the deleterious effects of doing so?"[105] In answering this final question, the judge should consider the importance of the religious practice to the witness, the degree of state interference with that practice, and the actual situation in the courtroom—most importantly, who will see the witness's face if she is not permitted to wear the niqab when giving evidence. The judge should also take into consideration "broader societal harms," most significantly whether requiring removal of the niqab will discourage women from reporting offences or otherwise participating in the justice system.[106] On the other side, the judge must consider whether the witness's evidence is peripheral or central to the case and whether the credibility of the witness is a significant issue in the case.

There are a number of problems with the approach proposed by the majority in NS. First, the Chief Justice refused to confront the question of whether or not demeanour evidence is reliable or useful. She declared that the courts have long relied on such evidence and noted that no expert opinion was provided to the Court to refute the assumption that

---

101 Ibid at para 9.

102 One assumes that credibility will almost always be an issue.

103 Above note 30 at para 9.

104 The Chief Justice used the term "accommodation" in a very limited way. A religious practice will be accommodated when it can coexist with the government's policy—with no trade-off or compromise to that policy (i.e., "minimal impairment" in the strictest or most formal sense).

105 Above note 30 at para 9.

106 Ibid at para 37. This seems like a general rather than a case-specific factor. Indeed, there are a variety of obvious reasons why it would not be appropriate to treat this as a case-specific consideration. I would note here also that the Court's approach seemed to assume that a witness might choose not to give evidence. But what if a witness was subject to a subpoena? Would a court compel her to give evidence?

demeanour evidence has an important role to play in the assessment of witness credibility and the conduct of cross-examination. Because this assumption is so deeply embedded in the common law system, the Chief Justice thought that the burden fell on the witness (whose rights were being restricted) to demonstrate that it was unfounded:

> On the record before us, I conclude that there is a strong connection between the ability to see the face of a witness and a fair trial. Being able to see the face of a witness is not the only—or indeed perhaps the most important—factor in cross-examination or accurate credibility assessment. But its importance is too deeply rooted in our criminal justice system to be set aside absent compelling evidence.[107]

The Chief Justice's observation that the system has historically treated demeanour evidence as important substitutes for a judgment that demeanour is, in fact, important evidence of a witness's credibility. She appeared to reverse the ordinary requirement in *Charter* cases that the state demonstrate the need for a restriction on the right.

Second, in declining to establish a rule and leaving the issue to be resolved by the trial judge, based on her assessment of the circumstances of the particular case, the majority has created a situation in which the trial judge's decision will be difficult to review. Review is made particularly difficult since, as I will suggest in a moment, the majority offered no real guidance about what the judge is to balance in these cases or how this balancing is to be done. When the Court handed the issue back to the trial judge to decide whether, in the particular circumstances, a witness should be allowed to wear a niqab when giving evidence, it may have been doing one of two things. First, it might simply have been advancing a rule that a witness must testify without a niqab unless her credibility is not in issue. Indeed the majority judgment was reasonably clear that the right to a fair trial should take precedence and that the religious practice should be accommodated only if it does not present an actual risk to a fair trial. The other possibility is that the Court was giving the trial judge the authority to decide the general issue of whether demeanour evidence has value—the issue that it was

---

107 *Ibid* at para 27. The use of the word "importance" reflects the Court's evasion of the issue. Earlier, McLachlin CJ said: "The common law, supported by provisions of the *Criminal Code*, RSC 1985, c C-46, and judicial pronouncements, proceeds on the basis that the ability to see a witness's face is an important feature of a fair trial. While not conclusive, in the absence of negating evidence this common law assumption cannot be disregarded lightly" (*ibid* at para 21). If the evidence on the issue was inadequate, the Court might have called on the parties to bring forward more evidence.

unwilling to directly address. The trial judge, in a particular case, is left to make her own decision on the general issue of the value of demeanour evidence based on her personal experience with, or assumptions about, such evidence.[108] I suspect that most trial judges believe that demeanour evidence has value and that they are capable of managing its problems or limits and so will decide that the witness must remove the niqab if her credibility is at issue.

Third, in the final stage of the proposed approach, the trial judge is asked to balance the competing rights claims. However, many of the factors that the majority judgment said ought to be weighed in the balance have no clear content. For example, the majority thought that the most significant consideration weighing on the side of the religious freedom claim is the importance of the religious practice to the witness. But how is this to be measured? The majority recognized that "[i]t is difficult to measure the value of adherence to religious conviction, or the injury caused by being required to depart from it. The value of adherence does not depend on whether a religious practice is a voluntary expression of faith or a mandatory obligation under religious doctrine: *Amselem* . . . ."[109] (Yet when the Court in *Amselem* said that the practice's value did not depend on whether it was mandatory, the Court was considering the scope of section 2(a) protection and not the weight of the practice's value at the section 1 stage.) The practice has no value from a secular perspective. What objective weight can be attached to the subjective experience of the believer? A judge can determine that the practice matters deeply to the individual because the individual has told him so or has adhered to this practice in the past. But it is not clear how a subjective commitment to a particular belief or practice (deep or shallow) is to be compared with the individual's right to (and the public interest in) a fair trial.

At the end of its analysis, the majority judgment seemed to say that the right to a fair trial must take precedence. According to the majority, "[w]here the liberty of the accused is at stake, the witness's evidence is central to the case and her credibility vital, the possibility of a wrongful

---

108 The majority judgment suggested that expert evidence may be relevant in deciding whether, as a general matter, demeanour evidence is reliable or useful. But if the judge is making a contextual judgment about the relevance and risks of demeanour evidence (or the risks to a fair trial if a witness is permitted to wear a niqab), then the relevance of expert evidence may be limited.

109 Above note 30 at para 36.

conviction must weigh heavily in the balance . . . ."[110] Despite the Chief Justice's frequent references to balancing, it appears that a witness will be permitted to wear a niqab only when witness credibility is not at issue, so that there will be no impact on the fairness of the trial. The pretense that the issue will be resolved through "balancing" can be maintained only because the Court has given trial judges the authority to decide the matter based on their reading of the particular facts or circumstances of the case before them. The majority's unwillingness to create a general exception for witnesses who sincerely believe that they must cover their faces in public settings is surprising given the other situations, described by the majority, in which witnesses may be excused from giving evidence in person.[111] The majority's refusal to recognize an exemption for the niqab seemed to rest on an assumption that wearing the niqab is a choice that lies within the witness's control and so is different from other situations in which a witness may be allowed to give testimony away from the courtroom or without being seen by the judge or lawyers.

K. *POLYGAMY REFERENCE*

In *Reference re: Criminal Code of Canada (BC)*, the British Columbia government asked the Supreme Court of British Columbia for its opinion concerning the constitutionality of the *Criminal Code* ban on polygamy.[112] Section 293(1) of the *Code* provides as follows:

(1) Every one who

(*a*) practises or enters into or in any manner agrees or consents to practise or enter into

(i) any form of polygamy, or

---

110 *Ibid* at para 44. Furthermore,

[o]n an individual level, the cost of an unfair trial is severe. The right to a fair trial is a fundamental pillar without which the edifice of the rule of law would crumble. No less is at stake than an individual's liberty—his right to live in freedom unless the state proves beyond a reasonable doubt that he committed a crime meriting imprisonment. This is of critical importance not only to the individual on trial, but to public confidence in the justice system (*ibid* at para 38).

111 See Natasha Bakht, "Objection, Your Honour! Accommodating *Niqab*-Wearing Women in Courtrooms" in Ralph Grillo et al, eds, *Legal Practice and Cultural Diversity* (Farnham, Surrey; Burlington, VT: Ashgate, 2009) 115 at 129: "[I]t should not be forgotten that there are circumstances where judges will take evidence without being able to see the witness's face: for example, where evidence is taken over the telephone or where the judge is visually impaired."

112 2011 BCSC 1588.

(ii) any kind of conjugal union with more than one person at the same time, whether or not it is by law recognized as a binding form of marriage, or

(b) celebrates, assists or is a party to a rite, ceremony, contract or consent that purports to sanction a relationship mentioned in subparagraph (a)(i) or (ii),

is guilty of an indictable offence and liable to imprisonment for a term not exceeding five years.[113]

After hearing an unprecedented amount of expert evidence concerning the practice of polygamy, the judge held that the ban breached section 2(a) but was justified under section 1. The ban was justified, said the judge, because Parliament had "a very strong basis for a reasoned apprehension of harm to many in our society inherent in the practice of polygamy . . . ."[114]

The judge found that the criminal ban on polygamy was not the "product of religious animus."[115] While the impetus for the original ban may have been the arrival in Canada in the late 1800s of members of the Mormon community, its purpose was not to suppress a religious practice or community but rather to prohibit a harmful activity, which was at the time associated with the Mormons. The judge found that the harms "arising out of the practice of polygamy" included "harm to women, to children, to society and to the institution of monogamous marriage."[116] The judge determined that women in polygamous relationships face a greater risk of physical and psychological harm. Relationships between co-wives may be difficult because they must compete for emotional and material support from their shared husband. Women in polygamous relationships often have more children and tend to live shorter lives than women in monogamous relationships. They also do less well economically. More generally, they "tend to have less autonomy . . . and lower levels of self-esteem."[117] Children "tend to suffer more emotional,

---

113 RSC 1985, c C-46. Section 293(2) of the *Code, ibid,* provides as follows:

Where an accused is charged with an offence under this section, no averment or proof of the method by which the alleged relationship was entered into, agreed to or consented to is necessary in the indictment or on the trial of the accused, nor is it necessary on the trial to prove that the persons who are alleged to have entered into the relationship had or intended to have sexual intercourse.

114 Above note 112 at para 6.

115 *Ibid* at para 896.

116 *Ibid* at para 5.

117 *Ibid* at para 8.

behavioural and physical problems, as well as lower education achieve-ment than children in monogamous families."[118] This is due to conflict among co-wives as well as "[t]he inability of fathers to give sufficient affection and disciplinary attention to all of their children. . . ."[119] Chil-dren are also exposed to "harmful gender stereotypes."[120] Girls in po-lygamous communities often marry at a young age and to much older men. Young men unable to find wives because of the "sex ratio im-balance inherent in polygamy . . . are forced out of polygamous com-munities. . . ."[121] Polygamy's harms to society in general include larger, impoverished families and the creation of a class of unmarried, poorly educated men, who are "statistically predisposed" to violent and other anti-social behaviour.[122] Because "patriarchal hierarchy" and "authori-tarian control" are standard in polygamous communities, the members "tend to have fewer civil liberties than their counterparts in societies which prohibit the practice."[123]

The judge rejected the argument that these harms could be ad-dressed effectively through more targeted legal measures, such as the existing restrictions on child abuse or sexual coercion. In the judge's view, most of the harms described are "inherent" in the practice; they are not simply "the product of individual misconduct; they arise in-evitably out of the practice."[124] These inherent harms include "harm to children (for example, from divided parental investment or as a result of less genetic-relatedness of family members), to the psychological health of the spouses, and to the institution of monogamous marriage."[125] Yet at least some of these harms seem to be related to, or at least aggra-vated by, the insularity of polygamous communities, and as the judge observed, this insularity is wholly or partly due to the criminalization of polygamy.[126] The "lost boys" problem, for example, would be less se-vere if the young men, who were unable to find wives in their religious community, did not find themselves effectively exiled into an unfamiliar world. Concern about sexual coercion or denial of education could be

---

118 *Ibid* at para 9.
119 *Ibid*.
120 *Ibid* at para 12.
121 *Ibid* at para 11.
122 *Ibid* at para 13.
123 *Ibid*.
124 *Ibid* at para 1045.
125 *Ibid*.
126 *Ibid* at para 310: "Wary of legal prohibitions against polygamy, Mormon funda-mentalists tend to live covertly in isolated communities . . . ."

more easily addressed if the group were less insulated from the larger community.

But even if some of the harms to women and children could be addressed without banning polygamy, the judge thought there were other significant harms inherent in the practice of polygamy. In the judge's view, "the positive objective" of the polygamy ban is "the protection and preservation of monogamous marriage."[127] "For that," said the judge, "there can be no alternative to the outright prohibition of that which is fundamentally anathema to the institution."[128] According to the judge, the institution of monogamous marriage is valuable—a "public good"—because "[t]he mutuality inherent in the dyadic structure habituated children to notions of equality and other important norms of citizenship."[129] In the judge's view, "exclusive and enduring monogamous marriage best ensured that men and women were treated with equal dignity and respect, and that husbands and wives, and parents and children provided each other with mutual support, protection and edification throughout their lifetimes."[130] The judge's claim, though, was not that the existence of polygamy undermines the institution of monogamous marriage and will lead to a decline in the number of such marriages, but was, simply, that polygamy is inferior to monogamy because it is structured as an unequal relationship. While inequality may be part of many monogamous marriages, it is not a structural feature of such relationships.

A preliminary issue for the judge was the scope of the polygamy prohibition. It had been argued that the ban applied broadly to any form of conjugal relationship (that is "committed, interdependent and of some permanence") involving more than two persons.[131] As a practical matter, such a broadly defined prohibition would be difficult to enforce. The judge, however, read the ban's scope narrowly so that it extended only to relationships in which the parties were "married" ("conjugal unions"), whether or not the "marriage" was legally binding. According to the judge, there must be a "voluntary joining together of two individuals with the requisite intent to 'marry' and the recognition and sanction by the couple's community."[132] The requirement of some kind of formal "sanctioning event" limited the scope of the ban and avoided

---

127 Ibid at para 1343.
128 Ibid. He continued, "there is no such thing as so-called 'good polygamy'" (ibid).
129 Ibid at para 174.
130 Ibid at para 209.
131 Ibid at para 916.
132 Ibid at para 1020.

at least some of the potential enforcement problems. It also directed the ban's focus toward religious or cultural communities that support or mandate polygamous relationships. The judge acknowledged that many of the harms associated with polygamy (and, in particular, the harm to the institution of monogamous marriage) may occur in (or result from) other multi-party intimate relationships; nevertheless he thought that the harms will be more severe in the case of a relationship that is religiously or culturally sanctioned and is embedded in a religious and cultural community, particularly one that is relatively insular. The inequ lity in the relationship may be reinforced, and less apparent, within a larger cultural or religious community that regards such relationships s morally appropriate or even required. Women in such a community may be pressured into polygamous relationships or may be unable to imagine any alternatives.

The principal argument against the polygamy ban is that it interferes with the religious freedom of members of the Fundamentalist Church of Jesus Christ of Latter-Day Saints and other religious groups that either permit or require polygamy. Yet, at the same time, the judge defined the ban so that its focus is on multi-party relationships within religious or cultural communities. The harm addressed by the ban is tied to the religious or cultural character of the practice. This, as we shall see in the next chapter, is a recurring tension in the religious freedom jurisprudence. The deep communal connections that are part of the value of religious life and commitment may also be the source of what the courts regard as harm—the perceived lack of choice or opportunity open to the members of such communities. The state may sometimes decide to intervene in the affairs of a religious community characterized by hierarchy and insularity when the prevailing practices in that community are thought to be harmful to some of its members, even though the members have, in a formal sense, chosen to participate in those practices. In the next chapter, I will return to the issue of state regulation of the internal operations of a religious community or organization.

L. RE MARRIAGE COMMISSIONERS APPOINTED UNDER THE MARRIAGE ACT

In *Re Marriage Commissioners Appointed Under The Marriage Act*, the Saskatchewan Court of Appeal held that a legislative proposal permitting provincially appointed civil marriage commissioners to refuse on religious grounds to perform same-sex marriage ceremonies would violate the section 15 equality rights of gays and lesbians and could not be justified under section 1.[133] At the time the case was heard, there were 372 marriage commissioners in the province. The provincial Marriage Unit did not assign commissioners to perform particular marriage ceremonies but, instead, provided the names and contact information of local commissioners to any couple inquiring about civil marriage services. A couple who wished to be married in a civil ceremony would directly approach a commissioner in their general geographic area. As the majority of the court noted, "commissioners are the route—the only route—by which individuals who wish to be married by way of a non-religious ceremony may have their union solemnized."[134]

The majority of the court recognized that if the government enacted such a law, a same-sex couple, who approached a marriage commissioner, could be told by the commissioner that she is unable to perform their marriage because of their sexual orientation. This, said the majority, will have the effect of "drawing a distinction based on sexual orientation," a ground the Supreme Court of Canada has identified in earlier cases as "analogous" to those specifically listed in section 15.[135] The majority accepted that the harm from such a denial would be significant:

> It is not difficult for most people to imagine the personal hurt involved in a situation where an individual is told by a governmental officer "I won't help you because you are black (or Asian or First Nations) but someone else will" or "I won't help you because you are Jewish (or Muslim or Budd[h]ist) but someone else will." Being told "I won't help you because you are gay/lesbian but someone else will" is no different.[136]

---

133 Above note 69. The proposed exemption provided that "[n]otwithstanding *The Saskatchewan Human Rights Code*, a marriage commissioner is not required to solemnize a marriage if to do so would be contrary to the marriage commissioner's religious beliefs": *ibid* at para 17. A second version of the exemption put before the court "grandfathered" the current group of commissioners allowing them not to perform same-sex marriages but did not extend this exemption to newly appointed commissioners: *ibid* at paras 17–18. Before this reference case, three marriage commissioners had filed a complaint under the provincial human rights code in which they argued that the provincial policy requiring them to perform same-sex marriages amounted to religious discrimination. Their complaint was dismissed. Another human rights code complaint followed this. In *Nichols v MJ*, 2009 SKQB 299, the Saskatchewan Court of Queen's Bench upheld the decision of the provincial human rights tribunal that a marriage commissioner breached the human rights code when he refused to marry a same-sex couple.

134 *Marriage Commissioners*, above note 69 at para 9.

135 *Ibid* at para 39.

136 *Ibid* at para 41.

Moreover, said the majority, a significant number of commissioners might decide that they are unable to perform same-sex marriages, and the law provides no assurance that a "minimum complement of commissioners will always be available to provide services to same-sex couples."[137] The majority had no difficulty concluding that the legislative proposal would have "the effect of creating a negative distinction based on sexual orientation" and that given the "historical marginalization and mistreatment of gay and lesbian individuals," the proposal would be discriminatory contrary to section 15.[138]

In its section 1 analysis, the majority accepted that a requirement that all marriage commissioners solemnize same-sex marriages would breach the religious freedom of those commissioners who regarded such relationships as sinful. The issue "at bottom," said the majority, is "managing the intersection of the freedom of religion of marriage commissioners on the one hand, and the equality rights of gay and lesbian individuals on the other."[139] The majority found that the proposed restriction on the section 15 rights of gay and lesbian couples failed both the minimal impairment and proportionality components of the *Oakes* test. There were other ways in which the state might protect the commissioners' religious freedom without impairing, at least to the same degree, the right to equality. The majority identified as a less restrictive measure "a 'single entry point' system under which a couple seeking the services of a marriage commissioner would proceed, not by directly contacting an individual commissioner, but by dealing with the Director of the Marriage Unit or some other central office."[140] Such a system would ensure that no couple would be denied services because of their sexual orientation. Any accommodation for marriage commissioners would occur "behind the scenes" and would not be apparent to the couple.[141] The majority did not decide whether a single entry point system would restrict the equality rights of gay and lesbian couples and if it did, whether it would be a reasonable limit on those rights; the majority decided only that it would be "less restrictive of s. 15 rights" than the proposed law.[142] The majority also found that the "freedom of religion interests" accommodated by the proposed law "do not lie at the heart of s. 2(a)," because they concern only the ability of the commissioners "to act on their beliefs in the world at large" and not their freedom "to hold the

---

137 *Ibid* at para 42.
138 *Ibid* at paras 44 & 45.
139 *Ibid* at para 66.
140 *Ibid* at para 85.
141 *Ibid*.
142 *Ibid* at para 89.

religious beliefs they choose or to worship as they wish."[143] Moreover, said the majority: "Persons who voluntarily choose to assume an office, like that of marriage commissioner, cannot expect to directly shape the office's intersection with the public so as to make it conform with their personal religious or other beliefs."[144]

The issue before the court was whether the proposed law breached the section 15 rights of same-sex couples. In addressing this issue, the majority accepted that a state requirement that all marriage commissioners perform same-sex civil marriages breached their religious freedom. However, the majority did not determine whether this requirement would be a justified restriction of their religious freedom, since the issue was not directly before the court. The majority decided only that a system in which couples wishing to be married in a civil ceremony applied to a centralized government service, which then assigned a commissioner to perform their marriage, would not interfere with the equality rights of gay and lesbian couples to the same extent as the proposed law. But if a centralized—single point of entry—system would protect the religious rights of the commissioners without significantly impairing the equality rights of same-sex couples, then the requirement that all marriage commissioners perform same-sex marriages (which would breach the section 2(a) rights of certain commissioners) might not be justified under section 1.

Yet, as the concurring judgment of Smith J suggested, it is not obvious that the requirement that the commissioners (who are public officials) perform same-sex civil marriages would interfere with their religious beliefs or practices. The marriage commissioners are not "compelled to engage in the sexual activity" to which they object; rather, "[t]heir objection is that it is sinful for *others* to engage in such activity."[145] "It is far from clear," said Smith J, "that officiating at a civil marriage ceremony carries any implication or connotation at all that the marriage commissioner who officiates necessarily *approves* of the particular union."[146] According to Smith J, any "interference with the right of marriage commissioners to act in accordance with their religious belief . . . is [at most] trivial or insubstantial, in that it is interference that does not threaten actual religious beliefs or conduct."[147] In the judge's view, then, the decision by a marriage commissioner not to perform a same-

---

143 *Ibid* at para 93.
144 *Ibid* at para 97.
145 *Ibid* at para 148.
146 *Ibid* at para 142.
147 *Ibid* at para 148.

sex marriage (based on the commissioner's belief that it would be wrong to perform such a marriage) would fall outside the scope of section 2(a), and so its "restriction" would require no justification under section 1.

Ordinarily in a civil service accommodation case, an individual who is employed by the government seeks an exemption from a job requirement that is inconsistent with his personal religious practice—an exemption, for example, from a police uniform requirement for a Sikh man who wears a turban or from a Saturday work requirement for a practising Jew or Seventh-day Adventist. The marriage commissioners, however, are not asking to be exempted from a restrictive law or practice. They are asking, instead, to be exempted from a job requirement that in their view associates them with an immoral practice. The law does not require them to directly engage in such a practice (as in the case of a "conscientious objector" being conscripted into military service) but instead requires them to "condone" the "sinful" activity of others, in this case homosexuality or same-sex relationships.

When a commissioner performs a marriage ceremony, he does so as a public official and not as a private person. The "restriction" in such a case is not a direct interference with his religious practice. The commissioner is simply required, as part of his public duties, to perform an act that extends legal recognition to a same-sex marriage. The performance of a public function by a civil servant should not be regarded as personal support for, or association with, the activity he regards as immoral. Moreover, the commissioner holds powers that others do not. The commissioner has chosen to serve in a public capacity. If he does not wish to be associated with an activity he regards as sinful, then he can give up the state-delegated power he holds to perform marriages. The commissioner's situation is different from that of an individual employee who cannot meet a formal requirement of her job, because it conflicts with her religious practices (e.g., she cannot work on Saturday). The commissioner is not being prevented from practising his personal faith. His complaint, instead, is that the performance of his public duties associates him with a practice or activity engaged in by others. He is asking that his morally based opposition to the legal recognition of same-sex marriages be "accommodated." A civil servant who is morally opposed to government policy (the legal recognition of same-sex marriage), or to basic public values (sexual-orientation equality), has no claim to be excused from performing the tasks, and exercising the powers, associated with his position.

M. STATE REGULATION OF RELIGIOUSLY MOTIVATED DISCRIMINATION

Should private actors who provide market services be exempted from non-discrimination requirements when they have religious objections to serving a particular group—or, what they might describe as, supporting an immoral practice?[148] In *Brockie v Ontario (Human Rights Commission)*, the Canadian Lesbian and Gay Archives [CLGA], a registered charity "with a mandate to acquire, preserve, organize, and give public access to publications, information, records and artifacts by and about homosexuals in Canada," ordered letterhead and business cards from a small printing business.[149] The owner of the business, Mr Brockie, refused to do the work because he believed that homosexuality is sinful and that "he must not assist in the dissemination of information intended to spread the acceptance of a gay or lesbian . . . lifestyle."[150] Mr Brockie indicated that he was willing to provide printing services to gay and lesbian customers but not to an organization that "was involved in furthering and supporting the homosexual 'lifestyle.'"[151] The CLGA responded by bringing a human rights code complaint against Mr Brockie's business. The Human Rights Tribunal of Ontario held that Mr Brockie's refusal to provide printing services (which were otherwise available to the public) to a gay and lesbian group amounted to discrimination under the Ontario *Human Rights Code*. The case was appealed to the Divisional Court of Ontario, which upheld the tribunal's decision. The court rejected as "specious" the distinction proposed by Mr Brockie "between discrimination because of the presence of or association with a human characteristic referred to in s. 1 [of the Ontario Code] per se and discrimination because a person engages in the political act of promoting the causes of those who have such characteristics."[152] The court said that even if Mr Brockie's objection was to the "Archives' objects and political purposes" rather than to "its mere

---

148 A related issue concerns the authority of the state, or a state-established professional regulatory body, to require a medical professional to perform a procedure that is contrary to her religious beliefs. Provided the refusal to provide the particular service does not amount to discrimination, the professional may be excused from direct participation. See, for example, "Physicians and the Ontario *Human Rights Code*," Policy Statement 5-08 (Toronto: College of Physicians and Surgeons of Ontario, 2008). See also Mary Anne Waldron, *Free to Believe: Rethinking Freedom of Conscience and Religion in Canada* (Toronto: University of Toronto Press, 2013) at 210.

149 *Brockie*, above note 70 at para 4.

150 *Ibid* at para 3.

151 *Ibid* at para 15.

152 *Ibid* at para 29.

association with people who bear such characteristics," the purpose of the Code is to create "a climate of understanding and mutual respect."[153] In the court's view, "efforts to promote an understanding and respect for those possessing any specified characteristic should not be regarded as separate from the characteristic itself."[154] The court found that although the tribunal's order breached Mr Brockie's section 2(a) rights under the *Charter*, it was nevertheless justified under section 1. According to the court, claims to religious freedom "in the commercial marketplace" are "at the fringes" of section 2(a).[155]

Yet, in its section 1 analysis, the court said that if the tribunal's order were read as requiring Mr Brockie to print not just the CLGA's letterhead and business cards but also "brochures or posters with editorial content espousing causes or activities clearly repugnant to [his] fundamental religious tenets," it would fail the section 1 proportionality requirement.[156] In the court's view, the Code prohibits only "discrimination arising from denial of services because of certain characteristics of the person requesting the services . . . ."[157] More particularly, said the court:

> If any particular printing project ordered by Mr. Brockie (or any gay or lesbian person, or organization/entity comprising gay or lesbian persons) contained material that conveyed a message proselytizing and promoting the gay and lesbian lifestyle or ridiculed his religious beliefs, such material might reasonably be held to be in direct conflict with the core elements of Mr. Brockie's religious beliefs. On the other hand, if the particular printing object contained a directory of goods and services that might be of interest to the gay and lesbian community, that material might reasonably be held not to be in direct conflict with the core elements of Mr. Brockie's religious beliefs.[158]

The court seemed to distinguish between material that assists group members and material that proselytizes or promotes the gay lifestyle, or ridicules religion. But it is not clear how a court is to distinguish between aid and promotion. Such a distinction is imaginable only because sexual orientation, like religion, is viewed as both an identity and a choice. If sexual orientation is seen as an identity, then "promotion" of homosexuality will be indistinguishable from support for gays and lesbians. The purpose of the CLGA's activities, whether described as sup-

---

153 *Ibid.*
154 *Ibid* at para 31.
155 *Ibid* at para 54.
156 *Ibid* at para 49.
157 *Ibid.*
158 *Ibid* at para 56.

port or promotion, is to protect or advance the interests of gays and lesbians. On the other hand, if homosexuality is viewed, in the way Mr Brockie views it, as an immoral "lifestyle choice," then any support for, or advocacy of, the interests of gays and lesbians will amount to the promotion or proselytization of the gay lifestyle—the attempt to encourage this lifestyle in the community. The court's reference to "proselytizing" this lifestyle suggested some sympathy for Mr Brockie's view, or at least an ambivalence about sexual orientation as an identity, and a troubling uncertainty about how to fit sexual orientation into the framework of antidiscrimination laws.

In *Smith v Knights of Columbus*, a Roman Catholic organization that made its hall available for rental to the general public cancelled an existing rental arrangement after discovering that the renters were a same-sex couple who intended to use the hall for their wedding reception.[159] The couple brought a complaint against the organization under the British Columbia *Human Rights Code*, arguing that it had discriminated against them on the grounds of their sexual orientation. The tribunal found that a *prima facie* case of discrimination had been made out against the organization. Under the British Columbia *Code*, a religious organization that was primarily engaged in serving the members of its group would not be considered to have breached the discrimination ban simply because it gave preference to the members of that group.[160] The

---

159 Above note 71. But see also *Eadie v Riverbend Bed and Breakfast (No 2)*, 2012 BCHRT 247 [*Eadie*], in which a couple operating a B & B cancelled a reservation after discovering that the double room had been reserved by a gay couple. The tribunal found at para 165 that "this case falls more towards the commercial end of the spectrum [in contrast to *Knights of Columbus*]. The Riverbend was not operated by a Church or religious organization. While the business was operated by individuals with sincere religious beliefs respecting same-sex couples, and out of a portion of their personal residence, it was still a commercial activity. It was the Molnars' personal and voluntary choice to start up a business in their personal residence. In this respect, the Molnars were not compelled by the state to act in a manner inconsistent with their personal religious views." See also the decision of the UK Supreme Court in *Bull and another (Appellants) v Hall and another (Respondents)*, [2013] UKSC 73, in which the facts were similar to those in the *Eadie* case. The UK court found that the cancellation amounted to unlawful discrimination and noted that "[s]exual orientation is a core component of a person's identity which requires fulfilment through relationships with others of the same orientation" (at para 52). The court considered both the *Eadie* and the *Knights of Columbus* decisions but said: "We cannot place too much weight on these cases, decided upon under different legislation and in a different constitutional context" (at para 50).

160 RSBC 1996, c 210, s 41(1):

If a charitable, philanthropic, educational, fraternal, religious or social organization or corporation that is not operated for profit has as a primary purpose

tribunal, though, found that the exemption was not applicable in this case, because the organization rented its hall to members of the general public. However, the tribunal went on to find that the organization had a *bona fide* and reasonable justification for its action. While the Knights of Columbus did not limit the rental of the hall to Roman Catholics, it had an informal policy of not renting the hall for events that were inconsistent with the Roman Catholic faith, or would compromise the organization's relationship with the Roman Catholic Church. The tribunal accepted that the organization should not be required to rent the hall for a function that was contrary to its "core" religious beliefs and to "indirectly condone" activities it regards as sinful.[161]

The tribunal, though, held that the organization, having initially agreed to rent the hall to the couple, had an obligation to help the couple find another location. The tribunal said:

> Although we have accepted that the Knights could refuse access to the Hall to the complainants because of their core religious beliefs, in the Panel's view, in making this decision they had to consider the effect their actions would have on the complainants . . . . [T]he Knights could have taken steps such as meeting with the complainants to explain the situation, formally apologizing, immediately offering to reimburse the complainants for any expenses they had incurred and, perhaps offering assistance in finding another solution. There may have been other options that they could have considered without infringing their core religious beliefs . . . . In the circumstances of this case, including the fact that the Hall was not solely a religious space, and the existence of the agreement between the parties for its rental, the Panel finds that the Knights should have taken these steps, which would have appropriately balanced the rights of both parties.[162]

In seeking to balance the competing interests at stake without giving priority to one over the other, the tribunal made several determinations that do not sit easily together. The tribunal found that an organization linked to the Roman Catholic faith that rented its hall to members of the general public for a wide range of purposes could refuse to rent

---

the promotion of the interests and welfare of an identifiable group or class of persons characterized by a physical or mental disability or by a common race, religion, age, sex, marital status, political belief, colour, ancestry or place of origin, that organization or corporation must not be considered to be contravening this Code because it is granting a preference to members of the identifiable group or class of persons.

161 *Knights of* Columbus, above note 71 at para 113.
162 *Ibid* at paras 120 and 124.

the hall to individuals who intended to use it for a purpose that was lawful, but inconsistent with Roman Catholic teaching. The scope of this "exemption" or justification is not clear. Would the "exemption" allow the organization to refuse to rent the hall to a couple for a wedding reception following a civil or Protestant ceremony? Or will this "exemption" or justification apply, in practice, only to events involving a same-sex couple or a gay organization? At the same time, the tribunal also found that the Knights of Columbus, having initially but mistakenly rented the hall to a same-sex couple, had an obligation to help that couple find another location for their reception—an activity that the organization considered to be immoral. There seems to be little justification for this compromise. Either the organization has a duty not to discriminate on the grounds of sexual orientation in the rental of its hall or it does not, because it should not be required to support activities it regards as immoral.

The organizations in *Brockie* and *Knights of Columbus* (a printing company and a men's group) argued that they should not be compelled by law to support an activity that according to their faith is immoral. There are obvious reasons why the provision of a market service should not be seen as support for the activities of the customer. In each case the service is provided in an impersonal fashion, and since the law requires that it be made available in a non-discriminatory way, no one should see the organization or business as choosing to support these groups and their activities. But there is a deeper issue here. The *Code's* ban on discrimination does not restrict the organization's religious practice; nor does it require the organization to engage in a practice it regards as immoral. The *Code* simply prohibits the organization from discriminating in the provision of market services. The organization argues that it should be exempted from the law and permitted to discriminate against gays or lesbians (or their activities, in the organization's view of the matter) because it regards homosexuality as immoral and does not accept the decision of democratic institutions to prohibit sexual-orientation discrimination.

N. THE QUEBEC *CHARTER OF VALUES*: CIVIL SERVANTS AND RELIGIOUS SYMBOLS

Religious dress has been a relatively minor issue in Canada, at least in comparison to France and other European countries. However, the proposed Quebec *Charter of Values* has recently given this issue greater prominence.[163] To ensure the neutral or secular character of the state, the proposed *Charter of Values* would prohibit provincial civil servants from wearing "objects such as headgear, clothing, jewelry or other adornments which, by their conspicuous nature, overtly indicate a religious affiliation."[164] The government has said that such a ban would apply to religious dress or symbols, such as the turban, hijab, and kippa. The ban on wearing conspicuous religious dress or symbols may, in some circumstances, be extended to businesses that provide public services under contract with the government. The *Charter of Values* also provides that civil servants "must exercise their functions with their face uncovered" and that individuals "must ordinarily have their face uncovered when receiving [government] services."[165]

In applying the ban on religious dress or symbols, a court, or other decision making body, would have to decide whether an item of clothing or jewelry is *conspicuous* and overtly *religious*. The proposed ban does not exclude symbols that are visible as long as they are not conspicu-

---

163 Shortly before the completion of this book, the Government of Quebec introduced into the legislature Bill 60 with the awkwardly long title of *Charter affirming the values of State secularism and religious neutrality and of equality between women and men, and providing a framework for accommodation requests*, 1st Sess, 40th Leg, Quebec, 2013 [*Charter of Values*]. The following are some of the more significant provisions in the Bill:

5. In the exercise of their functions, personnel members of public bodies must not wear objects such as headgear, clothing, jewelry or other adornments which, by their conspicuous nature, overtly indicate a religious affiliation.

6. Personnel members of public bodies must exercise their functions with their face uncovered, unless they have to cover their face in particular because of their working conditions or because of occupational or task-related requirements.

7. Persons must ordinarily have their face uncovered when receiving services from personnel members of public bodies. How this obligation applies must be specified by the public body in its implementation policy, in accordance with the second paragraph of section 22.

When an accommodation is requested, the public body must refuse to grant it if, in the context, the refusal is warranted for security or identification reasons or because of the level of communication required.

10. A public body may require that any person or partnership with whom it has entered into a service contract or subsidy agreement fulfill one or more of the duties and obligations set out in Chapters II and III, if such a requirement is warranted in the circumstances in particular because of the duration, nature or place of performance of the contract or agreement.

164 *Ibid*, s 5.
165 *Ibid*, ss 6 & 7.

ous. For example, the government has said that a small cross or crucifix would not be caught by the ban. But what turns on this distinction between visible and conspicuous? Why is one a concern and the other not? To answer this question, though, we may first have to understand better the distinction between visible (but discrete) and conspicuous. Why would a kippa (or headscarf or turban) be considered conspicuous—or at least any more conspicuous than a small cross? A kippa may be conspicuous only because it is less familiar, less common, in Quebec society than a cross or crucifix. For if wearing a kippa was common practice in the community, it would hardly be noticed. A large cross may be conspicuous only because it is out of the ordinary. Many practising Roman Catholics in Quebec wear small crosses, but few wear larger (than "normal") crosses. Indeed, the dominant faith, Christianity (in most forms), does not generally require the wearing of religious dress or symbols. The proposed *Charter of Values*, then, would not interfere with established or dominant religious practices in Quebec, which are familiar and therefore inconspicuous. The impact of the ban would fall most heavily on the practices of minority communities that are conspicuous against the background of the Roman Catholic or secular-Catholic status quo.

A second application issue concerns the *religious* character of an item of clothing such as a headscarf or hat. When is an item of clothing a religious symbol? Would the traditional dress of the Old Order Mennonites be seen as conspicuous religious dress? Mennonites are required to dress in a manner that is plain and not ostentatious. However, the fulfillment of this obligation has taken a particular form that is now identified with the religious community. The simple dress of the Old Order Mennonites, which is based on peasant dress styles in the eighteenth and nineteenth centuries, has become a marker of membership in the group. Is this style of clothing a conspicuous religious "symbol," or is it simply the particular way in which the members of the community satisfy a more general religious duty? What about the wig worn by an Orthodox Jewish woman, who is forbidden to expose her hair? Is her wig a form of religious dress or simply the established way in which she fulfills her duty of modesty? It seems unlikely that her wig would be classified as religious dress, because it is not the only way in which Orthodox Jewish women may fulfill their duty of modesty (they may also wear scarves or hats) and because wigs are worn for many nonreligious reasons—and most often for reasons other than modesty. Even if the wig is viewed as religious, it may not be viewed as "obviously" religious or as conspicuous, unless it is a bad wig. The hijab, like many other forms of religious dress, is worn to fulfill a duty of modesty. It has become the established or conventional way in which this duty is fulfilled, and as a result it has also become a marker of group identity for those inside and outside the group. However, because wigs, beards, and headscarves are worn for nonreligious reasons, it may be necessary, in applying the *Charter of Values*, to determine why a wig, beard, or headscarf is being worn in a particular case—whether it is for religious or other reasons.[166]

The wearing of a particular "symbol" or item of clothing may identify the individual as a member of a subgroup in the political community, a group that may command significant loyalty from its members and may support values that are seen as incompatible with the province's civic culture. That, at least, seems often to be the concern that lies behind restrictions on religious dress. As long as anxiety about national identity and the cohesiveness of the cultural community remains significant in Quebec society, the presence of identifiable minority groups that are seen as resistant to integration into the larger civic culture will be regarded as a threat to civil society. And so while the proposed ban focuses on the visibility of religion in the public sphere, its appeal is based on anxieties about religious pluralism in the province, and in particular the presence of a Muslim minority. The concern behind the ban is not the religious or spiritual nature of a symbol but rather the civic meaning or significance of particular symbols such as the Muslim headscarf which is viewed by many in the province as an expression of gender inequality.[167] The significant, and often regressive, political role of the Roman Catholic Church in Quebec before the Quiet Revolution has contributed to a general wariness in the province toward the visibility of religion in the public sphere, although the historical significance of Catholicism in the province, as well as its continued importance to many of the province's residents, means that the "neutrality" requirement applies differently to it.

The Quebec government says that the ban on civil servants wearing conspicuous religious symbols is necessary to ensure state neutrality. The claim does not seem to be that when civil servants wear religious symbols, ordinary citizens might think that their government is supporting, or affirming the truth of, a particular religion. Indeed, it would

---

166 As noted earlier, Locke argues that it is a clear breach of religious freedom when an activity that is otherwise permissible is banned when it is performed for religious reasons.

167 Indeed, it seems likely that one purpose behind the ban on conspicuous religious symbols is to limit Muslim visibility or practice and that the ban is framed in general terms to avoid the complaint, and the constitutional claim, that it is discriminatory.

be difficult to see this as a concern given that relatively few civil servants wear religious symbols and that the few who do wear them come from a variety of religious groups. However, the Quebec government suggests two ways in which the neutrality of the state may be compromised if civil servants are permitted to wear religious symbols. The first, and most often mentioned, is that when a civil servant wears a religious symbol, he may be seen as promoting his faith. The second way is that civil servants who display their religious affiliation may be perceived by others as nonneutral or partial in the performance of their duties.

To begin with the first claim, how might wearing a religious symbol (either discrete or conspicuous) promote religion? If a civil servant wears a religious symbol, others will know that she belongs to a particular group or faith tradition. But in the absence of active proselytization by the individual, it is difficult to see how simply wearing a symbol would amount to religious promotion. As the *Bouchard-Taylor Report* insists, "it is proselytism that should be prohibited and not the wearing of a religious sign, which in itself is not an act of proselytism."[168] The case of teachers, though, does cause the authors to pause: "[S]ome people maintain that a student in the first cycle of elementary school has not yet developed the autonomy necessary to understand that he does not have to adopt the religion of his female teacher, who is in a position of authority."[169] But the *Bouchard-Taylor Report* goes on to say "that young people who are exposed at a very early age to the diversity that they will encounter outside the school can more readily demystify the differences and will consequently be less likely to perceive them as a threat. Successful cohabitation in a diversified society demands that we learn to perceive as normal an array of identity-related differences."[170] A teacher is an authority figure, but as long as she does not actively promote her faith (which she could do without religious symbols), her form of dress will be viewed simply as a personal practice. This seems even more obvious when we recognize that few teachers in any school will wear such symbols.

The connection the Quebec government makes between wearing a symbol and promoting religion may reflect a Christian perspective on symbols and symbol wearing. While the cross and crucifix are important symbols in Christianity of the resurrection and sacrifice of Jesus, in most versions of Christianity there is no requirement that a believer wear a symbol of any kind. And so when a Christian chooses to wear

---

168 Gérard Bouchard & Charles Taylor, *Building the Future: A Time for Reconciliation* (Government of Quebec, 2008) at 150 [*Bouchard-Taylor Report*].

169 *Ibid.*

170 *Ibid.*

a cross or other symbol, he may be seen not just as signalling a personal faith commitment but also as advertising his faith to others. In other faith traditions there is a requirement that the adherent dress in a particular way, but this is most often understood as simply the way in which she is expected to live her faith or to submit to divine authority. An Orthodox Jewish man and a Muslim woman may cover their heads in obedience to divine authority. At the same time, of course, they signal to others their membership in a religious community. Those who wear these "symbols" (or adhere to these practices) may wish to encourage others to do the same, but their principal purpose is not to promote their faith. They are fulfilling an obligation. They may also be signalling their membership in a particular religious community or asserting a spiritual identity. The concern most often expressed by non-Muslims about the headscarf is that it represents a particular form of Islam that is reactionary or austere in character. According to this view, when a woman covers her head in this way, she is signalling to others her submission to male domination.[171] The evidence, though, indicates that women in the West who wear hijab do so for a variety of reasons related to modesty and identity.[172]

The other reason offered in support of the Quebec government's proposed ban is that civil servants who wear conspicuous religious symbols will not be, or at least will not appear to be, impartial in the exercise of their civic responsibilities. This claim may take one of two forms. It might be argued that a devoutly religious individual may feel driven to apply the tenets of his faith (supreme law) rather than state law when performing his duties. The wearing of a turban or kippa makes visible the individual's loyalty to another belief system. But does wearing a religious symbol mean that the individual is more likely to ignore her legal responsibilities and rely on religious law? There is no reason to think so. The most that can be said is that some in the community might think there is a link; but this perception rests on prejudice rather than experience. In the words of the *Bouchard-Taylor Report*:

> Why should we think that the person who wears a religious sign would be less likely to display impartiality, professionalism and loyalty to the institution than the person who does not wear such a sign? Why, therefore, dwell on external displays of faith? Should we not also demand of State employees that they relinquish any conviction of

---

171 The other claim, which is not directly relevant to the general exclusion of religious symbols (but will be discussed below), is that women should be protected from being forced by men to wear hijab.

172 See text accompanying notes 176 & 177.

conscience? It would obviously be absurd to do so. Why think a priori that people who display their religious affiliation are less likely to
take things into consideration than those who do not externalize their
convictions of conscience or who externalize them in a much less visible manner (the wearing of the Catholic cross comes to mind)? Why
refuse one person the presumption of impartiality and grant it to the
other one?[173]

The other version of the partiality claim is that the members of one
religious group may be seen as biased against the members of another
group. The *Bouchard-Taylor Report* suggests this might be a concern in
the case of judges, Crown prosecutors, police officers, and other civil
servants who exercise coercive power over dependent or vulnerable individuals.[174] Again the issue is one of perception since a religious adherent who wears a symbol of his faith is no more likely to be biased against
others than one who does not. An example given in the *Bouchard-Taylor
Report* involves an Orthodox Jewish judge who wears a kippa when pre-
siding over a case in which one of the parties is a Muslim: "It is essential that the parties involved in a trial, especially the respondent, who
may be punished, can assume the judge's impartiality. Could a Muslim
respondent assume the impartiality of a Jewish judge wearing a kippah
or a Hindu judge displaying a tilak?"[175] The Muslim litigant, it is suggested, may be concerned that the judge will not be impartial. But does
this concern about impartiality relate to the judge's religious beliefs?
Are Judaism and Islam, as belief systems or religious traditions, so at
odds that a Jewish judge might not render an impartial decision in such
a case? Surely agnosticism and atheism are more fundamentally at odds
with Islam and other faiths? The concern in the example given in the
Bouchard-Taylor Report is based not on religious incompatibility, or at
least not directly, but instead on the political views associated with each
group—particularly, one assumes, their views on the issue of Israel and
Palestine. If that is the concern, not only is it irrelevant whether the
judge wears a religious symbol but the degree of her religious devotion
may also be irrelevant. In North America some of the strongest defenders of Israel are secular Jews, who do not ordinarily wear kippas but
care deeply about the viability of a Jewish state. Similarly, some of the
strongest advocates for the rights of Palestinians are nonreligious.

---

173 Above note 168 at 149.
174 *Ibid* at 150.
175 *Ibid.*

O. THE EUROPEAN HEADSCARF DEBATE

Many of the arguments made in support of the proposed Quebec *Charter of Values* have been rehearsed in debates concerning religious dress restrictions in France and other European countries. Civil servants in France are not permitted to wear religious symbols when performing their duties. The French government has imposed a ban on students wearing conspicuous religious symbols in the public schools. A few years ago the French government prohibited the wearing of the niqab—religious face covering—in the general public sphere.[176] The French restrictions are said to be based on the principle of *laïcité*, the requirement of state or public neutrality. The Belgian government has prohibited certain civil servants such as police officers and judges from wearing religious symbols and has also banned the niqab from the public sphere. More narrowly defined bans have been imposed in other countries, such as a ban on teachers wearing hijab (or headscarf).[177]

---

176 In *Singh v France*, Communication No 1852/2008, UN Doc CCPR/C/106/D/1852/2008 (4 December 2012), a decision released in February 2013, the Human Rights Committee held that the exclusion of a Sikh student from a state school in France for wearing a keski (a small turban) violated his freedom of religion under the *ICCPR*. According to the Committee, the French government failed to demonstrate that wearing the turban "posed a threat to the rights and freedoms of other pupils or to order at the school" (at para 8.7). The European Court of Human Rights in the case of *SAS v France*, Application no 43835/11, is currently considering whether the general ban on the niqab breaches art 9 of the *Convention for the Protection of Human Rights and Fundamental Freedoms*, Rome, 4 November 1950, online: www.echr.coe.int/Documents/Convention_ENG.pdf.

177 For a discussion of the headscarf controversy, see Carolyn Evans, "The 'Islamic Scarf' in the European Court of Human Rights" (2006) 7 Melbourne Journal of International Law 52. In *Dahlab v Switzerland*, Application no 42393/98, Eur Ct HR, 15 February 2001, the European Court of Human Rights dismissed the freedom of religion claim of a primary school teacher who was prohibited from wearing a headscarf in the classroom. The restriction was justified, said the court, to protect the interests of her young students. The principal concern seemed to be that the headscarf might have a proselytizing effect even though the teacher said nothing to her students about her religion. In 2 BvR 1436/02 BverfGE 108, 24 September 2003 [*Headscarf Decision*], a German court struck down a restriction that prevented a teacher from wearing a headscarf. In *Sahin v Turkey*, Application no 44774/98, Eur Ct HR, 10 November 2005 [*Sahin*], the European Court of Human Rights upheld a prohibition on the wearing of headscarves in universities and other public institutions in Turkey. In *Denbigh*, above note 87, the UK House of Lords upheld the decision of a school authority to exclude a student who sought to wear, for religious reasons, a jilbab (a long cloak that completely covers the person's body) contrary to the school's uniform policy. The members of the Court, in concurring judgments, noted that the school's uniform had been

While the arguments in defence of these bans take a slightly different shape depending on the jurisdiction and the particular restriction, some common themes are apparent. The first is that religious symbols, such as the headscarf, should be banned because they represent, and may even promote, a fundamentalist form of Islam that is regressive, sexist, and perhaps even violent. The second, but related, theme is that the women who wear hijab often do so because of pressure or compulsion from the men in their families or communities. A ban on wearing hijab then is viewed as necessary to protect the autonomy of Muslim women. A ban on the niqab, or face covering, in various settings is sometimes justified as necessary to ensure security or identification, although such bans often seem to be motivated by a more basic discomfort with face covering, an anxiety about "extreme" religion, and a concern that men are forcing women to engage in this discriminatory practice.

The women who wear the headscarf are viewed as both the victims and the promoters of radical Islam and gender subordination. Yet the meaning of hijab and the reasons why women wear it are more complex and numerous. See, for example, the findings of the German Federal Administrative Court in the *Headscarf Decision*, which overturned the decision to dismiss a teacher who wore a headscarf for religious reasons:

> The expert witness Dr. Karakasoglu, who was heard in the oral hearing, carried out a survey of about 25 Muslim students at colleges of education, twelve of whom wore a headscarf, and on the basis of this survey she showed that the headscarf is also worn by young women in order to preserve their own identity and at the same time to show consideration for the traditions of their parents in a diaspora situation; in addition, another reason for wearing the headscarf that had been named was the desire to obtain more independent protection by signalling that they were not sexually available and integrating themselves into society in a self-determined way. Admittedly, the wearing of the headscarf was intended to document in public the value one placed on religious orientation in one's own life, but it was understood as the expression of an individual decision and did not conflict with a modern lifestyle. As understood by the women questioned, preserv-

---

established following a consultation with parents and students, a majority of whom were Muslim, and was perceived by most members of the community to meet their cultural and religious requirements. It was also noted that the student lived outside the school's ordinary catchment area and that other state schools that were closer to where she resided permitted the jilbab. And finally, concern was expressed that if the school permitted this more austere form of religious dress, other Muslim students might feel pressured to conform to this standard to be regarded as good or devout Muslims.

ing their difference is a precondition for their integration. It is not possible to make any statements that are representative of all Muslim women living in Germany on the basis of the interviews conducted and evaluated by the expert witness, but the results of the research show that in view of the variety of motive, the interpretation of the headscarf may not be reduced to a symbol of the social repression of women. Rather, the headscarf can for young Muslim women also be a freely chosen means to conduct a self-determined life without breaking with their culture of origin. Against this background, there is no evidence that the complainant, merely because she wears a headscarf, might for example make it more difficult for Muslim girls who are her pupils to develop an image of woman that corresponds to the values of the Basic Law or to put it into effect in their own lives.[178]

All individuals, and teenagers in particular, are subject to various forms of pressure from friends and family. There is never an absence of pressure or encouragement to conform to social or community standards and expectations. Yet there is plenty of evidence that the headscarf is often worn by women, and particularly high school students, as a personal statement, sometimes over the objections of parents or family members. Certainly the women in the various headscarf cases described in the notes were educated, professional women who were prepared to go to court to resist pressure to remove their headscarves and who insisted that it was their decision to wear a headscarf.[179]

Even if the headscarf conveyed a message of gender subordination and even if it were worn by women only because they were pressured to do so by overbearing men, it is not clear how banning the headscarf would prevent male oppression or support female autonomy. The ban addresses the symbols but not the sources of oppression and will more likely than not contribute to the isolation of Muslim women from mainstream society. As Joan Wallach Scott observes, "The veil, according to the Stasi commission . . . was an expression of Islam's strict segregation of the sexes. In fact, at least in the case of schools, the opposite was

---

178 *Headscarf Decision*, above note 177 at para 52. See also the dissenting judgment of Tulkens J in *Sahin*, above note 177 at para 10.

179 Joan Wallach Scott, in *The Politics of the Veil* (Princeton, NJ: Princeton University Press, 2007) at 126, notes that a variety of studies have shown that many of the girls in France who wear the headscarf describe their action "as a personal choice . . . made in the face of parental opposition . . . ." It is for them "part of an individual search for the spiritual values they found lacking in their communities and society at large" (*ibid*). Wallach Scott endorses the conclusion of sociologist Oliver Roy that "this kind of religiosity among Muslims is already a sign of their modernity and of their adoption of the values of Western individualism" (*ibid*).

true: wearing a headscarf allowed girls to attend co-educational schools who otherwise would have been unable to."[180] The headscarf ban in France and elsewhere reflects an anxiety about the presence of Muslims in these countries and concerns about the erosion of national identity and public values.[181] The ban affirms French social values (established and imagined) and seeks to encourage the assimilation of new immigrants into France's secular culture. Yet there is reason to believe that this approach has been counterproductive. Some girls have removed the headscarf to continue in the state school system, but many others have switched to private religious schools where they continue to wear hijab and have even less contact with students outside their religious community. More generally, the ban is experienced as part of a general practice of discrimination against Muslims (or individuals with a Muslim background) and so contributes to a greater sense of separation from mainstream French society and of identification with the (diverse) Muslim community and Islamic faith.

P. REASONABLE ACCOMMODATION AND BALANCING

The Canadian courts' adoption of a weak standard of justification for the restriction of religious practices reflects the practical concern identified by McLachlin CJ in the *Wilson Colony* case that given the innumerable ways in which religion may conflict with law, a significant duty to accommodate would severely limit the state's ability to act in the public interest. However, it also, and more fundamentally, reflects the courts' uncertainty about whether religious beliefs and practices are different from other beliefs and practices in a way that justifies their insulation from political decision making.

Law and religious practice can conflict in several ways. The conflict between religion and law may be described as indirect when the religious practice conflicts with the means chosen to advance a public purpose and not with the purpose itself.[182] For example, the govern-

---

180 *Ibid* at 157. Similarly, the Quebec *Charter of Values* will keep some Muslim women out of the public service.

181 Jacques Chirac, when serving as president of France, said that wearing a headscarf is "a kind of aggression that is difficult for the French to accept" (quoted in John R Bowen, *Why the French Don't Like Headscarves: Islam, the State, and Public Space* (Princeton, NJ: Princeton University Press, 2007) at 127).

182 In the discussion that follows, I have drawn a distinction between indirect and direct restrictions on religious practice. I recognize, though, that these two

ment may have decided on a particular route for a new highway only to discover that its preferred route runs through an area that is sacred to an Aboriginal group.[183] In such a case it may be possible for the state to advance its purpose as, or almost as, effectively in a different way, through different means, so that it does not interfere with the religious practice or interest. If that is so, then it may be said that the lawmakers should have taken into account the interests and circumstances of the different religious (and other) groups in the community and designed the law (selected a highway route) so as to avoid unnecessary interference with a religious belief or practice. Indeed, it may reasonably be asked whether the state would have enacted the same law (adopted the same means) had the religious practices of a more politically influential group been similarly affected.[184] It is important to recognize, though, that even in the case of what might be described as an indirect conflict between law and religion, the adoption of different means will often detract to some extent from the law's ability to advance a particular policy. In the example given, an alternative highway route may add to construction costs or detract from ideal road conditions.[185] In the case of an indirect or incidental conflict between law and religious practice, "reasonable accommodation" might be the appropriate response (or an appropriate way to describe the response).[186] The issue for the court, in

categories are sometimes difficult to distinguish and might more accurately be viewed as part of a continuum.

183 Such a claim was rejected in the US Supreme Court judgment of *Lyng v Northwest Indian Cemetery Protective Association*, 485 US 439 (1988).

184 See Christopher L Eisgruber & Lawrence G Sager, *Religious Freedom and the Constitution* (Cambridge, MA: Harvard University Press, 2010). However, they mistakenly believe that this test can be applied in a way that does not depend on the special character or value of religion. For an effective critique of their position, see Jeremy Webber, "Understanding the Religion in Freedom of Religion" in Peter Cane, Carolyn Evans, & Zoë Robinson, eds, *Law and Religion in Theoretical and Historical Context* (Cambridge; New York: Cambridge University Press, 2008) 26.

185 Conflict may occur more frequently in the case of "lived" religions that put greater emphasis on public ritual or that govern significant elements of the individual's life. For a discussion, see Lori G Beaman, "Is Religious Freedom Impossible in Canada?" (2010) 6 Law, Culture and the Humanities 1. For a discussion of the courts' problems in fitting Aboriginal spirituality within the framework of "freedom of religion," see John Borrows, "Living Law on a Living Earth: Aboriginal Religion, Law, and the Constitution" in Richard Moon, ed, *Law and Religious Pluralism in Canada* (Vancouver: UBC Press, 2008) 161.

186 I am less troubled than others by the use of the term "reasonable accommodation." The term may be appropriate once we recall the following: (1) religious beliefs often involve truth claims, and in many cases (particularly the institutional autonomy cases discussed in the next chapter) the individual or group is seeking exemption from the application of a public norm such as the right to sexual-

such cases, is whether the state can pursue its objective as, or almost as, effectively in another way that does not interfere to the same extent with the religious practice. When applying this test, and determining whether a religious practice should be accommodated, there may be disagreement about the extent to which government policy should be compromised.

Sometimes, though, the conflict between law and religious practice is more direct in the sense that the law is pursuing a policy (a public value) that is directly at odds with the religious practice. In such a case the conflict between the law and the religious practice cannot be avoided or reduced by the state simply adjusting the means it has chosen to advance its civic purpose. If lawmakers have decided, for example, that corporal punishment of children is wrong and should be banned or that sexual-orientation discrimination is wrong and ought to be prohibited, how is a court to decide whether an exception to these norms should be granted to a religious individual who believes that corporal punishment is mandated by God or that same-sex relationships are sinful and should not be supported? The issue for the court in the corporal punishment example is not whether physical discipline is effective or whether the value or utility of physical discipline outweighs its physical and emotional harm to children. Nor is the issue whether parents should have the right to make judgments about the welfare of their children without state interference, which if resolved in favour of parental autonomy, would result in the striking down of the ban and not just the creation of an exception for some parents. In other words, the court is not questioning the public norm and considering whether physical discipline is, in fact, sometimes right or justified. Instead, the issue is whether some parents—*religious* parents—should be exempted from an otherwise justified ban on physical discipline because they believe that God has mandated them to discipline their children in a way that the law has forbidden. The court must decide whether space should be given to a different normative view—a view that the legislature has rejected.

orientation equality; (2) although some of the public requirements from which the individual is seeking exemption reflect Christian practice (statutory holidays, for example), the state is not precluded from taking account of private religious practice in the formulation of public policy; and (3) a court is not in a position to broadly restructure social practices or the public distribution of burdens and benefits; its role, instead, is to adjudicate rights' claims that are necessarily limited in scope—that focus on a particular state measure to determine if it interferes with a protected right and if so whether it is justified in the public interest or if an exception should be made to it.

In such a case, then, the court's task is not to decide the proper balance or trade-off between competing interests or values (in accordance with the ordinary justification process under section 1 of the *Charter*). As noted earlier, the court has no way to attach specific value or weight to a religious practice. From a secular or public perspective, such a practice has no intrinsic value; indeed, it is said that the court should take no position concerning its value. The practice matters only because it is important to the individual; but there is no way to balance this "value" against the purpose or value of the restrictive law. The court's task instead is to determine whether a religious individual or group should be exempted from the law. But if, as a democratic community, we have decided that a particular activity should be restricted as harmful or that a particular policy should be supported in the public interest, why should the issue be revisited for an individual or group that holds a different view on religious grounds? If religious belief is understood as an opinion or choice, then we may reasonably expect the believer to bear some or all of the costs of his belief and not to place them onto the general public. There are several related reasons, though, why it might sometimes be appropriate to exempt religious adherents from the application of ordinary law—or to treat religion as an identity rather than a choice. We may be aware that the interests of religious minorities are often undervalued in the political process, particularly if religion is regarded as a private matter. We may believe that a degree of respect should be shown to the traditional or evolving responses of different religious communities to fundamental moral issues.[187] We may be concerned that minority religious groups will become alienated or marginalized in the political order.[188] Or our concern may be that if religious

---

187 Religious beliefs or practices connect the individual to a community of believers who participate in a common set of rituals and to a tradition that seeks to respond to the most fundamental issues of collective and spiritual life. See Bruce Ryder, "The Canadian Conception of Equal Religious Citizenship" in Moon, above note 185, 87 at 94: "Religious and conscientious belief systems are closely related to community formation and people's sense of membership in their communities. These communities are sources of strength, support, and normative authority that provide a counterpoint to the role of the state in people's lives." For a discussion of the importance of religious association, see also David Schneiderman, "Associational Rights, Religion, and the *Charter*" in *ibid*, 65.

188 The courts' approach to state restrictions on religious practice has been shaped by earlier private-sector religious discrimination cases. The seminal Canadian case was *Ontario (Human Rights Commission) v Simpsons-Sears Ltd*, [1985] 2 SCR 536, in which the Supreme Court held that under provincial antidiscrimination legislation, a private employer had a duty to accommodate the religious practices of an employee unless this would cause undue hardship to the employer. In that case, Mrs O'Malley had converted to Seventh-day Adventism and as a

adherents are required to act in a way that is contrary to what they believe is right or necessary, they will engage in acts of civil disobedience. Each of these reasons rests on the idea of religion as a cultural identity and religious communities as identity groups. For both principled and pragmatic reasons, it may be important to avoid the marginalization of such groups.

The courts have said that section 2(a) is breached any time the state restricts a religious practice in a nontrivial way. According to the courts, the state must justify the restriction under section 1 and the *Oakes* test, and this is said to involve a balancing of competing interests, the individual's freedom to practise his religion weighed against the state's ability to advance what it understands to be the public good. Yet despite their formal commitment to "reasonable accommodation" or "proportionality," the Canadian courts have been unwilling to require the state to compromise its policy in any significant way. While the courts do not engage in anything that could properly be described as the "balancing" of competing public and religious interests (in which the state's objectives might sometimes be subordinated to the claims of a religious community), they have sometimes sought to create space for religious practices at the margins of law, by adjusting the boundary between private liberty and civic action. First, accommodation may sometimes be granted to religious practices that conflict indirectly with the law (that conflict not with the law's objective but with the means chosen to advance that objective). In such a case the court may require the state to compromise, in a minor way, its pursuit of a particular objective to make space for a religious practice. This is most likely to occur at the minimal impairment stage of the section 1 justification process, where the courts consider whether the government's purpose can be pursued almost as effectively in another way that will not limit the right or freedom to the same extent.[189] However, even in the case of an indirect restriction, the

---

consequence was no longer able to work on Saturdays. Saturday, of course, was Simpsons-Sears's busiest day, and the store had a policy that all full-time retail employees must work on that day. The store's policy was not meant to exclude those who kept Saturday as the Sabbath, and it was not arbitrary; nevertheless Simpsons-Sears was required to accommodate her — to exempt her from the Saturday work requirement. The contrasting results in the *Amselem* and *Wilson Colony* cases may show that the courts are more willing to compromise private or local purposes rather than public or civic objectives.

189 Chief Justice McLachlin, however, has adopted a strict reading of the minimal impairment test so that a law will only fail this test if its objective can be pursued just as effectively without impairing (to the same degree) the right or freedom. Under her approach any form of balancing or trade-off between the policy or purpose of the law and the *Charter* right or freedom should take place at the final

concern expressed by McLachlin CJ in the *Wilson Colony* case (that the number of individuals who may claim a particular exemption is impossible to predict in advance and is potentially unlimited) may lead the court to refuse any form of exemption. Second, in the case of a more direct conflict between a religious practice and a legal norm, the court will require the state to exempt (accommodate) a religious individual or group from the law only if the exempted activity is "self-regarding" and will have no significant impact on others in the community. In such a case the practice will be treated as personal to the individual or internal to the group and insulated from the application of the law.

At issue in the "religious accommodation" cases, then, is the line between the political sphere (of government action) and the private sphere (of religious practice). The courts may sometimes draw the line so that a religious practice is exempted from the application of an otherwise justified law. In this way they may create some "private" space for religious practice without directly challenging the state's authority to govern in the public interest and to establish public norms. A religious practice will be accommodated only if it can be seen as private—as not impacting the rights and interests of others in any significant way. Accommodation, though, will not be extended to beliefs or practices that explicitly address civic matters (the rights or welfare of others in the community) and are directly at odds with democratically adopted public policies. There is, however, no test or standard for determining when an exemption should be granted—when the line between private and civic should be adjusted to make space for a religious practice.[190] Because there is no principled way for the courts to determine the appropriate "balance" between democratically selected public values or purposes and the spiritual beliefs or practices of a religious individual or community (an alternative normative system), the insulation of religion from public decision making will be at best minor and pragmatic. However, a pragmatic response to the competing claims of state policy and religious practice does not fit well with the court's commitment to resolving issues in a principled way, a commitment that underpins the legitimacy of judicial review.[191]

---

balancing stage of the court's s 1 analysis. Such an approach makes it less likely that an exemption will be granted.

190 A religious practice is more likely to be subject to legal restriction if it impacts others; yet the more the "practice" affects others or relates to civic interests, the more likely it will be viewed not as a religious practice but as a political act or position and a proper subject for political support or restriction.

191 Recognition of this may lie behind the often-made argument that it is best left to religious individuals or groups and public institutions to work out the appro-

The difficulty in determining whether an exemption should be granted is apparent in the cases dealing with paternalistic laws. A religious exemption might seem appropriate in the case of a paternalistic law that precludes individuals from engaging in "risky" activities that are required by their faith, for example, an exemption for Sikh men from a law that requires everyone to wear a helmet when riding a motorcycle or bicycle. Paternalistic laws are intended to protect individuals from their own bad decisions. A commitment to religious freedom might, at least, limit the state's power to treat "self-regarding" religious practices as unwise—as something against which the individual needs to be protected. Yet, even in the case of apparently paternalistic laws, the courts have been hesitant to recognize exceptions and treat the practice as a private matter.[192] The reluctance to recognize a religious exception in such cases appears to be based on a realization that no action is entirely private or personal in its impact, and so no law is simply paternalistic. Any time an individual is injured, there will be an impact on others, including friends and family members, employers, co-workers, and of course the general community, which must cover the injured person's medical costs.

Q. THE MYTH OF BALANCING

The structure of *Charter* adjudication is built on the idea that the fundamental rights protected by the *Charter* are the basic conditions of individual autonomy that must be protected from the demands of collective welfare or the common good.[193] These rights, though, may sometimes conflict with other valuable interests, and so in exceptional situations, they may be subject to limits that protect the rights of other individuals. The two-step structure of *Charter* adjudication assumes a bright line

---

priate accommodations or compromises. See Jeremy Webber, "The Irreducibly Religious Content of Freedom of Religion" in Avigail Eisenberg, ed, *Diversity and Equality: The Changing Framework of Freedom in Canada* (Vancouver: UBC Press, 2006) 178.

192 See *R v Badesha*, 2011 ONCA 601, in which the Ontario courts rejected a Sikh man's claim to be exempted from a provincial motorcycle helmet requirement. But see also *Dhillon v British Columbia (Ministry of Transportation and Highways, Motor Vehicle Branch)*, [1999] BCHRTD No 25, in which it was held that an accommodation should be granted because the risk of harm was to the motorcycle rider and not to the general public.

193 The discussion in this section draws on Richard Moon, "Justified Limits on Expression: The Collapse of the General Approach to Limits on *Charter* Rights" (2002) 40 Osgoode Hall LJ 335.

between the protected right or interest of the individual (for example, in expression) and the conflicting rights or interests of other individuals or of the collective (for example, in privacy or in being free from manipulation). At the first stage of the adjudication, the court determines whether the restricted activity falls within the scope of the right. At the second stage, the court balances the right against the competing interest to determine whether the restriction should be upheld. In R v Oakes, the Supreme Court of Canada sought to establish a rigorous test for the assessment of limits on all Charter rights.[194] This generic approach rests on the idea that the rights protected in the Charter have the same basic structure, each right representing a zone of individual privacy or independence that the state should not interfere with except in very special circumstances.

But many of the Charter's rights do not fit this individual liberty model and are better understood as social or relational in character.[195] If the rights protected by the Charter are diverse in character, representing different aspects of human flourishing or dignity within the community, then the form or character of "limitations" on these rights may differ in significant ways. Or, better perhaps, the issues and questions that must be addressed in the adjudication of a religious freedom claim will be different from those that must be addressed in a freedom of expression case. There can be no single generic test for limits on rights, such as the Oakes test.[196] What counts as a "limit" on freedom of expression may be very different from what counts as a limit on religious freedom, or the right to equality. This may account for the rather vague and malleable character of the Oakes test.

Another implication of the social or relational understanding of rights is that the two steps of Charter adjudication (the determination of the right's scope and the justification of limits) may often be difficult to separate. For example, the constitutional right to freedom of expression does not simply protect individual freedom or liberty from state interference. Rather, it protects the individual from state interference with her liberty or freedom to communicate with others—to engage with others and participate in community life. Expression is valuable because individual identity and agency emerge in communicative interaction—because our understanding of self and the world develops through communication with others.[197] Because freedom of expression

---

194 Above note 10.
195 See Richard Moon, The Constitutional Protection of Freedom of Expression (Toronto: University of Toronto Press, 2000).
196 See Moon, ibid at 367.
197 See Moon, ibid, ch 1.

rests on the social character of agency, it will not quite fit within the *Charter*'s adjudicative process, which regards the individual as distinct from the community and her interests as separate from, and potentially in opposition to, those of others or of the larger community. In the leading Canadian freedom of expression cases, the issue for the court is not the correct or reasonable balance between separate but competing interests – is not simply whether the harm "caused" by the expression outweighs its value. Instead, the critical issue in these cases seems to be whether the form of expression (e.g., hate speech, obscenity, election spending, or commercial advertising) contributes to insight and understanding or whether it manipulates or appeals to the irrational. But the audience's freedom from manipulative or irrational appeals is not a competing interest. When it assesses the "manipulative" impact of expression, the court is not simply balancing the distinct interests of separate individuals, the interest in communicating or receiving information and ideas against the interest in not being manipulated or deceived. It is instead making a contextual judgment about the character or quality of the communicative relationship. In these cases, the "value" of expression and the "harm" of expression are not distinct issues but are, instead, two sides of the same basic issue. This is why all of the analysis in the freedom of expression cases occurs at the section 1 stage.

In contrast, in section 15 equality rights cases, all of the analysis seems to take place at the section 15 stage—the determination of whether the section has been breached—leaving no space for section 1. The state breaches section 15 when it fails to show the individual the respect or recognition that he is owed as a member of the community. The right to equality rests on the social character of individual identity and dignity. It rests on a recognition that the individual's identity, self-esteem, and dignity depend on how that person is regarded and treated relative to others in the community. The state does not discriminate simply because it withholds a benefit or imposes a burden on a particular individual or group. Nor does it discriminate simply because it has made a less than fully rational policy choice. A finding of discrimination depends on larger social practices or circumstances—on the context of the particular state act. Given the relational character of the right to equality and the requirement that the courts look to the larger context to determine whether an act is discriminatory, it is not surprising that the courts have struggled to develop a coherent approach to section 1 limits on equality rights. In equality cases, the courts' section 1 analysis often repeats, in a fairly perfunctory way, the considerations that led to the decision that the state act is discriminatory, contrary to section 15. While the significant analysis by the courts in freedom of expression cases takes place at the section 1 stage, the focus of the courts' analysis in equality cases is at the first stage of the adjudication, the issue of whether the right has been breached. In both cases the analysis takes place at one stage of the adjudication because the court is addressing a single, complex question about the individual's connection with the community. It is not simply balancing separate and competing interests, as contemplated by the two-step structure of adjudication.[198]

In section 2(a) cases, the courts have been quick to find a breach of the right. Any nontrivial restriction on a religious practice will amount to a breach of the section. Yet, at the section 1 stage, the standard of justification in freedom of conscience and religion cases seems to be very weak. Any public interest pursued in a rational way may be sufficient to justify a breach of the right. In these cases, then, the courts do not engage in any significant balancing of competing interests. The tension in the courts' understanding of religion and religious freedom—as both social identity and individual judgment—is manifested in the two-step structure of *Charter* adjudication. At the section 2(a) stage of analysis, the courts acknowledge the importance of religion as an identity that should be treated with equal respect, while at the section 1 stage, they recognize that religious beliefs involve judgments about truth and right that often affect others in the larger community and so cannot simply be insulated from state action or treated with equal respect.[199]

Most modern defences of judicial review regard constitutional rights as basic conditions of individual autonomy or citizenship that should be protected from the give-and-take of ordinary preference-based politics.

---

198 The Canadian courts have interpreted the s 15 ban on discrimination as including both intentional (or direct) discrimination and effects (or constructive) discrimination. There are good reasons for this including, most significantly, the difficulty in distinguishing between them in practice. When a court decides that the state has engaged in intentional discrimination—has been motivated by prejudice—there is no way in which the breach of right can be justified. On the other hand, when a court decides that the state has discriminated because it enacted a law that has a disadvantaging impact on the members of a historically marginalized group, the law may sometimes be justified, despite its impact. And so in the case of effects discrimination, s 1 might have a role to play. However, the courts have sought (for good reason) to address these two forms of discrimination in a single analytic framework and have incorporated justificatory considerations into this framework making s 1 redundant. For a discussion, see Richard Moon, "A Discrete and Insular Right to Equality: Comment on *Andrews v. Law Society of British Columbia*" (1989) 21 Ottawa L Rev 563.

199 Benjamin L Berger, in "The Cultural Limits of Legal Tolerance" (2008) 21 Can JL & Jur 245 at 257, describes the shift in analysis in a slightly different way noting that at the justification stage, the limit is assessed on the basis of the norms and assumptions of the "rule of law."

Because they are insulated from direct political pressure, the courts can serve as a "forum of principle," a place where issues of principle or basic value can be debated and resolved.[200] However, if constitutional rights protect the individual's connection or relationship with others and are about the realization of self within community, judgments about their scope and limits may involve complex social and economic considerations. The issue in most freedom of religion cases is whether a religious individual or group should be exempted from ordinary law. An exemption will be allowed only when its impact on state policy will be relatively minor. This would seem to involve a pragmatic trade-off of interests rather than a principled reconciliation of rights.

---

200 See Ronald Dworkin, "The Forum of Principle" (1981) 56 NYU L Rev 469.

CHAPTER 4

THE AUTONOMY
OF RELIGIOUS
ORGANIZATIONS

A. INTRODUCTION

When an individual believer claims exemption from the law for her religious practice, the key issue for the court is whether the exception—the accommodation—will negatively affect the public interest or the rights of others. In some cases, though, the accommodation claim is made not by an individual, who is seeking exemption for a specific practice, but by a religious organization or institution, which is seeking a degree of autonomy in the governance of its affairs—in the operation of its internal decision making processes, and the application of what Alvin Esau refers to as "inside law" to its members.[1] As Ayelet Shachar observes, most individual accommodation claims are about inclusion within society—a claim for exemption that enables the individual to participate more fully in the general community—while institutional "autonomy" claims are about "opting out of, or seceding from the effects of the polity's public laws or norms."[2] In these institutional autonomy cases, the court must determine not only whether the exemption from state law

---

1   Alvin J Esau, "Living by Different Law: Legal Pluralism, Freedom of Religion, and Illiberal Religious Groups" in Richard Moon, ed, *Law and Religious Pluralism in Canada* (Vancouver: UBC Press, 2008) 110 at 110.
2   Ayelet Shachar, "Privatizing Diversity: A Cautionary Tale from Religious Arbitration in Family Law" (2008) 9 Theor Inq L 573 at 581. See also José Woehrling, "L'obligation d'accommodement raisonnable et l'adaptation de la société à la diversité religieuse" (1998) 43 McGill LJ 325.

will impact the rights and interests of others (i.e., whether the group's application of "inside law" will negatively affect outsiders to the group) but also whether the members of the group should be protected by state law from internal rules that are unfair and contrary to public policy. The courts' judgment about when intervention into the "internal" operation of the group is necessary will be affected by their understanding of the nature and value of religious association—whether it is seen as a collective bond or identity or, instead, as a voluntary alliance of individuals pursuing common ends and whether it is viewed as a source of meaning and value for its members or as potentially oppressive and confining.

In a variety of ways, the law acknowledges the importance of religious community as a source of meaning or identity for the individual and as a centre of social life, public charity, and community action. Religious institutions are generally exempted from property taxes and, as charitable organizations, from income tax.[3] Religious organizations are also given significant autonomy in the conduct of their affairs, sometimes through specific legal exemptions from ordinary law.

B. MEMBERSHIP, IDENTITY, EXIT, AND INTERVENTION

The general assumption is that those who choose to become, or to remain, members of a religious group do not require protection from intragroup rules, even rules that are harsh and discriminatory. If the "members" of a group have voluntarily submitted to the group's rules or decision making processes, then the state ought not to intervene. The individual's membership in the group may be seen as voluntary as long as he is free to leave the group, and live under ordinary state law, if he disagrees with the group's actions.

Yet exit from a religious group is seldom costless. There may be a variety of barriers or impediments to the individual's withdrawal from such a group. As part of its commitment to religious freedom, the state should endeavour to remove or lower these barriers to enable individ-

---

3   For a more detailed account of church tax exemptions, see MH Ogilvie, *Religious Institutions and the Law in Canada*, 3d ed (Toronto: Irwin Law, 2010) at 258ff [*Religious Institutions*]; and Janet Epp Buckingham, *Fighting Over God: A Legal and Political History of Religious Freedom in Canada* (Montreal; Kingston: McGill-Queen's Press, 2014). Another way in which the law may recognize and support religious communities is the protection granted to the confidentiality of the priest and penitent relationship, which is established by statute in some provinces and given some protection in the common law (*R v Gruenke*, [1991] 3 SCR 263).

ual members, if they choose, to leave the group and either join another group or associate with no particular group in civil society. Whether such a barrier should be removed or overridden was the issue in several cases concerning exit and expulsion from Hutterite colonies. Property in these colonies is collectively owned, and so if a member decides to leave the colony or is expelled from the colony, she leaves with nothing, in theory not even "personal" property. The courts have recognized that this rule or practice is a potential deterrent to individuals who might want to leave the community. The problem, though, is that collective ownership is not just a barrier to exit; it is a central tenet of the group's belief system. If a court were to override this practice, it might undermine the group's belief system and its organizational structure.[4]

In *Hofer et al v Hofer et al* (a pre-*Charter*[5] case), the Supreme Court of Canada had to decide whether members of a Hutterite colony had been lawfully expelled.[6] In addressing this issue, the Court considered whether the members had voluntarily agreed (in contract) to the collective ownership rule and so were bound by this rule when they were expelled from the colony. The majority of the Court found that the expelled members had voluntarily agreed to the colony's articles of association and were therefore subject to its terms. However, Pigeon J in his dissenting judgment questioned whether the appellants' assent to the colony's rules should be described as voluntary:

> [F]reedom of religion includes the right for each individual to change his religion at will. While Churches are otherwise free like other voluntary associations to establish whatever rules they may see fit, freedom of religion means that they cannot make rules having the effect of depriving their members of this fundamental freedom. In my view, this is precisely what these Hutterians have been attempting to do. . . . The evidence shows that the rules and practices of this religious group make it as nearly impossible as can be for those who are born in it to do otherwise than embrace its teachings and remain forever within it. . . . They have no right at any time in their life to leave the colony where they are living unless they abandon literally everything. Even the clothes they are wearing belong to the colony and, according to

---

4   A point also made in Dwight G Newman, "Exit, Voice, and 'Exile': Rights to Exit and Rights to Eject" (2007) 57 UTLJ 43 at 65. But it is important not to jump too quickly to this hard response since there may be ways in which individuals who "exit" the colony could be "bought out" without the colony collapsing.

5   *Canadian Charter of Rights and Freedoms*, Part 1 of the *Constitution Act, 1982*, being Schedule B to the *Canada Act 1982* (UK), 1982, c 11 [*Charter*].

6   [1970] SCR 958 [*Hofer*]. The appellants in the case sought an order winding up the colony and dividing its assets.

the judgments below, they are to be returned to it as its property by anyone who ceases to be a member of the Church.[7]

The difficulty with treating colony membership as voluntary—as a matter of agreement—is that most members have been born into the community. The majority judgment of Ritchie J, though, glossed over this problem: "[I]f any individual either through birth within the community or by choice wishes to subscribe to such a rigid form of life and to subject himself to the harsh disciplines of the Hutterian Church, he is free to do so."[8] Insofar as they could be said to have agreed to the terms of the "association," they did so as members who were already embedded in a form of life and association defined by these rules.

Indeed, the barriers to exit are often less tangible than a simple financial penalty and so may be difficult, if not impossible, to remove.[9] A religious community may be so insular that even if its members are "free" to exit, they may be unable to imagine living outside the group. An individual who was born into a particular group will feel bound to that group by ties of friendship and kinship. More significantly, her identity may be tied to the group so that exit is difficult even when there are few material barriers. In other words, the individual's exit from her religious community may be difficult for the very same reason that community autonomy is important. Exit is difficult precisely because religious community plays a central role in the individual member's life and identity—because it is a source of meaning and significance for him. The individual's social and psychological ties to his community are sometimes described as barriers to his exit, similar to the economic costs that may deter him from leaving the community. The term "barrier," though, suggests that these ties interfere with the individual's judgment, preventing him from making the choices he would otherwise make, and, like material restrictions, ought to be removed. Yet the claim most often made in cases involving religious communities (or identity groups) is not that the courts or the state should nullify these "barriers to exit," as if that were possible or desirable. Instead the claim is that the courts or the state should intervene to protect the individual from unjust or oppressive internal group rules because she should not have to choose

---

7   *Ibid* at 984 & 985: "Such a construction of the contractual relationship between the members of the Colony means that they really cannot exercise their right of freedom of religion." Justice Pigeon also noted that "it is unusual for Hutterian children to be allowed to go beyond Grade 8 education" (*ibid* at 985).

8   *Ibid* at 975.

9   See the discussion of *Bruker v Marcovitz*, 2007 SCC 54 [*Bruker*], in Section D(3), below in this chapter.

between leaving the community to which she is deeply connected and remaining within the community but subject to its unfair rules.[10]

C. EXEMPTION FROM HUMAN RIGHTS CODES

Whether the state should be permitted to regulate the "internal" operations of a religious organization has been an issue in a number of cases involving human rights and labour laws. In these cases, the central question is whether the organization is performing a religious function, either serving the members of a spiritual community or carrying out a religious mission within the larger community, or whether instead it is providing nonreligious services to the general community and is more appropriately viewed as a public or market actor. If the organization is performing a religious function, then it may be exempted from antidiscrimination and other laws that are inconsistent with its religious character and mission. But, as will become apparent, it is not always easy to determine whether the function being performed by the organization is exclusively or even primarily religious.[11]

Each of the human rights codes in Canada includes an exemption from its ban on employment discrimination for a "bona fide occupational qualification" [bfoq], an exemption that has been applied to religion-based requirements for employment at religious organizations.[12] Some of these codes also include more specific exemptions for organiza-

---

10   For a discussion of the importance of respecting group differences while protecting vulnerable group members, see Ayelet Shachar, *Multicultural Jurisdictions: Cultural Differences and Women's Rights* (Cambridge; New York: Cambridge University Press, 2001); and Howard Kislowicz, "Judging the Rules of Belonging" (2011) 44 UBC L Rev 287. The rules in the *Divorce Act*, RSC 1985, c 3 (2d Supp), s 21.1, dealing with religious divorce may be an example of this. These rules were discussed in *Bruker v Marcovitz*, but they were not applied in that case, and so their constitutionality was not directly addressed. However, the majority judgment of Abella J implied that these rules would be upheld. They empower a judge in a civil divorce case to exert pressure on a spouse who refuses to give his consent to a religious divorce by dismissing any application by that spouse and striking out any other pleadings and affidavits filed by the spouse. For a discussion of these rules, see John T Syrtash, *Religion and Culture in Canadian Family Law* (Toronto: Butterworths, 1992).

11   For example, when a religious authority performs a marriage, the marriage is recognized as a civil marriage, which creates legal rights and duties.

12   In the absence of such a provision, an exemption claim could be made directly under the *Charter*.

tions that serve "the interests of persons identified by their . . . creed."[13] Most obviously a church community will not be found to have breached the ban on religious discrimination in employment when it selects a minister or pastor based on her commitment to a particular religious belief system. A more difficult case arises when an organization requires that all its employees, regardless of the specific tasks they perform, adhere to certain religious practices. For example, in *Caldwell et al v Stuart et al*, the Supreme Court of Canada held that a Roman Catholic high school could dismiss a teacher who, although a member of the church, had married a divorced man in a civil ceremony contrary to church doctrine.[14] The Court found that the school's requirement that all teachers adhere to church doctrine was a bfoq. According to the Court, because teachers are role models for their students, it was reasonable for a religious school to expect them to conform to the doctrines of the church, regardless of the courses they teach.[15] The Court observed that "[i]t will be only in rare circumstances that such a factor as religious conformance can pass the test of *bona fide* qualification. In the case at bar, the special nature of the school and the unique role played by the teachers in the attaining of the school's legitimate objects are essential to the finding that religious conformance is a *bona fide* qualification."[16]

In *Ontario (Human Rights Commission) v Christian Horizons*, the Divisional Court of Ontario had to determine whether the dismissal of a lesbian employee by an evangelical Christian group that operated group homes for developmentally disabled individuals amounted to employment discrimination under the Ontario *Human Rights Code*.[17] The *Code* prohibits employment discrimination on the grounds of sexual orientation but recognizes an exception to this ban:

> 24. (1) The right under section 5 to equal treatment with respect to employment is not infringed where,
>   (a) a religious, philanthropic, educational, fraternal or social institution or organization that is primarily engaged in serving the inter-

---

13   For example, the Ontario *Human Rights Code*, RSO 1990, c H.19, s 24(1)(a). Section 18 provides a similar exception to the ban on discrimination in the provision of services.

14   [1984] 2 SCR 603. There may be some unease in insulating religious schools from human rights laws. They may be seen as religious in character or as advancing a religious purpose, but because they educate children, they may also be seen as performing a public role, as educating democratic citizens.

15   A number of these cases are discussed in Alvin J Esau, "Islands of Exclusivity: Religious Organizations and Employment Discrimination" (2000) 33 UBC L Rev 719. See, for example, *Schroen v Steinbach Bible College*, [1999] MHRBAD No 2.

16   Above note 14 at 625.

17   2010 ONSC 2105.

ests of persons identified by their race, ancestry, place of origin, colour, ethnic origin, creed, sex, age, marital status or disability employs only, or gives preference in employment to, persons similarly identified if the qualification is a reasonable and *bona fide* qualification because of the nature of the employment . . . .[18]

The court held that even though Christian Horizons was a religious organization "serving the interests of persons identified by their . . . creed," the group's religiously based prohibition on homosexual behaviour was not a bfoq for the particular job performed by the employee. The organization's decision to dismiss the employee because she failed to conform to the ban on same-sex relationships amounted to employment discrimination on the grounds of sexual orientation, contrary to the *Code*.

In the court's view, Christian Horizons was a religious organization operating group homes "for religious reasons — in order to carry out a Christian mission."[19] The organization would not be "assisting people with disabilities in a Christian home environment but for the religious calling of those involved."[20] According to the court, the organization's charitable work was "undertaken as a religious activity through which those involved could live out their Christian faith and carry out their Christian ministry to serve people with developmental disabilities."[21] The court concluded that the organization was "primarily engaged in serving the interest of persons identified by their creed" with beneficial consequences for the individuals residing in the group homes.[22] I am doubtful, though, that the members of the organization would say that their purpose was to serve themselves — to satisfy their desire to perform Christian service. While their motivation may have been to do God's will, their purpose was to help others. The court, however, was concerned that if the organization, or any "religious group" doing charitable work in the community, were found not to be "primarily" engaged in serving the interests of persons identified by their creed, the organization would not be covered by section 24(1) and so "could not require even its senior officers, who constitute the organization's directing mind, to be adherents to its religious beliefs."[23] But ought this to be a concern if the organization provides general services, pays its employees, and receives government funding?

---

18   Above note 13.
19   Above note 17 at para 75.
20   *Ibid.*
21   *Ibid* at para 77.
22   *Ibid.*
23   *Ibid* at para 65.

The court, however, went on to find that the requirement that employees refrain from same-sex relationships was not a bfoq for the particular job performed by Ms Heintz, since she was not involved in religious teaching or conversion.[24] In determining that the organization had a religious mission, the court focused on the shared spiritual commitment of the staff; however, when deciding that conformity with religious doctrine was not a bfoq for nonmanagement positions, the court's focus shifted to the actual services provided by Ms Heintz and other employees. The court's conclusion is an awkward one: the organization is serving a religious group—its workers—but its workers need not conform to all of the organization's religious tenets. The court appeared to accept that the organization's practice of hiring only evangelical Christians did not breach the *Code*. "There was no question," said the court, "that religious commitment is seen by the organization as fundamental to both its approach to service delivery and to the carrying out of the job responsibilities."[25] The court emphasized that Ms Heintz continued to identify herself as an evangelical Christian and "viewed her work with Christian Horizons as the fulfillment of her calling to do Christian ministry" even if she did not accept or conform to the organization's particular beliefs about same-sex relationships.[26] She was, said the court, "a follower of Christian Horizon's ethos in every other way, and is committed and quite capable of performing the job functions of a support worker with the love and care that has typically characterized Christian Horizon's service to people with developmental disabilities and with respect for the Christian activities in the homes."[27] And so the court found that even though a commitment to Christianity might be a legitimate job requirement, it was not necessary for Ms Heintz to accept, and live in accordance with, the organization's religious views about homosexuality. A general commitment to the religious ethos of

24   The court insisted (*ibid* at para 90) that

> [t]he qualification, to be valid, must not just flow automatically from the religious ethos of Christian Horizons. It has to be tied directly and clearly to the execution and performance of the task or job in question. A focus that is only on the religious organization and its mission, without regard to how it is manifested in the particular job in issue, would deprive the final element of s. 24(1)(a) . . . of any meaning.

The court found (quoting from the decision of the Ontario Human Rights Tribunal) that the "primary role of a support worker is not to help all residents to adopt a Christian way of life, or to carry out a mission of salvation, or to convert residents to the faith beliefs of the organization" (*ibid* at para 92).

25   *Ibid* at para 99.
26   *Ibid* at para 82.
27   *Ibid* at para 104.

the organization was sufficient to enable her to perform her job properly. The court seemed to decide that the rejection of homosexuality was not an essential part of the organization's Christian commitment.

There is, however, a larger issue lurking in the background of this case. Christian Horizons employs only Christians, and according to the court it advances a Christian mission. Even if the court is right, and the organization does not engage explicitly in religious proselytization, its activities in the group homes are infused with religious content.[28] Yet Christian Horizons is the principal operator in the province of group homes for the developmentally disabled and is almost entirely funded by the province. If the organization is viewed as "religious," then the province's support for it as the main provider of these services may run afoul of the section 2(a) neutrality requirement.

D. THE ENFORCEMENT OF PRIVATE LAW ARRANGEMENTS

1) Cautious Enforcement

The courts will not ordinarily enforce religious rules on those inside or outside the group. To do so would breach the requirement of religious neutrality or the ban on state compulsion of religious practice. However, when religious rules or practices are incorporated into contractual and other private law arrangements, the situation is different. The courts have been cautiously willing to enforce contracts made between religious group members that give legal form to the norms or practices of the group.

There are several reasons why the courts may hesitate or decline to enforce agreements that are based on religious norms or that address religious matters. When enforcing a contract that is based on a religious norm, the court may be drawn into disputes about the proper meaning of the norm with no secular or "objective" standard upon which to base its interpretation. The court may be forced into the role of "arbiter" of religious doctrine and find itself enforcing contested doctrine on dis-

---

28   See *ibid* at para 101:

> The evidence shows that the "Christian environment" that was provided in the homes by the support workers mainly manifested itself through prayer, hymn singing and Bible reading. There is no evidence that Ms. Heintz refused to participate in these activities. In doing so, the support workers are not engaged in converting the residents to Evangelical beliefs or lifestyle.

senting members of the group.[29] Yet when interpreting commercial and other contractual arrangements, the courts are often required to consider the customs and norms of different subgroups within the larger community. The contracting parties may have relied on such norms or customs even though they may have (slightly) different views about their meaning and implications. Why then is it unacceptable for the courts to enforce a contract when the norms underlying it (and subject to contest) are religious? The problem, I think, is that religious norms, particularly when they are in dispute, cannot be viewed as simply social conventions to be determined by an examination of group practice. They are, for the adherent, part of a higher law and must be respected because they are true or because they are God given. Any dispute between the contracting parties about the proper understanding of these norms is a dispute about spiritual truth. The resolution of such a dispute involves a judgment not about the best interpretation of a social practice but about the proper reading of divine law—about what God has truly commanded. The democratic and secular state, though, is expected to remove itself from such issues and avoid making determinations about spiritual truth.

Another reason for judicial reluctance to enforce religious contracts is that both the subject matter of the contract and the relationship between the contracting parties may make legal enforcement inappropriate. Such a contract may be based on norms that are faith based, deeply held, and "religiously" binding on the members of a spiritual community. When entering an agreement or "contract," the parties may not understand themselves as creating legal obligations. They may consider themselves bound not by secular law but by the spiritual norms of their community—by higher law—and by their commitment to each other as members of a spiritual community. And to this, we might add that the legal enforcement (or the threat of legal enforcement) of such an agreement, or undertaking, may undermine the deeper spiritual connections between community members. The courts may be reluctant to enforce "religious" agreements for the same reasons they have sometimes declined to enforce "family bargains"—because these agreements are embedded in larger relationships and are inseparable from deeper obligations. The reluctance to enforce both family and religious bargains may also rest on a recognition that legal intervention will damage the deeper

---

29   In *Syndicat Northcrest v Amselem*, 2004 SCC 47 at para 50, Iacobucci J declared that "the state is in no position to be, nor should it become, the arbiter of religious dogma. Accordingly, courts should avoid judicially interpreting and thus determining, either explicitly or implicitly, the content of a subjective understanding of religious requirement . . . ."

relationship between family members or religious adherents. Moreover, the particular norm or practice that is the subject of the contract may be embedded within (and understandable in relation to) a larger system of religious norms and practices. For example, the husband's promise in a Muslim marriage contract to pay his wife (deferred) *mahr* if they divorce is tied to his power to divorce his wife unilaterally.[30] Even when religious parties explicitly make use of private law forms—and may reasonably be understood as creating legal rights and obligations—they may believe that it would be wrong, a breach of their faith and their commitment to their community, to resort to the courts when disputes arise about the meaning or implementation of the agreement.[31]

Finally, the courts may be reluctant to enforce religious contracts because they are concerned that one or both of the parties have not made a free and independent decision to enter into a legally binding agreement. The parties to a religious contract may be connected by a common history and a shared commitment to a set of faith-based norms and practices. They may be materially and psychologically tied to their spiritual community. In this context, family and friends may apply significant pressure to agree.[32] This pressure may be explicit, and involve demands and threats, or it may be more subtle.[33] The individual may feel "compelled" to agree to contractual terms that are presented as morally binding or as elements of community membership or identity. However, we should not confuse the inner pressure that an individual may feel to live up to certain values or obligations with the different forms of external pressure that may be brought to bear on her in an attempt to get her

---

30   For a discussion of this, see Pascale Fournier, "In the (Canadian) Shadow of Islamic Law: Translating *Mahr* as a Bargaining Endowment" in Moon, above note 1, 140. The Canadian cases dealing with the enforcement of an agreement to pay *mahr* are inconsistent in their results, for example, *Kaddoura v Hammoud*, [1998] OJ No 5054, in which the court refused to enforce the agreement, and *Amlani v Hirani*, [2000] BCJ No 2357, in which the agreement was enforced.

31   For a discussion of the Hutterite prohibition on resort to secular courts, see Alvin J Esau, *The Courts and the Colonies: The Litigation of Hutterite Church Disputes* (Vancouver: UBC Press, 2004).

32   See Lindsey E Blenkhorn, "Islamic Marriage Contracts in American Courts: Interpreting *Mahr* Agreements as Prenuptials and Their Effect on Muslim Women" (2002) 76 S Cal L Rev 189 at 198, which notes that in the case of an agreement to pay *mahr*, "the bride herself has little to no involvement in the negotiation . . . . "

33   Some of those who proposed the establishment of a system of sharia arbitration under the private arbitration law in Ontario expressed the view that an individual could not be regarded as a good Muslim if he submitted his disputes to the secular courts rather than arbitration under sharia rules. For a discussion of this, see Lorraine E Weinrib, "Ontario's Sharia Law Debate: Law and Politics under the *Charter*" in Moon, above note 1, 239.

to agree to certain practices or norms. Each of us is affected by an array of deeply held values, commitments, and associations. We should not be too quick to decide that religious commitments negate agency.

The Canadian courts have been cautiously willing to enforce private law arrangements between religious community members even when these arrangements are based on religious norms or require the interpretation of such norms. In the recent case of *Bruker v Marcovitz*[34] and in earlier cases involving disputes within Hutterite colonies and other religious communities, the courts have adopted a pragmatic response to the enforceability of such contracts. The courts have been willing to enforce these arrangements if they have a legal form and can be interpreted without the courts' being drawn (deeply) into a debate about the proper understanding of religious doctrine. The courts have been willing to do this because they recognize that the parties have relied on these private legal forms and organized their affairs accordingly and because the courts accept that there is a public interest in resolving disputes about these arrangements. In many of these cases, the courts are called upon to determine who "owns" or controls church property. Because this issue has civic consequences, judicial abstinence may not be a practical option.

2) Church Property Disputes

Generally speaking, the property of a religious organization "is understood to be held in trust, whether express or implied, for the purposes of that organization."[35] When a dispute arises concerning the control or ownership of church property, resulting from division in the church, the role of the courts in resolving the dispute has been to determine the terms of the trust.[36] In a series of cases beginning with the decision of the House of Lords in *General Assembly of the Free Church of Scotland v Overtoun*,[37] British and Canadian courts found that the property was

---

34   Above note 9.

35   *Religious Institutions*, above note 3 at 292.

36 See MH Ogilvie, "Church Property Disputes: Some Organizing Principles" (1992) 42 UTLJ 377; Alvin J Esau, "The Judicial Resolution of Church Property Disputes: Canadian and American Models" (2003) 40 Alta L Rev 767; and *Religious Institutions*, above note 3 at 291–95. In her book *Religious Institutions*, Ogilvie also discusses the courts' role in overseeing the discipline and dismissal of clergy, which is confined to ensuring that the church follows its internal rules and the standards of procedural fairness (*ibid* at 302). See, for example, *McGaw v United Church of Canada* (1991), 82 DLR (4th) 289 (Ont CA). But see also *Hart v Roman Catholic Episcopal Corp of the Diocese of Kingston*, 2011 ONCA 728.

37   [1904] AC 515 (HL) [*Free Church*].

held in trust for a church identified by its adherence to a particular set of religious doctrines. The beneficiary of the property trust in such cases was the group that remained committed to the established (and fundamental) doctrines of the church. In some cases, this meant that the beneficiary of the trust was the group that was splitting from the main body of the organization because it did not agree with significant revisions to established doctrine. More recently, however, the courts have been less inclined to see the trust as based on adherence to traditional doctrine and more likely to find that the property is held in trust for the benefit of the general organization, which has the authority to interpret and revise doctrine.

This more contemporary approach was applied in the recent case of *Bentley v Anglican Synod of the Diocese of New Westminster*.[38] In that case, the British Columbia Court of Appeal had to determine who was entitled to hold and use church property following a doctrinally based schism in a diocese of the Anglican Church of Canada. The appellants, who were members and clergy of several Anglican parishes, sought to withdraw from the Diocese of New Westminster of the Anglican Church while retaining the right to use church property in the parish for their worship. The appellants wished to withdraw from the diocese because they disagreed with the synod's decision to bless same-sex marriages. They argued that parish property was held for purposes consistent with historic, orthodox Anglican doctrine. They further argued, relying on the *Free Church* decision, that because they adhered to traditional church doctrine, they most closely conformed to the conditions of the trust under which parish property was held. The court, however, was unwilling in this case to follow the *Free Church* approach, which did "not allow for the institution in question to adopt changes in doctrine, or at least fundamental doctrine. . . ."[39] The court found that the property was held in trust for purpose of "further[ing] Anglican ministry in accordance with Anglican doctrine, and that in Canada, the General Synod has the final word on doctrinal matters."[40] The court recognized that the Anglican church is a hierarchical body and that Anglicanism cannot be separated from the church organization's episcopal authority.[41] The rules of the Anglican Church of Canada provided that doctrinal matters fell within the jurisdiction of the bishop and the synod and that these doctrinal determinations governed all parishes. The court dismissed the appellants' claim to the property.

38　[2010] BCCA 506.
39　*Ibid* at para 66.
40　*Ibid* at para 76.
41　*Ibid* at para 74.

Courts in different jurisdictions have responded to church property disputes in different ways, trying to resolve these disputes while minimizing their involvement in matters of doctrine. The commitment in the United States to the separation of church and state has led to two responses to this dilemma: 1) deference to the determination of the highest decision making body in a hierarchical church, without asking whether this body (the mother or central church) has deviated from traditional doctrine, and even without asking whether this body has adhered to its own rules, including process rules; or 2) the application of "neutral principles" with the court or other civil authority determining the property issue on the basis of the express terms of title deeds, contracts, and perhaps even the church's charter and bylaws, provided these documents can be read in exclusively secular terms without requiring any judgment about religious doctrine.[42]

In *Lakeside Colony of Hutterian Brethren v Hofer*, the Supreme Court of Canada reviewed the decision by a Hutterite colony to expel some of its members from the religious community and from the community's collectively owned property.[43] Justice Gonthier, for the Court, found that the colony was a voluntary association and that its members had agreed to the articles of association. He further found that the colony had the power under these articles to expel members who deviated from the religious beliefs and practices of the community. However, in this case, he thought that the decision making authorities in the colony had failed to adhere to the requirements of procedural fairness, and so the expulsion decision was ineffective. Justice Gonthier said that while the Court would not review the merits of the colony's decision to expel members, it would consider whether the association had followed its own rules when making such a decision. Justice Gonthier was aware of the entanglement issue but did not seem unduly troubled by it. He noted that the courts will not generally intervene in doctrinal or spiritual matters but may do so when civil or property rights are involved. According to Gonthier J, once the court assumes jurisdiction over a dispute with religious components, "there is no alternative but to come to the best understanding possible of the applicable tradition and custom."[44]

---

42   See, for example, *Watson v Jones*, 80 US (13 Wall) 679 (1871); and *Jones v Wolf*, 443 US 595 (1979).

43   [1992] 3 SCR 165 [*Lakeside Colony*]. See also the pre-*Charter* case of *Hofer*, above note 6. These and other cases involving the Hutterite colonies in Canada are considered in Esau, above note 31.

44   *Lakeside Colony*, above note 43 at para 64. Justice Gonthier continued, "[T]radition or custom which is sufficiently well established may be considered to have the status of rules of the association, on the basis that they are unexpressed terms

3) *Bruker v Marcovitz*

The same pragmatic approach was adopted by the majority of the Supreme Court of Canada in *Bruker v Marcovitz*.[45] At the time of their civil divorce, Mr Marcovitz and Ms Bruker entered into an agreement concerning custody, access, division of property, and support. Their agreement also included an undertaking by each to appear before the Beth Din (rabbinical court) for the purpose of obtaining a *get*, or divorce, under Jewish law.[46] For their marriage to be dissolved under Jewish law, it was necessary for Mr Marcovitz to provide and Ms Bruker to accept a "bill of divorce," or *get*. Without a *get*, neither party could remarry in the faith, and any subsequent intimate relationship entered into by either of them would be considered adulterous, and any children born of that relationship would be viewed as illegitimate. Mr Marcovitz did not appear before the Beth Din immediately following the civil divorce, despite his promise. Indeed, his consent to a religious divorce came fifteen years later and then only after Ms Bruker had commenced an action for breach of contract. Once Mr Marcovitz gave his consent, and the couple were divorced under Jewish law, Ms Bruker amended her action to seek compensation for the loss she had suffered as a consequence of his failure to give his consent at the time of the civil divorce.

A majority of the Supreme Court of Canada, in a judgment written by Abella J, held that Mr Marcovitz's promise to consent to a religious divorce was legally enforceable and that Ms Bruker was entitled to damages for the loss she had suffered as a consequence of her husband's

---

of the Articles of Association. In many cases, expert evidence will be of assistance to the Court in understanding the relevant tradition and custom" (*ibid* at para 65).

45 Above note 9. For a discussion of the *Bruker* case, see Rosalie Jukier & Shauna Van Praagh, "Civil Law and Religion in the Supreme Court of Canada: What Should We Get Out of *Bruker v. Marcovitz*?" (2008) 43 Sup Ct L Rev (2d) 381; John C Kleefeld & Amanda Kennedy, "'A Delicate Necessity': *Bruker v. Marcovitz* and the Problem of Jewish Divorce" (2008) 24 Can J Fam L 205; Richard Moon, "Divorce and the Marriage of Law and Religion: Comment on *Bruker v. Marcovitz*" (2008) 42 Sup Ct L Rev (2d) 37; and MH Ogilvie, "*Bruker v. Marcovitz*: (Get)ting Over Freedoms (Like Contract and Religion) in Canada" (2009) 24 NJCL 173.

46 Clause 12 of their agreement provided as follows: "The parties [agree to] appear before the Rabbinical authorities in the City and District of Montreal for the purpose of obtaining the traditional religious *Get*, immediately upon a Decree Nisi of Divorce being granted" (*Bruker*, *ibid* at para 107). Strictly speaking, the *get* is not the divorce itself but rather the "bill of divorce," which the husband presents to his wife in the presence of a rabbi and witnesses. When she accepts the bill, the marriage is terminated. Because there is no additional requirement, involving the consent of a religious authority, the term "*get*" is often used to refer to the divorce itself.

failure to do as he had promised. Justice Abella thought that a contract could have a religious object provided that object was not "prohibited by law" or "contrary to public order."[47] In her view, the religious character of Mr Marcovitz's undertaking did not "immunize it from judicial scrutiny."[48] The promise by Mr Marcovitz to remove the religious barriers to remarriage by providing a *get* was negotiated between two consenting adults, each represented by counsel, as part of a voluntary exchange of commitments intended to have legally enforceable consequences. A court, said Abella J, may take jurisdiction so long as the dispute concerns the legal rights of the parties. She observed that in this case, "[w]e are not dealing with judicial review of doctrinal religious principles, such as whether a particular *get* is valid. Nor are we required to speculate on what the rabbinical court would do."[49] Justice Abella seemed to assume that the contract in this case could be enforced without the Court's having to delve into religious doctrine. She noted that Mr Marcovitz had offered no religious reasons for his failure to perform his undertaking and that, in any event, Judaism recognized no reasons to refuse consent. According to Abella J, the enforcement of the undertaking did not breach Mr Marcovitz's religious freedom, because "[h]is religion does not require him to refuse to give Ms. Bruker a *get*. . . . There is no doubt that at Jewish law he *could* refuse to give one, but that is very different from Mr. Marcovitz being prevented by a tenet of his religious beliefs from complying with a legal obligation he voluntarily entered into and of which he took the negotiated benefits."[50] She concluded that the enforcement of his promise to consent to a divorce did

---

47   *Ibid* at para 59.

48   *Ibid* at para 47.

49   *Ibid*. Earlier, Abella J observed: "The fact that a dispute has a religious aspect does not by itself make it non-justiciable" (*ibid* at para 41).

50   *Ibid* at para 69 (emphasis in original). A fuller quotation follows (*ibid* at paras 68–69):

> It is not clear to me what aspect of his religious beliefs prevented him from providing a *get*. He never, in fact, offered a religious reason for refusing to provide a *get*. Rather, he said that his refusal was based on the fact that, in his words: "Mrs. Bruker harassed me, she alienated my kids from me, she stole some money from me, she stole some silverware from my mother, she prevented my proper visitation with the kids. Those are the reasons . . . ." This concession confirms, in my view, that his refusal to provide the *get* was based less on religious conviction than on the fact that he was angry at Ms. Bruker. His religion does not require him to refuse to give Ms. Bruker a *get*. The contrary is true. There is no doubt that at Jewish law he *could* refuse to give one, but that is very different from Mr. Marcovitz being prevented by a tenet of his religious beliefs from complying with a legal obligation he voluntarily entered into and of which he took the negotiated benefits.

not breach his freedom of religion—did not compel or pressure him to act in a way that is inconsistent with his religious beliefs. But, of course, Abella J could make this determination only after considering the rules and practices of the religious community.

Justice Abella's judgment involved more (and perhaps less) than a determination that religious contracts are legally enforceable. She held that Mr Marcovitz's promise to consent was enforceable not simply because it was a voluntary obligation but because public policy supported the removal of barriers to religious divorce and remarriage. The enforcement of Mr Marcovitz's promise, she said, was supported by a public policy favouring the removal of such barriers and, more generally, by a public commitment to gender equality and freedom of choice in marriage. Moreover, while Abella J was prepared to enforce Mr Marcovitz's promise to consent, there is more than a suggestion in her judgment that a husband may not use his consent power as a bargaining lever to obtain, or extort, concessions from his spouse, and in particular concessions relating to custody, support, and the division of property. Underlying her judgment was a desire to mitigate the harshness of the Jewish community's divorce rules. She accepted that religious community members may sometimes require legal protection from the rules and practices of their community. Not far in the background of Abella J's judgment is the issue of the constitutionality of section 21.1 of the *Divorce Act*,[51] an issue

---

51   Above note 10. Section 21.1 of the *Divorce Act* provides as follows:

21.1 (2) In any proceedings under this Act, a spouse (. . . "deponent") may serve on the other spouse and file with the court an affidavit indicating . . . .

(c) the nature of any barriers to the remarriage of the deponent within the deponent's religion the removal of which is within the other spouse's control;
   . . .

(e) that the deponent has, in writing, requested the other spouse to remove all of the barriers to the remarriage of the deponent within the deponent's religion the removal of which is within the other spouse's control; . . . .

(g) that the other spouse, despite the request described in paragraph (e), has failed to remove all of the barriers referred to in that paragraph.

(3) Where a spouse who has been served with an affidavit under subsection (2) does not

(a) within fifteen days after that affidavit is filed with the court or within such longer period as the court allows, serve on the deponent and file with the court an affidavit indicating that all of the barriers referred to in paragraph (2)(e) have been removed, and

(b) satisfy the court . . . that all of the barriers referred to in paragraph (2)(e) have been removed,

the court may, subject to any terms that the court considers appropriate,

(c) dismiss any application filed by that spouse under this Act, and

that the Court did not specifically address. Nevertheless, Abella J drew from this legislative provision a public policy supporting the removal of barriers to remarriage. While she insisted that nothing in her reasons "purports in any way to decide the constitutionality of s. 21.1," her judgment would seem to support the constitutionality of the provision.[52]

Justice Abella was prepared to enforce Mr Marcovitz's undertaking because it had been voluntarily made and because, she believed, its interpretation did not require the court to consider contested religious doctrine. While conscious of the inaccessibility of religious reasons or doctrines to secular institutions, she accepted that religious agreements (or agreements dealing with religious matters) could not lie entirely outside law's purview. She thought that instead of refusing to enforce all religious contracts, the courts should address concerns about undue influence or contractual intention on a case-by-case basis. The courts should decline to enforce a particular contract when there is genuine dispute about the relevant religious values or practices or when there is real concern that the consent of the parties was not given voluntarily. This approach seems both reasonable and necessary. A general decision by the courts not to enforce religious contracts might unfairly deny religious individuals the power to make binding legal arrangements based on their values, practices, and interests. More practically a general exclusion would require the courts to distinguish religious from nonreligious agreements. Given the subtle and significant ways in which religious belief shapes individual action, the line between these might be very difficult to draw. The problem remains, though, that every time a religious contract is contested, the courts will be drawn, to some extent, into the interpretation (and enforcement) of religious practice or doctrine.

(*d*) strike out any other pleadings and affidavits filed by that spouse under this Act.

(4) . . . [T]he court may refuse to exercise its powers under paragraphs (3)(*c*) and (*d*) where a spouse who has been served with an affidavit under subsection (2)

(*a*) . . . serves on the deponent and files with the court an affidavit indicating genuine grounds of a religious or conscientious nature for refusing to remove the barriers referred to in paragraph (2)(*e*); and

(*b*) satisfies the court . . . that the spouse has genuine grounds of a religious or conscientious nature for refusing to remove the barriers referred to in paragraph (2)(*e*) . . . .

(6) This section does not apply where the power to remove the barrier to religious remarriage lies with a religious body or official.

52 *Brucker*, above note 9 at para 35.

In her dissenting judgment, Deschamps J held that Mr Marcovitz's promise was not legally binding, because it lacked a justiciable "object," one of the essential elements of an enforceable agreement at civil law. According to Deschamps J, a contract with an exclusively religious object (or an object that could only be understood in religious terms) was not legally enforceable under the Quebec *Civil Code*. In contrast to the *Lakeside Colony* case (and other church property cases), the contractual obligation at issue in the *Bruker* case had no civic consequences. It related to Ms Bruker's position or status within the religious community and not to her legal status or property rights. The religious nature of the contractual right raises questions about both the appropriateness and the effectiveness of state intervention. In a case such as this, in which the court is not removing a material barrier to exit but is instead seeking to mitigate the unfairness of an internal practice or norm, the court cannot be sure of the effectiveness of its intervention. The religious divorce rules at issue in the *Bruker* case affect the status of Ms Bruker within the Jewish community as married or divorced (and the status of her subsequent relationships). But the state does not have the power to determine her status in the religious community and so is limited in its ability to prevent internal status harm. If the religious community (and in particular the religious authorities) took the view that state pressure on the husband to give a *get* negated its effectiveness, it would be difficult to see what the state could do to protect the interests of Ms Bruker. State intervention appears to be effective in this case because many in the Jewish community — and not just the affected women — are willing to say that indirect state pressure on a husband to give a *get* is acceptable and does not make his "consent" involuntary.

4) Sharia Arbitration in Ontario

In late 2003 a heated debate began in Ontario concerning the arbitration of family disputes on the basis of sharia law under the province's arbitration legislation. The Ontario *Arbitration Act, 1991* provides for the resolution of disputes in commercial, family, and other areas by an arbitrator chosen by the disputing parties.[53] The decision of the arbitrator is binding on the parties. At the time the sharia arbitration issue arose, the Act provided that the arbitrator was to resolve the dispute on the basis of the relevant provincial law unless the parties agreed to the application of another set of norms or laws, which might include religious laws. The Act further provided that the parties must voluntarily

---

53   SO 1991, c 17.

consent to the arbitration process and that the arbitration hearing must conform to basic standards of procedural fairness.[54] Before the public controversy about sharia arbitration, several religious groups, including Orthodox Jews and Ismaili Muslims, had made use of the legislative framework to resolve family disputes in their communities on the basis of religious laws. However, when a member of the Sunni Muslim community publicly announced the establishment of an Islamic arbitration institute that would resolve family disputes through the application of sharia law, a strong public reaction followed. Contributing to this reaction was the assertion by the institute's founder that all "good Muslims" would be expected to submit their disputes to the "Sharia courts."[55] A variety of concerns were expressed in the public debate about religious arbitration. The principal concern was that Muslim women might feel pressured to submit their family disputes to this process and thereby surrender their rights under Canadian law. Because arbitration decisions made in accordance with the Act are legally enforceable, there was also concern that the state would be implicated in the enforcement of decisions based on religious standards that were inconsistent with public values such as gender equality.

The province appointed former provincial attorney general Marion Boyd to examine and make recommendations concerning the use of arbitration based on religious norms in family and inheritance matters. The *Boyd Report*, which was released in December 2004, recommended that the *Arbitration Act, 1991* continue to permit the arbitration of family and inheritance disputes based on religious norms.[56] The report found no "evidence to suggest that women are being systematically discriminated against as a result of arbitration of family law issues."[57] The report also identified certain benefits to maintaining a legal framework for the resolution of private disputes between the members of a religious group:

[I]ncorporating cultural minority groups into mainstream political processes remains crucial for multicultural, liberal democratic societies. By availing itself of provincial legislation that has been in place for over a decade, and that has been used by others, the Muslim community is drawing on the dominant legal culture to express itself. By

---

54   Most importantly the parties must each be given a fair opportunity to present their arguments and hear and respond to the arguments of the other side (*ibid*, s 19).

55   Marion Boyd, *Dispute Resolution in Family Law: Protecting Choice, Promoting Inclusion* (Toronto: Ontario Ministry of the Attorney General, 2004) at 55ff [*Boyd Report*].

56   *Ibid.*

57   *Ibid* at 133.

using mainstream legal instruments minority communities openly engage in institutional dialogue. And by engaging in such dialogue, a community is also inviting the state into its affairs, particularly since the *Arbitration Act*, even in its present form, specifically sets out grounds for state intervention in the form of judicial oversight. Use of the *Arbitration Act* by minority communities can therefore be understood as a desire to engage with the broader community.[58]

Oversight mechanisms would help to mitigate the unfairness that might sometimes occur in an otherwise private process. More generally, the interaction between state and religious law may contribute to the integration of minority religious groups into mainstream society.

The *Boyd Report* recommended that the Act be amended to include a number of additional safeguards to protect the interests of vulnerable members of religious groups. The report suggested giving the courts authority to set aside an arbitral award in several circumstances: if the award is unconscionable, if it is not in the best interests of any children affected by it, if either of the parties did not receive independent legal advice or did not waive their right to such advice before the arbitration, or if either of the parties did not receive "a statement of principles of faith-based arbitration" before agreeing to arbitration.[59] The report also recommended that mediators or arbitrators be required "to screen the parties separately about issues of power imbalance and domestic violence prior to entering into an arbitration agreement. . . ."[60] The Government of Ontario, though, rejected the report's central recommendations and instead amended the legislation to exclude "faith-based" arbitration. The premier declared that "[t]here will be no Sharia law in Ontario. There will be no religious arbitration in Ontario. There will be one law for all Ontarians."[61]

But, of course, religious "arbitration" is still taking place in Ontario, even if the decisions made by religious authorities are not enforceable in the Ontario courts.[62] More significantly, individuals are still able to enter legally binding pre-nuptial or separation agreements, dealing with

---

58   *Ibid* at 93.
59   *Ibid* at 134.
60   *Ibid* at 136.
61   Quoted in Jennifer A Selby & Anna C Korteweg, "Introduction: Situating the Sharia Debate in Ontario" in Anna C Korteweg & Jennifer A Selby, eds, *Debating Sharia: Islam, Gender Politics, and Family Law Arbitration* (Toronto: University of Toronto Press, 2012) 12 at 23.
62   For an examination of this debate and the complex issues it raised about the relationship between law and religion, most of which were either ignored or distorted in the public debate, see Korteweg & Selby, eds, *ibid*.

the division of property and the provision of support in the event of marriage breakdown. These agreements may be based on religious principles that differ significantly from the values that underlie family law rules. They will be legally binding as long as they have been entered into voluntarily. As Audrey Macklin points out:

> [T]he question was never whether Muslim men and women could lawfully rely on religious authorities to negotiate domestic contracts, to mediate disputes or to arbitrate the consequences of marital dissolution. They have done so in the past, they do so now, and they will continue to do so in the future. They may participate more or less voluntarily, and abide by more or less fair outcomes. The state possesses neither will nor resources to police whether and how people resolve disputes outside the formal judicial system. In fact, unless one of the parties deliberately engages the formal legal system, the agreement will be insulated de facto from judicial scrutiny.[63]

The government, understandably, wanted to avoid being implicated in the enforcement of rules or practices that were inconsistent with public values. The question, though, is whether the withdrawal of legal recognition reduces the reliance of religious community members on religious norms and processes in the resolution of family disputes and encourages the integration of religious minorities into the larger community—or whether, as we have seen in other contexts, the "principled" exclusion of religious value systems (or practices) from the public sphere impedes the process of community integration. Religious arbitration (like other religious practices) does not come to an end when it is denied legal recognition but, instead, is pushed into the private sphere, where it operates free of legal oversight and contact with public norms.

---

63   Audrey Macklin, "Multiculturalism Meets Privatisation: The Case of Faith-Based Arbitration" (2013) 9 International Journal of Law in Context 343 at 361. Macklin also makes the point that "the deficiencies attributed to faith-based arbitration are actually instantiations of larger tensions between private ordering and public justice in the specific context of family law dispute resolution" (*ibid* at 345).

CHAPTER 5

RELIGIOUS SCHOOLS

A. INTRODUCTION

The courts have held that section 2(a) of the *Charter*[1] prohibits state support for the practices or institutions of a particular religion but does not prevent the state from providing general support for religious practices or institutions. A province, then, may fund religious schools as long as it does so in an even-handed way. Whether or not a province funds religious schools, parents are understood to have the right to send their children to such schools. The province retains the power to regulate religious (and other) schools, establishing curriculum requirements and instruction standards.[2]

B. SECTION 93 AND SEPARATE SCHOOLS

There is, however, a constitutional exception to the requirement of equal treatment. Section 93 of the *Constitution Act, 1867*, as well as the Acts establishing provinces that later entered the union, protect the rights of "Separate" or "Dissentient" schools (principally Roman Catholic schools)

---

1 *Canadian Charter of Rights and Freedoms*, Part 1 of the *Constitution Act, 1982*, being Schedule B to the *Canada Act 1982* (UK), 1982, c 11 [*Charter*].

2 See, for example, the judgment of Iacobucci J in *Adler v Ontario*, [1996] 3 SCR 609 at para 15, and of Sopinka J in *ibid* at para 171 [*Adler*].

that existed in a province at the time of its entry into Confederation.[3] The courts have described section 93 as "part of a solemn pact resulting from the bargaining which made Confederation possible."[4] The opening words of section 93 state that the provinces have exclusive legislative jurisdiction in relation to education. The section, though, goes on to say that the provinces may not "prejudicially affect any Right or Privilege

---

3   See the *Constitution Act, 1867* (UK), 30 & 31 Vict, c 3, reprinted in RSC 1985, App II, No 5, s 93. See also the *Saskatchewan Act*, SC 1905, c 42, s 17, and the *Alberta Act*, SC 1905, c 3, s 17. The constitutional terms under which each of the provinces entered the union included a recognition of the rights of denominational schools; however, the courts found that in many provinces the provision had no application since at the time of their entry into the union, they had no legally established denominational schools. While the provinces of Quebec and Newfoundland were originally bound under the Constitution to provide support for denominational schools, these obligations were ended (in the case of Quebec) or substantially removed (in the case of Newfoundland) by constitutional amendment.

The full text of s 93 of the *Constitution Act, 1867, ibid*, is as follows:

93. In and for each Province the Legislature may exclusively make Laws in relation to Education, subject and according to the following Provisions:

(1) Nothing in any such Law shall prejudicially affect any Right or Privilege with respect to Denominational Schools which any Class of Persons have by Law in the Province at the Union;

(2) All the Powers, Privileges, and Duties at the Union by Law conferred and imposed in Upper Canada on the Separate Schools and School Trustees of the Queen's Roman Catholic Subjects shall be and the same are hereby extended to the Dissentient Schools of the Queen's Protestant and Roman Catholic Subjects in Quebec;

(3) Where in any Province a System of Separate or Dissentient Schools exists by Law at the Union or is thereafter established by the Legislature of the Province, an Appeal shall lie to the Governor General in Council from any Act or Decision of any Provincial Authority affecting any Right or Privilege of the Protestant or Roman Catholic Minority of the Queen's Subjects in relation to Education;

(4) In case any such Provincial Law as from Time to Time seems to the Governor General in Council requisite for the due Execution of the Provisions of this Section is not made, or in case any Decision of the Governor General in Council on any Appeal under this Section is not duly executed by the proper Provincial Authority in that Behalf, then and in every such Case, and as far only as the Circumstances of each Case require, the Parliament of Canada may make remedial Laws for the due Execution of the Provisions of this Section and of any Decision of the Governor General in Council under this Section.

4   *Reference re Bill 30, An Act to Amend the Education Act (Ontario)*, [1987] 1 SCR 1148 at para 27, Wilson J [*Reference re Bill 30*]. See also *Reference re Education Act (Quebec)*, [1993] 2 SCR 511 at para 24, Gonthier J: "Section 93 is unanimously recognized as the expression of a desire for political compromise. It served to moderate religious conflicts which threatened the birth of the Union."

with respect to Denominational Schools which any Class of Persons have by Law in the Province at the Union."[5] The effect of section 93 is that the legal rights of denominational schools at the time of Confederation are constitutionally entrenched and cannot be removed or reduced except through constitutional amendment. The rights or privileges of these separate schools may be added to by a province, but such additions are not entrenched and may be withdrawn by the province. Section 93 provides for an appeal to the federal government from any act or decision of a province that affects the rights and privileges of these schools, including any rights that have been granted by the province after Confederation and so are not entrenched.

At the time of Confederation, Ontario had a legally established system of Roman Catholic schools, which received funding on the same basis as the non-denominational common schools.[6] In Quebec both Roman Catholic and Protestant schools were established before Confederation; however, the rights of religious schools in that province were removed by constitutional amendment in 1997. At the time of Confederation, Nova Scotia and New Brunswick did not have legislatively established separate schools, and so the courts found that section 93(1) had no application in these provinces. Similarly Prince Edward Island and British Columbia at the time they joined Confederation did not have legally established separate schools. The Acts establishing the provinces of Manitoba, Saskatchewan, and Alberta each contained provisions similar to section 93, and so the separate school rights that existed in each of these provinces at the time of their entry into the union were constitutionally protected. The courts, though, found that no such rights were established in Manitoba when it joined the union. At the time of its entry into Confederation, Newfoundland was also required to maintain its existing separate schools, but the right of these schools to state support was substantially removed in 1998.[7] The constitutional protection granted to separate schools in a particular province depends on the legal status of these schools at the time of the province's entry into the

5   Above note 3, s 93(1). Section 93(2), *ibid*, which ensured that Protestant (and Roman Catholic) schools would have the same rights as those granted to Roman Catholic schools in Ontario, is no longer operative.

6   At the time of Confederation, there were a number of dissentient Protestant schools in Ontario protected under s 93. These schools were later folded into the public school system.

7   For a discussion, see John P McEvoy, "Denominational Schools and Minority Rights: *Hogan v. Newfoundland (Attorney-General)*" (2001) 12 NJCL 449.

union, and so there is some variation among the provinces in the rights established.[8]

The Supreme Court of Canada in *Reference re Bill 30, An Act to Amend the Education Act (Ontario)* considered both the scope of separate school rights under section 93 and the relationship between section 93 rights and the *Charter*'s protection of religious freedom and religious equality.[9] The issue in that case was whether the decision of the Government of Ontario to fund high school grades in Roman Catholic schools (separate schools) without providing equivalent funding to other religious schools breached either section 2(a) or section 15 of the *Charter*. Seventy years earlier in 1915, when the province began funding high school grades in the public school system, it declined to fund the same grades in the Catholic system arguing that section 93 only entitled the separate school system to funding for the grades that existed at the time of Confederation.[10] In the decision of *Tiny Roman Catholic Separate School Trustees v The King*, the Judicial Committee of the Privy Council held that this differential funding did not breach section 93, because at the time of Confederation, the separate schools in Ontario had had no guaranteed right to state funding for high school grades.[11] When the Government of Ontario decided to reverse its earlier decision and fund high school grades in the separate schools to the same extent that it funded these grades in the public system, it referred to the courts the question of whether this extension of funding (Bill 30) was constitutional.

In *Reference re Bill 30*, the courts were asked whether the practice of funding the upper grades of the Roman Catholic schools, which according to the *Tiny School Board* decision was not required by section 93 of the Constitution, while declining to fund other religious schools, breached section 2(a), freedom of religion, and section 15, religious equality, of the *Charter*. The Supreme Court of Canada assumed that in the absence of section 93, the exclusive support of Roman Catholic religious schools would breach section 2(a) of the *Charter*.[12] It followed then that if the funding of high school grades in the separate school sys-

---

8   For a history (up to 1964) of the application of s 93 in each of the provinces, see Douglas A Schmeiser, *Civil Liberties in Canada* (Oxford: Oxford University Press, 1964) ch 4.

9   Above note 4.

10   The province had also prohibited the separate schools from providing these grades of schooling.

11   [1928] AC 363 [*Tiny School Board*]. According to the court, since the province retained the power in 1867 to regulate separate schools, these schools had no established right to determine what grades could be offered.

12   Justice Wilson, quoting the Ontario Court of Appeal, observed that "[t]hese educational rights . . . make it impossible to treat all Canadians equally. The country

tem was not mandated by section 93, the province would be improperly favouring the schools of one religion over those of another contrary to section 2(a). A majority of the Court, in a judgment written by Wilson J, held that the *Tiny School Board* decision was wrong and that the province was obligated under section 93 to fund high school grades in the separate schools. Justice Wilson noted that at the time of Confederation, separate school trustees in Ontario held the same powers as common school trustees, including the power to provide advanced education. As well, in 1867 separate schools in Ontario had been entitled to a proportion of the funding granted to the common schools.[13] Justice Wilson concluded that Bill 30 simply "return[ed] rights constitutionally guaranteed to separate schools by s. 93(1) . . . ."[14] However, Wilson J also said that even if *Tiny School Board* was correctly decided, and the province was not constitutionally required to fund these grades, it was entitled to do so under section 93(3), which contemplates the expansion of separate school rights.[15] Justice Wilson then referred to section 29 of the *Charter*, which specifically provides that the section 93 rights and privileges of separate schools are insulated from *Charter* review. She noted that the effect of section 29 is that the preferential treatment of Roman Catholic schools, whether constitutionally required or permitted under section 93, does not breach the *Charter*.[16] Moreover, said Wilson J, even without section 29 of the *Charter*, the province's exclusive support for Roman Catholic schools will not breach section 2(a). As a matter of constitutional interpretation, a specific right or power established in the *Constitution Act, 1867* is not repealed or nullified by the later but more general provisions of the *Charter of Rights*.[17]

---

was founded upon the recognition of special or unequal educational rights for specific religious groups in Ontario and Quebec" (above note 4 at para 64).

13   In *Reference re Bill 30*, Wilson J thought that the narrow reading of s 93 adopted by the court in the *Tiny School Board* decision made the constitutional protection of separate schools "illusory" and "undermine[d] this historically important compromise" (*ibid* at para 58).

14   *Ibid* at para 60.

15   *Ibid* at para 29, Wilson J: ". . . Bill 30 is a valid exercise of the provincial power to add to the rights and privileges of Roman Catholic separate school supporters under the combined effect of the opening words of s. 93 and s. 93(3) . . . ."

16   Section 29 of the *Charter*, above note 1, provides that "[n]othing in this *Charter* abrogates or derogates from any rights or privileges guaranteed by or under the Constitution of Canada in respect of denominational, separate or dissentient schools."

17   Above note 4 at para 623, Wilson J: "It was never intended, in my opinion, that the *Charter* could be used to invalidate other provisions of the Constitution, particularly a provision such as s. 93 which represented a fundamental part of the Confederation compromise." Section 29 served only to create greater certainty

The courts' interpretation of section 93, and its relationship to the *Charter*, is based on the idea that the protection of separate school rights was a political bargain or compromise necessary for the achievement of Confederation. In *Adler v Ontario*, Iacobucci J described section 93 as "a child born of historical exigency" that does not "represent a guarantee of fundamental freedoms."[18] Justice Beetz, in *Protestant School Board of Greater Montreal v Quebec (AG)*, said that even though section 93 "may be rooted in notions of tolerance and diversity," it is not "a blanket affirmation of freedom of religion or freedom of conscience . . . [and] should not be construed as a *Charter* human right . . . ."[19] Justice Wilson, in *Reference re Bill 30*, agreed with this description of section 93 as a historical compromise but did not think that this "foreclose[d] a purposive approach" to the interpretation of the section.[20] She thought that while the courts must be careful not to give a wide interpretation to "a provision which reflects a political compromise . . . , it must still be open to the Court to breathe life into a compromise that is clearly expressed."[21] The courts have treated the constitutional protection of separate schools as an anachronism that only constitutional amendment can correct. The assumption is that, however unfair it may be for the state to fund only one religious school system, section 93 was part of the Confederation bargain, to which the parties are bound until they agree otherwise.

But does this view of section 93, as part of the Confederation bargain, preclude a liberal or principled interpretation of the provision—a reading of the provision as a minority right? Section 93 was included in the Constitution at a time when the dominant public or common school

---

about this. In *Waldman v Canada*, Communication No 694/1996, UN Doc CCPR/C/67/D/694/1996 (5 November 1999), the UN Human Rights Committee found that the preferential funding of Roman Catholic schools in Ontario amounted to a breach of Canada's obligations under the *International Covenant on Civil and Political Rights*. The committee said (*ibid* at para 10.6):

> [I]f a State party chooses to provide public funding to religious schools, it should make this funding available without discrimination. This means that providing funding for the schools of one religious group and not for another must be based on reasonable and objective criteria. In the instant case, the Committee concludes that the material before it does not show that the differential treatment between the Roman Catholic faith and the author's religious denomination is based on such criteria.

18   Above note 2 at para 30.
19   [1989] 1 SCR 377 at 401 [*Montreal Protestant School Board*].
20   Above note 4 at para 29.
21   *Ibid*. This purposive reading was necessary to her conclusion that the rights of separate schools in Ontario included the funding of high school grades.

system in Ontario had a clear Protestant ethos.[22] The section 93 protection of separate school rights ensured that Roman Catholic parents
would not be financially pressured to send their children to the Protestant common schools. But the character of the public school system
has changed dramatically since 1867, a change that has been hastened
by the *Charter*. The public schools are no longer permitted to advance
even a non-denominational religious perspective, and so the reason for
the special protection of Roman Catholic schools may no longer exist.[23]
A principled reading of section 93 might support the ending of separate school rights in Ontario now that the reason for these rights has
ceased to exist. However, for a variety of political reasons it is unlikely
that the courts will be prepared to bring about this change through
constitutional interpretation (despite their occasional references to the
Constitution as a "living tree"), and this change will only occur through
constitutional amendment.[24] In the alternative, if the purpose of section
93 was to create a right to religious education for the minority Roman
Catholic community in Ontario (a positive right to religious education
rather than simply a right not to be forced into the majority Protestant
school system), then a principled reading of the section would support
the extension of this right to other religious groups in the province. In
1867 there was only one significant religious minority in Ontario. The
right to state-supported religious schools should now be extended to
other religious groups that have grown since 1867.[25] If we believe that
section 93 protects the right of Roman Catholic parents to educate their
children in their faith, there is no reason why this right should not be

22 Justice Sopinka, in *Adler*, above note 2 at para 154, referred to the Christian
    character of the non-denominational common schools in Ontario at the time of
    Confederation.
23 A recognition that the reason for s 93(1) no longer exists led to the constitutional
    amendment ending religious school rights in Quebec. To view s 93 as granting
    Roman Catholic parents in Ontario the right to educate their children in their
    own belief system — to indoctrinate children into their faith or to insulate them
    from exposure to other beliefs, values, or groups — is to confuse the church's
    justification for separate schooling, which applies whether or not the main-
    stream schools are Protestant or secular, with the constitutional justification for
    the special funding of separate schools, which may simply have been to protect
    Catholics from being forced into the religious education system of the majority
    community. Of course, in 1867 this distinction would not have been obvious,
    since it would have been difficult at the time to envision an entirely nonreligious
    or "secular" school system.
24 Such an amendment would require only the consent of the federal government
    and the Government of Ontario.
25 While I favour the first reading, my former research assistant Matthew Macdonald
    made a strong case to me for the second.

extended to other religious groups. The irony may be that a "minority" group right was enlarged by the provincial government in 1986 and continues to be specially protected because of the increased political power of that group in the province. Other religious groups in Ontario do not receive state funding for their schools, because they lack sufficient political influence.[26]

C. THE RIGHTS OF SEPARATE SCHOOLS

A province is precluded from interfering with the rights or privileges of separate schools that were established by law at the time of the province's entry into the union. Despite the courts' description of section 93 as a bargain, they have not regarded the rights of separate schools as static. The Ontario Court of Appeal in *Ontario English Catholic Teachers' Assn v Ontario (AG)* insisted that section 93 be interpreted in a purposive way to ensure that it did not become "a historical strait-jacket."[27] In upholding the Court of Appeal's decision, the Supreme Court of Canada affirmed that "the rights guaranteed by s. 93(1) do not replicate the law word-for-word as it stood in 1867" and that "[i]t is the broader purpose of the laws in force which continues to be protected."[28]

In *Reference re Bill 30*, and several other section 93 cases, the rights claimed by separate school supporters related to the funding and organizational structure of the schools.[29] However, many of the section 93 cases that have come before the courts have been concerned with the right of separate schools to maintain their denominational or religious character. According to Beetz J in *Montreal Protestant School Board*, section 93 protects the "denominational aspects" of these schools as well as the "non-denominational aspects" that are necessary to give prac-

---

26   During the 2007 Ontario provincial election campaign, the Progressive Conservative Party under leader John Tory proposed an extension of provincial funding to faith-based schools. The defeat of the Conservatives in the election was attributed by many to this proposal. Opposition to the proposal appears to have come from both public school and separate school supporters. Both Saskatchewan and Alberta provide some support for other religious schools.

27   [1999] OJ No 1358 at para 18. A purposive approach, said the court, should be applied to "both the provincial power to legislate about education . . . and the denominational guarantee of separate schools" (*ibid*).

28   2001 SCC 15 at para 32 [*Ontario English Catholic Teachers' Assn*].

29   See also *ibid*, where the Court held that the system for funding could be altered as long as proportionality in funding between the two school systems was maintained.

tical effect to the denominational guarantees.[30] Significantly, the courts have said that the state may not interfere with the right of separate schools to hire and retain teachers based on their membership in the Roman Catholic Church and their adherence to Catholic doctrine.[31] For example, in *Daly v Ontario (AG)*, the Ontario Court of Appeal held that separate schools have the right to exclude non-Catholic teachers from administrative positions in the schools.[32] However, the most contentious cases in recent times have been concerned with the conflict or tension between Roman Catholic doctrine and publicly recognized equality rights—particularly those of gays and lesbians.

In *Hall (Litigation Guardian of) v Powers*, a separate school board in Ontario refused to allow a graduating student to attend the high school prom with his same-sex date.[33] The board defended its decision on the grounds that homosexual relationships are contrary to Roman Catholic teaching. The issue for the court was whether section 93 protected the school board's action from the application of the *Charter* ban on sexual-orientation discrimination. The judge found, among other things, that while the Roman Catholic Church regarded "homosexuality [as] contrary to natural law" and "homosexual acts [as] intrinsically disordered," there was "a substantial diversity of opinion within the Catholic community regarding the appropriate pastoral care and the practical application of [the] Church's teachings on homosexuality"—regarding how the church and its members should treat individuals who identify as gay or lesbian.[34] Even though the bishop with "hierarchical responsibility" for the region within which the school was located had taken the view that excluding same-sex couples from the dance was "an authentically Catholic position," the judge found that this was "not the only Catholic position" and perhaps not even "the majority position."[35]

---

30   Above note 19 at 415. The s 93 guarantee does not preclude the establishment of a common school curriculum in the province.

31   See *Casagrande v Hinton Roman Catholic Separate School District No 155* (1987), 38 DLR (4th) 382 (Alta QB). See also *Caldwell et al v Stuart et al*, [1984] 2 SCR 603, in which the Supreme Court of Canada held that a Roman Catholic school did not breach human rights legislation when it dismissed a teacher because she had married a divorced man contrary to Catholic doctrine.

32   (1999), 172 DLR (4th) 241 (Ont CA). See also *Ontario English Catholic Teachers' Assn v Dufferin-Peel Roman Catholic Separate School Board* (1999), 172 DLR (4th) 260 (Ont CA).

33   [2002] OJ No 1803 (SCJ) [*Hall*]. For a discussion of the case, see Bruce MacDougall, "The Separation of Church and Date: Destabilizing Traditional Religion-Based Legal Norms on Sexuality" (2003) 36 UBC L Rev 1.

34   *Hall, ibid* at para 23.

35   *Ibid* at para 30.

This enabled the judge to find that the board's stance was not an aspect of the denominational character of the separate schools in Ontario that was protected under section 93 and insulated from *Charter* challenge. The judge issued an interim injunction enabling Mr Hall to attend the prom with his date. There was no further litigation and no final determination of the issue.

The willingness of the judge in *Hall* to probe into Roman Catholic doctrine might seem inconsistent with the Supreme Court of Canada's admonition in *Syndicat Northcrest v Amselem* that a court should not decide what is accepted doctrine in a religious community but should consider only whether the individual's belief in a particular practice or value is sincere.[36] At issue in the *Hall* case, though, was not whether an individual's beliefs or practices should be accommodated under section 2(a). Instead, the court had to decide whether the school, a religious institution (and also paradoxically a state actor) that has special rights and privileges under section 93, could rely on a particular understanding of religious doctrine (that was not shared by all members of the religious community) to insulate itself from the application of the *Charter*. The bishop had taken the position that bringing a same-sex date to the prom was contrary to church doctrine; and as the judge noted, one of the bishop's "designated religious duties is to interpret the teachings of the church."[37] The judge's interpretation of church doctrine, or at least his finding that the application of this doctrine was contested (his bypassing of the bishop's interpretation), allowed him to avoid the uncomfortable conclusion that publicly funded schools (state actors) could engage in sexual-orientation discrimination. The judge interpreted the Roman Catholic prohibition on homosexuality narrowly so that it did not apply to general social activity and did not support the exclusion of individuals who identify as gay or lesbian. The judge in *Hall* found that while the Roman Catholic school board sincerely believed that homosexuality is sinful, it was mistaken in thinking that this belief or commitment was compromised, or interfered with, by Mr Hall's attendance at the prom.[38] At some point, however, the courts may have to address more directly the question of whether the separate school system

---

36   2004 SCC 47.

37   Above note 33 at para 30.

38   The judge's reasoning might be compared to that of the Supreme Court of Canada in the later judgment of *SL v Commission scolaire des Chênes*, 2012 SCC 7 (which is discussed in Chapter 3). The alternative argument was that simply permitting Mr Hall and his same-sex date to attend the prom (even if this activity was understood to be contrary to Catholic doctrine) would not amount to support for, or condonation of, a practice that was inconsistent with the school board's beliefs.

should be permitted to discriminate against gays and lesbians based on the constitutional right to operate publicly funded religious schools or whether, instead, the scope of section 93 should be defined more narrowly so that it does not insulate separate schools from basic equality requirements, even when these requirements are inconsistent with Roman Catholic doctrine.[39]

D. SECULAR AND RELIGIOUS SCHOOLS: *ADLER V ONTARIO*

In *Adler v Ontario*, the Supreme Court of Canada considered whether the provincial government's failure to fund religious schools (other than separate schools under section 93) breached either section 2(a) or section 15 of the *Charter*.[40] The Court concluded unanimously that the government's nonfunding of religious schools did not violate section 2(a). A majority of the Court also held that the government's practice of funding secular public schools but not religious schools did not breach the section 15 equality right. However, two judges, McLachlin and L'Heureux-Dubé JJ disagreed and found that this practice breached section 15. Justice McLachlin went on to hold that the breach was justified under section 1, while L'Heureux-Dubé J held that the section 15 violation was not justified.

Justice Iacobucci, writing for the majority of the Court, took the position that section 93 was a complete code for the funding of religious schools. He said that while the government could choose to fund other religious schools, it had no obligation to do so. According to Iacobucci J, section 93 established certain rights for religious schools, and section 2(a) could not be used to expand those rights.[41] In response to the appellants' section 15 claim, Iacobucci J observed that section 93 specifically

---

This, though, would have been a more difficult claim to make given the school's oversight of the event.

39 Legislation addressing the problem of bullying—particularly bullying based on sexual orientation or gender identity—may again bring the issue of sexual orientation in Roman Catholic schools before the courts. For an examination of bullying in the schools, see Donn Short, *"Don't Be So Gay!" Queers, Bullying, and Making Schools Safe* (Vancouver: UBC Press: 2013).

40 Above note 2.

41 Justice Iacobucci argued that "any claim to public support for religious education must be grounded in s. 93(1) which is a 'comprehensive code' of denominational school rights" (*ibid* at para 27). Later he said that to find that s 2(a) required extension of funding for other religious schools "would be to hold one section of the Constitution violative of another" (*ibid* at para 35).

envisioned state support for public schools. In his view, the reasoning of the Court in *Reference re Bill 30* that the rights and privileges granted to separate schools in Ontario under section 93 could not be challenged under the *Charter* applied also to public schools. According to Iacobucci J, the section 15 "claim fails because the funding of Roman Catholic separate schools and public schools is within the contemplation of the terms of s. 93 and is, therefore, immune from *Charter* scrutiny."[42] The provincial government had the power under section 93 to increase support for both public and separate schools, and the exercise of that power could not be viewed as a breach of the *Charter*.[43]

Justice Sopinka, in his concurring judgment, held that the nonfunding of religious schools did not breach section 2(a). As Sopinka J saw it, the appellants were asking for state support for their religious practices. In his view, section 2(a) prohibits state restrictions on religious practice but does not guarantee state support for such practices. According to Sopinka J, provincial support for public schools neither compels the parents in this case "to act in any way that infringes their freedom of religion" nor imposes upon them an unconstitutional burden.[44] He regarded the costs incurred by the parents in sending their children to religious schools as "a natural cost" of their religion and distinguished this case from *R v Edwards Books & Art Ltd*:[45]

> The legislation [in this case] is not the source of any distinction amongst all the groups whose exercise of their religious freedom involves an economic cost. This situation is distinguishable from Edwards Books, where one religious group was suffering an additional burden not imposed on other religious groups vis-à-vis non-observers.[46]

In *Edwards Books*, the challenged law had the effect (if not the purpose) of favouring one religious group over another. In contrast, the funding of secular schools in this case did not benefit or disadvantage a particular religious group.

In rejecting the parents' section 15 argument, Sopinka J pointed to earlier judgments, such as *Zylberberg v Sudbury Board of Education*,[47] that prohibited religious practices in the public schools. He thought that the courts, having ordered the removal of religion (and, more spe-

---

42   *Ibid* at para 27.
43   Justice Iacobucci's extension of the reasoning in *Reference re Bill 30* to public schools was criticized by Sopinka and McLachlin JJ, who pointed out that section 93 does not specifically grant any rights to public schools.
44   *Ibid* at para 171.
45   *Ibid* at para 176; [1986] 2 SCR 713 [*Edwards Books*].
46   *Adler*, above note 2 at para 174.
47   (1988), 52 DLR (4th) 577 (Ont CA).

cifically, Christian practices) from the public schools to ensure their religious neutrality, could hardly now say that the secular public schools
were religiously partisan and that state support for such schools (without equivalent support for religious schools) was unconstitutional.[48]

Justice McLachlin (with L'Heureux-Dubé J concurring on this point)
agreed with Sopinka J that the exclusive funding of public schools did
not breach section 2(a) of the *Charter*. Like Sopinka J, she thought that
freedom of religion prohibits the state from restricting or compelling
religious practice but does not require the state to support such practices: "Absence of state funding for private religious practices, as distinct
from prohibitions on such practices, has never been seen as religious
persecution."[49] However, McLachlin and L'Heureux-Dubé JJ both held
that the state's refusal to fund religious schools amounted to religious
discrimination contrary to section 15 of the *Charter*.[50] Justice McLachlin found that "while secular schooling is in theory available to all
members of the public, the appellants' religious beliefs preclude them
from sending their children to public schools."[51] It followed from this,

---

48 Above note 2 at para 181:

> While it is true that the appellants feel compelled to send their children to
> private school because of a personal characteristic, namely their religion, and
> therefore are unable to benefit from publicly-funded schooling, I fail to see
> how this is an effect *arising from the statute*. The reason why the public school
> system is not acceptable to the appellants lies in its secular nature. This secu-
> lar nature is itself mandated by s. 2(a) of the Charter as held by several courts
> in this country. [emphasis added]

49 *Ibid* at para 200. But this may not be quite so straightforward. The parents in *Adler*
argued that the exclusive funding of secular schools put pressure on their children
to adopt the "faith of secularism" or sent a message that religious adherents are
not full members of the political community. The only way to avoid this argument
was to find (as Sopinka J did) that secular (nonreligious) schools, in contrast to
religious schools, are religiously neutral or inclusive. But this does not fit easily
with McLachlin J's later finding that the funding of secular schools breached s 15.

50 According to the Supreme Court of Canada in *Law v Canada (Minister of Employment and Immigration)*, [1999] 1 SCR 497, and other decisions, the value or
interest protected by s 15 is compromised if a law or other government action
distinguishes between individuals on religious grounds (or another enumerated
or analogous ground) or has a differential impact on the members of a particular
religious group and if this differential treatment is discriminatory, that is, involves
stereotyping or reinforces the marginalized position of the group.

51 Above note 2 at para 209. Justice L'Heureux-Dubé found, *ibid* at para 68, that for
the appellants in this case:

> [m]embership in an identifiable group precludes their accessing the other,
> publicly funded options. Evidence . . . establishes that to remain a member
> of the particular religious communities in question, and to act in accordance
> with the tenets of these faiths, the appellants are required to educate their chil-

said McLachlin J, that the exclusive funding of secular public schools amounted to adverse discrimination against the appellants. They were denied a benefit that was available to others, because they believed they could not send their children to public secular schools.

According to McLachlin and L'Heureux-Dubé JJ, the exclusive funding of public (and separate) schools is discriminatory because the appellants believe their children must be educated in an environment in which their religious views are affirmed. But if public schools are seen as noninclusive simply because they do not affirm the beliefs and practices of a particular faith, there can be no such thing as an inclusive school, nor indeed can there be any sort of neutral or inclusive public program or institution. Equality on this view can only be achieved through separation — equal support by the state for the institutions or practices of different religions. Not surprisingly, in their section 1 analysis, McLachlin and L'Heureux-Dubé JJ were unwilling to follow to its logical conclusion the idea that the secular public schools are partisan or exclusive. At the section 1 stage, both judges recognized and valued the role of public schools in providing an educational environment in which children from different backgrounds can meet and develop a level of mutual understanding and tolerance toward others. Justice McLachlin described the benefits of a public system:

> Children of all races and religions learn together and play together. No religion is touted over any other. The goal is to provide a forum for the development of respect for the beliefs and customs of all cultural groups and for their ethical and moral values. The strength of the public secular school system is its diversity — diversity which its supporters believe will lead to increased understanding and respect for different cultures and beliefs.[52]

For McLachlin J, the value of the open and tolerant learning environment offered by the public schools (an environment in which no one religious belief system is favoured over another) justified the restriction of the parents' section 15 rights.

Justice L'Heureux-Dubé accepted that the state has an interest in supporting a public school system that is "intended to be universally open and free to all, without discrimination" and in fostering "the values of a pluralist, democratic society, including the values of cohesion,

---

dren in a manner consistent with this faith and therefore outside of the public or the separate schools.

52   *Ibid* at para 212.

religious tolerance and understanding."[53] However, she thought that the viability of the public system would not be compromised by partial state funding of religious schools, and so she concluded that the breach of section 15 was not justified under section 1. In her view, partial state support for religious schools (something less than full funding) would reduce the burden on parents who want to send their children to religious schools without at the same time leading to a mass exodus from the public schools and compromising the state's goal of maintaining a diverse public school system.

Justice L'Heureux-Dubé believed that parents should be able to send their children to (state-funded) religious schools, but she also thought that the secular public schools perform an important public function and should be protected. Her two concerns, though, are difficult to reconcile. In her view, if state funding of religious schools had a significant impact on public school attendance, the state might be justified in funding only secular public schools. But how does this fit with her earlier claim that the parents were disadvantaged (spiritually compromised) because they were forced for financial reasons to send their children to public schools? Why should the parents' right be limited in any way to protect the viability of public schools? Either it is objectionable, a form of discrimination, to (financially) pressure parents to send their children to a public school, because it supports a world view that is contrary to their faith, or it is not objectionable because public schools are inclusive and non-partisan and because it is important that children be exposed to other groups and perspectives in the larger community. On the one hand, if the government is right that exposure to other views and cultures is an important part of a child's civic education, we should be concerned about the removal of any child from the public system. The justification for the exclusive funding of public schools (and support for tolerance and respect) should not depend on the number of parents who would remove their children from the system if religious schools received state funding. On the other hand, if it is wrong for religious parents to be financially pressured into sending their children to a public school, is this not so for all religious parents, including those who could not afford to pay even partial fees for religious schooling?

The contradiction in the judgments of McLachlin and L'Heureux-Dubé JJ, between their view of public schools as partisan and noninclusive at the section 15 stage and as inclusive and neutral at the section 1 stage, reflects a deeper tension in the public conception of religion as both a cultural identity and a personal choice or commitment. At

---

53   *Ibid* at para 97.

the section 15 stage of their analysis, McLachlin and L'Heureux-Dubé JJ rely on a conception of religious belief as a cultural identity. A law that has a differential impact on a particular belief system may amount to discrimination against the believers—an identity group. Yet at the section 1 stage, the value that both judges attach to the public schools, of supporting tolerance and mutual understanding or of enabling children to make independent judgments, rests on this different conception of religion as a set of values—of truth claims—that may be right or wrong and may be adopted or rejected by an individual. It is noteworthy that section 1 seldom plays more than a perfunctory role in section 15 cases—that once a breach of section 15 is found, a court is unlikely to then find that the breach is justified under section 1. Yet, in this case section 1 may have a role because the Court is uncertain about whether or when to treat religious adherence as an identity and therefore as a ground of discrimination.

Children require a structure of values and customs—a cultural framework—to develop as moral and rational agents. As well, the survival of a religious or cultural community depends on its ability to pass its values and practices on to the next generation. At the same time, the development of children as agents and citizens (capable of making their own spiritual and other judgments) requires that they be exposed to different ideas, values, and ways of living. The fact that the public schools expose children to other views and values and encourage independent thought does not make these schools partisan or exclusive in the way these terms must be understood in a liberal democracy that is committed to religious freedom and tolerance. Even if there is some value in religious or cultural education, particularly in the early grades, the failure of the state to support religious schools should not be seen as an act of discrimination. The education of children in a separate religious environment is not simply a private or personal religious practice, similar to praying or wearing a religious symbol, which the state ought to accommodate. It concerns the development of children as agents and citizens and so has public significance.

CHAPTER 6

PARENTS AND CHILDREN

A. INTRODUCTION

It is not surprising that some of the most contentious freedom of religion cases involve the claim of parents to make religiously based decisions concerning their children. In these cases, the parents' claim to oversee the spiritual welfare of their children, and to transmit their faith to their children, is often pitted against their children's interest in developing as independent agents, capable of making their own judgments, including spiritual judgments, or the interest of the larger community in ensuring the development of children as citizens who are tolerant and able to contribute to society. In this way the debate about religious freedom in the family context exposes most starkly the central tension in the courts' understanding of religion, as both a personal commitment and a cultural identity, and of religious freedom as both the right of the individual to make spiritual choices and the right of religious believers or communities to be treated with equal respect.

B. PARENTS' RIGHTS

The right of parents to oversee the spiritual life of their children may simply be part of a more general right of parents to make decisions about the welfare of their children. It is sometimes argued that parents have this right because they are in the best position to make judgments about what is good for their children. Children require guidance and oversight. Because parents have intimate knowledge of their children and because they ordinarily have the best interests of their children in mind, they are able to provide this guidance. The right (and "right" may not be the proper term) or authority of parents to make decisions concerning the welfare of their child may also, and more substantially, rest on the positive value of the family relationship to the child's emotional and intellectual development and on a recognition that interference with this relationship may be harmful to the child and hinder her development.[1] The "right" of parents to oversee the spiritual life of their children, or to transmit religious values and customs, then may be based on the importance of the family relationship to the development of children. While it may sometimes be necessary to interfere with the family relationship to protect children from harm, we know that this is never an ideal option and that the costs to the children will be significant.[2]

---

1   See K Anthony Appiah, *The Ethics of Identity* (Princeton, NJ: Princeton University Press, 2005) at 201–2: "The intimacy of family life; the love of children for parents (and other relatives) and of parents (and other relatives) for children; the sense of a family identity, family traditions: all these would be lost. More than this, the state would be invested with a quite enormous power in the shaping of the citizenry; a power whose potential for abuse is obvious enough."

2   According to the courts, s 7 of the *Canadian Charter of Rights and Freedoms*, Part 1 of the *Constitution Act, 1982*, being Schedule B to the *Canada Act 1982* (UK), 1982, c 11 [*Charter*], ("the right to life, liberty and security of the person") also protects the right of parents to make decisions concerning the welfare of their children. See, for example, *RB v Children's Aid Society of Metropolitan Toronto*, [1995] 1 SCR 315 [*RB*].

   The justification for the restriction of the parents' right is most often based on the interests (or right) of the state or the larger community in the development of citizens who are capable of making independent decisions and tolerating the views of others. But to view this as simply a state interest is to confuse the actor with the reasons for action. The state or the larger community does have an interest in ensuring that children mature into responsible citizens, and contribute to the welfare of the larger community, but there is a more basic interest or good at stake here than the effective operation of the democratic process or the economic system, and that is the development of a child's capacity for reasoned judgment and emotional attachment.

C. HARM TO CHILDREN AND INTERNAL LIMITS TO SECTION 2(A)

As previously noted, the Canadian courts have said that section 2(a) of the *Charter* is breached whenever the state interferes (in a nontrivial way) with an individual's religious practice. Once the court finds a breach of section 2(a), it must then consider whether the restriction on the religious practice is justified under section 1 of the *Charter*. However, some members of the Supreme Court of Canada have said that a religious practice or decision that is "harmful" does not fall within the protection of section 2(a), and so the state will not be required to justify the restriction of such a practice under section 1. Notably, the claim that harmful religious practices should be excluded from the scope of section 2(a) arises principally in cases involving parental oversight of children and seems to reflect our ambivalence about parental "rights" and, more deeply, our complex understanding of religion as both a matter of cultural identity and personal judgment. In the recent judgment of *Saskatchewan (Human Rights Commission) v Whatcott*, the Supreme Court of Canada indicated that even if there is an exclusion of harmful religious practices from the scope of section 2(a), it should be narrowly defined: "Just as the protection afforded by freedom of expression is extended to all expression other than violence and threats of violence, in my view, the protection provided under s. 2(*a*) should extend broadly."[3]

In *RB v Children's Aid Society of Metropolitan Toronto*, Iacobucci and Major JJ held that the parents' refusal on religious grounds to consent to a potentially life-saving medical treatment for their infant child was not protected by section 2(a), so that the state's override of that decision did not breach the section:

> The parents['] . . . constitutional freedom includes the right to educate and rear their child in the tenets of their faith. In effect, until the child reaches an age where she can make an independent decision regarding her own religious beliefs, her parents may decide on her religion for her and raise her in accordance with that religion. However, the freedom of religion is not absolute . . . . [W]e are of the view that the right itself must have a definition, and even if a broad and flexible definition is appropriate, there must be an outer boundary. Conduct which lies outside that boundary is not protected by the Charter.[4]

---

3   2013 SCC 11 at para 154.
4   Above note 2 at para 223 & 224.

More specifically, Iacobucci and Major JJ found that "the appellants do not benefit from the protection of s. 2(a) of the Charter since a parent's freedom of religion does not include the imposition upon the child of religious practices which threaten the safety, health or life of the child."[5] However, this was not the approach adopted by the majority of the Court in that case. Justice La Forest, for the majority, observed that "[t]his Court has consistently refrained from formulating internal limits to the scope of freedom of religion in cases where the constitutionality of a legislative scheme was raised; it rather opted to balance the competing rights under s. 1 of the *Charter* . . . ."[6]

The particular issue before the Court in the *RB* case was the constitutionality of a crown wardship order granted to the children's aid society under provincial child welfare legislation. The parents, who were Jehovah's Witnesses, had refused for religious reasons to consent to a blood transfusion for their critically ill infant. The wardship order enabled the children's aid society to consent to the transfusion. The parents argued that the order breached section 2(a) and section 7 of the *Charter*. Justice La Forest, for the majority, agreed that parents had a right under section 2(a) to raise their children in accordance with their religious beliefs and that this included the right to make decisions about the medical treatment of their children; however, he went on to find that the state's breach of this right, to protect a child at risk, was justified under section 1. While the Court agreed that parents should be free to care for their children as they think proper and to pass their beliefs on to their children, it recognized that an infant who was denied necessary medical treatment because of her parents' religious beliefs would never reach an age at which she would be able to make her own judgments.

The issue is different when the child is old enough to express a view and indicates his opposition to treatment. Adults have a general right to refuse medical treatment, including life-saving treatment, and are not required to justify their refusal on religious or other grounds. The law in most provinces extends to "mature minors" this right to refuse treatment.[7] The Supreme Court of Canada considered the constitutionality

---

5 *Ibid* at para 225. Similarly, in *Young v Young*, [1993] 4 SCR 3 at para 218 [*Young*], (which is discussed later) McLachlin J said that "conduct which poses a risk of harm to the child would not be protected."

6 *RB*, above note 2 at para 109.

7 The history of the common law mature minor exemption is discussed in *AC v Manitoba (Director of Child and Family Services)*, 2009 SCC 30 at para 59ff [*AC*]. In *BH (Next Friend of) v Alberta (Director of Child Welfare)*, 2003 ABCA 109 [*BH*], the Alberta Court of Appeal upheld a medical treatment order under provincial child welfare law. While the *Child Welfare Act*, RSA 2000, c C-12 defined "child"

of a version of the mature minor exemption in *AC v Manitoba (Director of Child and Family Services)*.[8] The appellant in that case was almost fifteen years old when she was admitted into hospital with severe intestinal bleeding. She was a member of the Jehovah's Witness faith and refused to consent to a blood transfusion even though her doctor had told her that a transfusion was medically necessary. The Director of Child and Family Services for the province applied for a treatment order from the court. Under the province's child welfare law, a court may authorize treatment it judges to be in the child's "best interests." The presumption in the legislation is that if a child is sixteen or older, his "best interests" will be "most effectively promoted" by allowing his views about treatment to determine the issue. This presumption will be rebutted only if it is demonstrated that the child does not appreciate the consequences of his decision to refuse treatment. The legislation, though, says that no such presumption is to be made when the child is under the age of sixteen. The trial judge in *AC* held that because the appellant was under sixteen, the "best interests" test applied, and so he ordered that the transfusion be given. The child challenged the constitutionality of the legislative scheme arguing that it breached her section 2(a) rights. A majority of the Supreme Court of Canada, in a judgment written by Abella J, held that the "best interests" of the child test should include some consideration of the child's capacity for mature, independent judgment. The capacity of a child who is under the age of sixteen to make such decisions is a relevant consideration in the determination of her best interests. According to Abella J, "The more a court is satisfied that a child is capable of making a mature, independent decision on his or her own behalf, the greater the weight that will be given to his or her views when a court is exercising its discretion under [the legislation]."[9]

---

in s 1(1)(d) as "a person under the age of 18 years," it also provided in s 2(d) that a child who is "capable of forming an opinion, is entitled to an opportunity to express that opinion on matters affecting the child and the child's opinion should be considered by those making decisions that affect the child." The court accepted that H lacked the capacity to refuse medical treatment that was necessary to save her life. The court concluded that the treatment order did not breach the *Charter* "where there is no mature minor or no informed decision by one": *BH*, above note 7 at para 13. For a discussion of this case, see Lori G Beaman, *Defining Harm: Religious Freedom and the Limits of the Law* (Vancouver: UBC Press, 2008).

8   *AC*, above note 7.

9   *Ibid* at para 87. She continued (*ibid*):

> If, after a careful and sophisticated analysis of the young person's ability to exercise mature, independent judgment, the court is persuaded that the necessary level of maturity exists, it seems to me necessarily to follow that the adolescent's views ought to be respected. Such an approach clarifies that in the

She concluded that when the "best interests" test is interpreted in this way, as taking into account the child's capacity to make medical judgments, it will not be found to violate section 2(a). Because the medical emergency in the case had long passed, and the child was over sixteen when the case was heard, the only issue before the Court was the constitutionality of the legislation.

The courts have also held that parental practices such as physical discipline of children, even if grounded in religious belief, will not receive *Charter* protection if they are found to be harmful. In *Prince Edward Island (Director of Child Welfare) v SPL*, the Supreme Court of Prince Edward Island granted permanent guardianship of children in a religious commune to the province's Director of Child Welfare and rejected the religious group's argument that use of the "rod" to discipline children and other forms of abusive behaviour were protected by the *Charter* as religious practices.[10]

D. CUSTODY AND ACCESS

When resolving disputes about child custody and access, the courts are generally expected to avoid making judgments about the character or value of the parents' religious beliefs.[11] However, the courts will take into account a parent's religious beliefs when those beliefs create a risk of harm to the child. In such a case, a parent may be denied custody or access, or her access rights may be curtailed.[12] Religion most commonly plays a role in a court's decision about custody or access when the beliefs or practices of the separated (custody and access) parents conflict in a way that may cause stress to the children. When an access

---

context of medical treatment, young people under 16 should be permitted to attempt to demonstrate that their views about a particular medical treatment decision reflect a sufficient degree of independence of thought and maturity.

10   2002 PESCTD 74. In *Canadian Foundation for Children, Youth and the Law v Canada (AG)*, 2004 SCC 4, the Supreme Court of Canada upheld a narrowly defined exception to the prohibition on assault for the reasonable use of force by a parent in correcting the behaviour of his child.

11   See GD Chipeur & TM Bailey, "Honey, I Proselytized the Kids: Religion as a Factor in Child Custody and Access Disputes" (1994) 4 NJCL 101 at 116. But if religion is not a relevant consideration in the application of the child's best interests test in custody and access cases, it is only because we have decided that religion should be treated like a "trait" comparable to gender or race rather than a contestable belief.

12   See Shauna Van Praagh, "Religion, Custody, and a Child's Identities" (1997) 35 Osgoode Hall LJ 309 at 318.

parent seeks to teach his children beliefs or practices that are incompatible with the beliefs of the custodial parent, the courts may be willing to limit the access parent's ability to involve his children in his religious life. The courts, though, are prepared to curtail the access parent's right to expose his children to his faith only when the religious conflict (and the resulting stress to the children) is significant. The courts recognize that it is generally in the children's best interests to maintain a relationship with the access parent and to be connected as fully as is reasonably possible with his life.[13]

The issue of religious conflict between divorced or separated parents arose in two Supreme Court of Canada cases, *Young v Young*[14] and *P(D) v S(C)*.[15] In both cases, the Court considered whether it was in the best interests of the children to limit the non-custodial parent's ability to discuss his religion with them or to involve them in his religious practices and, if it was decided that the children's best interests test required the imposition of such a limit on the non-custodial parent, whether this limit breached his freedom of religion rights under the *Charter*.

In *Young*, following the breakdown of the couple's marriage, the mother was awarded custody of their three children, and the father was granted access subject to the condition that when he was with his children, he was not to discuss his religion (Jehovah's Witness), take them to any religious meetings, or involve them in religious canvassing. The father agreed not to take his children on canvassing excursions or to religious services but questioned the prohibition on discussing religious matters with them. The Court accepted that issues of custody and access were to be determined on the basis of the children's "best interests." Before deciding whether the lower court judge had properly applied the "best interests" test to the case, the Court considered whether this test breached section 2(a) and, if it did, whether it was justified under section 1. According to L'Heureux-Dubé J, "even if the Charter were to apply to custody and access orders, no infringement of religious freedoms would occur where such orders are made in the best interests of the child."[16] She argued that "[w]hile parents are free to engage in religious practices themselves, those activities may be curtailed where they interfere with the best interests of

---

13   The custody and access cases in which the parents' religious commitments are no longer in harmony make clear that "parent's rights" is just a term of convenience and that the focus is really on the child's interests.

14   Above note 5.

15   [1993] 4 SCR 141 [*P(D)*].

16   Above note 5 at para 137.

the child without thereby infringing the parent's religious freedoms."[17] Similarly McLachlin J said that "the Charter guarantee of freedom of religion does not extend to protect conduct which is not in the best interests of the child . . . ."[18] The majority of the Court found that, in this case, the best interests of the children did not require the father to refrain from any kind of "genuine discussion of religious belief" with his children and so ordered the removal of this particular condition of access.[19] The Court made clear that the maintenance of this relationship—and more particularly the parent's ability to teach his children about his faith—is protected because it is in the children's best interests and not because the parent has a right of some kind.

In a companion case from Quebec, P(D), the Court confirmed that the sole consideration in matters of custody and access is the child's best interests and that freedom of religion is "inherently limited by the rights and freedoms of others."[20] In this case, the Court upheld restrictions on the non-custodial parent's access that prohibited him from engaging in religious indoctrination. While insisting that religious differences between parents were not "automatically harmful" and indeed might be beneficial, Cory and Iacobucci JJ accepted the trial judge's determination that the father's religious practice (described as religious fanaticism) was the source of significant conflict with the children and contrary to their best interests.[21]

As these cases illustrate, judgments about the value or character of religious belief or practice may sometimes play a role in decisions about custody and access. Justice L'Heureux-Dubé in Young insisted that in these cases, "where there is conflict over religion, it is important to emphasize that the court is not engaged in adjudicating a 'war of religion' nor are the religious beliefs of the parties themselves on trial. Rather, as courts have often recognized, it is the manner in which such beliefs are practised together with the impact and effect they have on the child which must be considered . . . ."[22] Yet, for the father who is a practising member of the Jehovah's Witness community and shares its commit-

---

17   Ibid. "The Charter has no application to private disputes between parents in the family context, nor does it apply to court orders in the area of custody and access. While a child's exposure to different parental faiths or beliefs may be of value, when such exposure is a source of conflict and is not in the best interests of the child, such exposure may be curtailed": ibid at para 157.

18   Ibid at para 218.

19   Ibid at para 186.

20   Above note 15 at para 107.

21   Ibid at para 140.

22   Above note 5 at para 135.

ment to active proselytization, this distinction between the beliefs he holds and the manner in which he practises them will make little sense. Shared custody, or generous access for the non-custodial parent, may work when parents are affiliated with the same religious group or with different "mainstream" religious groups that are generally compatible or do not come into direct conflict. In such cases, the differences in religious outlook between the parents will not be particularly disruptive or confusing to the children. However, other belief systems that demand exclusive allegiance and regard competing faiths not just as mistaken but as sinful or blasphemous may generate significant tension between the parents and stress in the children. A court then may sometimes decide that it is in the best interests of a child to restrict the access of a parent who seeks to involve the child in religious practices that conflict with the beliefs of the custodial parent.[23]

---

23 In *Vojnity v Hungary*, Application no 29617/07, Eur Ct HR, 12 February 2013 at para 41, the European Court of Human Rights confirmed that "a measure as radical as the total severance of contact [access rights] can be justified only in exceptional circumstances . . . ."

CHAPTER 7

FREEDOM OF CONSCIENCE

A. INTRODUCTION

Despite the courts' formal definition of the scope of freedom of conscience and religion as encompassing both religious and nonreligious beliefs, religious beliefs have been at the centre of the section 2(a) *Charter*[1] jurisprudence. In their section 2(a) decisions, the courts seem to regard religious beliefs and practices as special or as different from other, nonreligious, beliefs and practices. The state should remain neutral in matters of religion. It should neither support particular religious practices nor restrict such practices without adequate reasons. While the courts have said that freedom of conscience may be breached when the state restricts a nonreligious practice, it is difficult to find cases in which section 2(a) has been successfully used to protect such a practice. Moreover, the courts appear not to have considered the possibility that section 2(a) may be breached when the state compels or supports a nonreligious practice. In other words, freedom of conscience may sometimes protect the individual's freedom to "conscience" (her freedom from interference with her fundamental commitments) but not

---

1   *Canadian Charter of Rights and Freedoms*, Part 1 of the *Constitution Act, 1982*, being Schedule B to the *Canada Act 1982* (UK), 1982, c 11 [*Charter*].

her freedom from "conscience" (her freedom from the imposition of the deeply held nonreligious beliefs of others).[2]

The problem of distinguishing religious beliefs and practices from secular beliefs and practices, which has bedevilled the US courts, was something that Canadian courts and commentators thought section 2(a) had avoided by creating a single "integrated" right to freedom of conscience and religion. If freedom of conscience and religion protects all deeply held commitments or beliefs about right and truth, then the courts do not need to embark upon the difficult task of determining when a belief or practice is religious rather than "secular." Yet in *Syndicat Northcrest v Amselem*, the case that established the basic test for determining a breach of section 2(a), the Supreme Court of Canada offered a tentative definition of religion:

> While it is perhaps not possible to define religion precisely, some outer definition is useful since only beliefs, convictions and practices rooted in religion, as opposed to those that are secular, socially based or conscientiously held, are protected by the guarantee of freedom of religion. Defined broadly, religion typically involves a particular and comprehensive system of faith and worship. Religion also tends to involve the belief in a divine, superhuman or controlling power. In essence, religion is about freely and deeply held personal convictions or beliefs connected to an individual's spiritual faith and integrally linked to one's self-definition and spiritual fulfilment, the practices of which allow individuals to foster a connection with the divine or with the subject or object of that spiritual faith.[3]

And, indeed, the test developed by the Court in *Amselem* for determining whether a practice falls within the scope of section 2(a), which asks whether the individual believes that the practice connects him to the

---

2   While it is true that some political theorists have argued that the state should remain neutral toward competing conceptions of the good or deep judgments of value, it may be enough to say here that this position appears to have no support in the s 2(a) cases. Perhaps the ban on state support for religion, at least in some cases, could be understood as protecting freedom of conscience. As earlier noted, the complainants in many of the contemporary cases in which state support for religion has been challenged have been agnostics or atheists. Their complaint in these cases has not been that the state is supporting one religion over another, the religion of the majority over that of the minority, but rather that it is supporting religious belief or practice generally and sending a message of exclusion to citizens who are not religious, or imposing religion on them, or treating them unequally.

3   2004 SCC 47 at para 39 [*Amselem*].

divine, seems to be concerned exclusively with religious matters.[4] It is worth recalling, though, that while the Court in *Amselem* indicated that this test was applicable in section 2(a) *Charter* cases, the law applied in that case was the Quebec *Charter of Human Rights and Freedoms*, which protected both freedom of religion and freedom of conscience but listed them as separate rights.

B. AN INTEGRATED RIGHT OR TWO RIGHTS?

The term "freedom of conscience" was once used interchangeably with freedom of religion to refer to the individual's freedom to hold beliefs that were spiritual or moral in character. At this earlier time the moral beliefs of most individuals were rooted in a religious system. However, freedom of conscience is now viewed as an alternative to religious freedom. While freedom of religion protects fundamental religious beliefs, freedom of conscience extends protection to fundamental beliefs that are not part of a religious belief system—to secular morality. Together, then, freedom of conscience and freedom of religion protect the individual's most fundamental moral beliefs. But if religious freedom is now understood as requiring the state to remain neutral in spiritual matters or to treat different religious belief systems or communities with equal respect (and not just as requiring the state to refrain from religious coercion), it may no longer be possible to see freedom of conscience and religion as two aspects of a single, integrated right. The state may extend a degree of liberty to nonreligious beliefs and practices, but it cannot practically remain neutral toward all such beliefs, taking no position as to their truth. Indeed, if the state were precluded from supporting or impeding any basic values or practices, meaningful public action would be impossible. State support for or restriction of religion can be viewed as illegitimate only if there are other grounds (nonreligious values or practices) that the state may legitimately support or restrict. "Secular" values and practices provide the neutral ground or baseline that enables the courts to determine whether the state has treated religious groups unequally or has imposed religious practices or values on others. The

---

4   *Ibid* at para 46:

> [F]reedom of religion consists of the freedom to undertake practices and harbour beliefs, having a nexus with religion, in which an individual demonstrates he or she sincerely believes or is sincerely undertaking in order to connect with the divine or as a function of his or her spiritual faith, irrespective of whether a particular practice or belief is required by official religious dogma or is in conformity with the position of religious officials.

neutrality requirement then can be applied to only a narrow category of beliefs and practices—to religious beliefs and practices (but, as noted earlier, not even to all religious beliefs and practices) and perhaps also to a narrow set of nonreligious beliefs and practices that resemble religious beliefs and practices in certain respects.

There are two ways in which freedom of conscience may be related to religious freedom if the latter is understood as an equality right. The first is simply as a lesser right, or a second tier of protection. While freedom of religion requires the state to treat religious beliefs and practices "equally," freedom of conscience may protect a limited form of liberty: the right to hold and live in accordance with nonreligious fundamental commitments that do not conflict with the rights of others or the welfare of the community. In other words, freedom of conscience may be understood as freedom of religion once was—as a dimension of the individual's basic liberty of thought and action. The most obvious problem with this understanding of freedom of conscience is that the text of section 2(a) appears to join freedom of conscience and religion together in what Dickson CJ described as a "single integrated right."[5] The more significant problem is that a liberty-based understanding of freedom of conscience seems insubstantial as a constitutional right. If the right simply protects the individual's freedom to hold and act on basic moral commitments or important practices subject to state regulation in the public interest, then any reasonable state interest will be sufficient to justify its restriction. The second way in which freedom of conscience may be understood is as a minor extension of religious freedom; or as described by Jeremy Webber, "freedom of religion is the primary category, conscience the derivative."[6] Freedom of conscience on this account extends the same protection (state neutrality) to a narrow category of nonreligious beliefs and practices that resemble in content and

---

5   *R v Big M Drug Mart Ltd*, [1985] 1 SCR 295 at para 120. Moreover, the two elements of s 2(a) have a common origin in the early writings of liberalism, in which the terms were used interchangeably. Of course, at this earlier time, freedom of religion involved a commitment to individual liberty or autonomy in spiritual (and other deeply personal) matters. It is our understanding of freedom of religion that seems to have changed.

6   Jeremy Webber, "The Irreducibly Religious Content of Freedom of Religion" in Avigail Eisenberg, ed, *Diversity and Equality: The Changing Framework of Freedom in Canada* (Vancouver: UBC Press, 2006) 178 at 179. See also *ibid* at 186: "But the remarkable thing about freedom of conscience is just how parasitic it remains on freedom of religion in all of its most difficult contemporary dimensions." For a different view see Jocelyn Maclure and Charles Taylor, *Secularism and Freedom of Conscience*, translated by Jane Marie Todd (Cambridge, Mass: Harvard University Press, 2011).

structure paradigmatic religious beliefs and practices. Because there are so few Canadian conscience cases, it is difficult to determine which approach the courts have taken, or will take; although the dearth of cases might suggest that the courts understand freedom of conscience in this second way.

If freedom of conscience is understood as an extension of religious freedom, then in what respects must a nonreligious belief or practice resemble a religious belief to receive protection under section 2(a)? The answer to this will depend on why we think the state should remain neutral in religious matters. But this is not a simple question. For, as we have seen, the courts have enforced the requirement that the state remain neutral in matters of religion in a partial or selective way. It appears that a religious belief will receive special treatment (be insulated and excluded from civic action) when it is viewed as a cultural practice (a form of worship) rather than a contestable judgment about proper moral or political action. How the courts view a particular belief, as cultural practice or political or moral judgment, will depend on whether they see it as otherworldly in its orientation or instead as addressing civic concerns, such as the rights of others or the welfare of the community. As noted earlier, this judgment, in turn, may depend on the decision maker's views about the ordinary forms of religious practice and the proper scope of political action.

In the public imagination, the conscientious objector is someone who takes a moral or political stand against the dominant assumptions of the culture. She refuses to conform to the norms of the general community and holds to her own judgment about what is right or just. But if her objection to the law is based on a moral view that the majority in the democratic community has considered and rejected, why should she be exempted from the law? In the democratic process some views will prevail over others. It cannot be enough, then, that the conscientious (or religious) objector is committed to views or values that are inconsistent with state policy. Instead "freedom of conscience" may extend only to conscientious beliefs that appear to stand outside ordinary political debate—that are at odds with the most basic and widely held moral assumptions of the general community. This may be what is meant when these beliefs are described as "deeply held"—not just that they are fundamental to the individual but that they are part of a distinctive world view or moral framework. A conscientiously held belief may fall within the scope of section 2(a) when it resembles a paradigmatic religious belief or practice (a faith-based commitment) that is fundamental in significance, specific in content, peremptory in force, and perceived by non-believers as inaccessible or unconventional.

Because it is not derived from widely accepted moral premises, the position of the conscientious objector may appear to others to be personal or cultural rather than universal in character.

A secular (nonreligious) commitment may be regarded as a matter of conscience under section 2(a) when it diverges at a foundational level from prevailing moral norms and seems to lie outside the scope of reasonable political debate. A belief of this kind, though, is less likely to be sustained outside a religious or cultural group. It is not an accident then that many nonreligious "conscientious" practices are historically linked to religious practices. The protection of section 2(a) will most often be extended to nonreligious beliefs or commitments that are similar in content to familiar religious practices such as vegetarianism or pacifism, and indeed that may have developed from these practices. Moreover, if the claim to accommodation is based not simply on liberty concerns (and in particular on reducing the situations in which the individual must choose between obeying the law or following his conscience) but also on equality concerns (on preventing the marginalization of particular identity groups resulting from state interference with their practices), then it may not apply with the same force to beliefs or practices that are idiosyncratic and have no link to a cultural or religious group.[7]

Finally it should be noted that, as is the case with religious beliefs and practices, conscientious beliefs and practices may be "accommodated" only when they do not have a direct or significant impact on the rights of others. Religious and nonreligious beliefs or practices may be insulated from state action only when they are viewed as private and can be treated as cultural or personal. Indeed, it appears that the conscientious commitments protected by the courts under section 2(a) relate to activities such as diet that are ordinarily thought to fall within the private sphere.

C. THE FREEDOM OF CONSCIENCE CASES

One of the only reported cases in Canada in which freedom of conscience under section 2(a) was found to have been breached involved a refusal by the federal prison authorities to provide an inmate with vegetarian meals. In *Maurice v Canada (AG)*, an inmate had previously received vegetarian meals on religious grounds, as a member of the

---

7   As well, the growth of more individualized views—associated with spiritualism—may make it more difficult to carve out exceptions to the law.

Hare Krishna community.[8] After he had disassociated himself from that community, he asked that he continue to receive vegetarian meals in the prison for moral rather than religious reasons. The prison authorities took the position that they were only obligated to provide vegetarian meals for religious reasons. The Federal Court of Canada (Trial Division), however, rejected this argument noting that section 2(a) protects both religious and nonreligious beliefs and practices. In the court's view, the prison could accommodate the inmate's vegetarianism without difficulty, particularly since it was already providing vegetarian meals to inmates on religious grounds.

Two factors may have been critical to the success of this claim, setting it apart from other (possible) claims to accommodation for nonreligious beliefs and practices. The first has to do with the character of the practice. The judgment provided little information about the inmate's commitment to vegetarianism; however, it appeared that the practice was basic for him and not derived from more general principles, the elaboration of which might have been the subject of debate and disagreement. The practice was both specific in content and peremptory in force and so looked much like a religious duty. The inmate's claim was helped by the similarity of his particular practice, vegetarianism, to a recognized religious practice and indeed by the fact that he had previously been provided with vegetarian meals on religious grounds. Second, the court may have been willing to protect a moral practice that in ordinary circumstances is regarded as a private matter. Outside the prison context, vegetarianism is a practice in which the individual is free to engage and that has no obvious impact on the rights or interests of others. The state ordinarily has no direct involvement in the individual's dietary choices. Within the prison, however, all aspects of an inmate's life are controlled by the prison authorities. The inmate can do nothing without the support or co-operation of the state.

A number of lower-court decisions have considered conscience-based claims to exemption from paternalistic laws such as the requirement that car passengers wear seatbelts or that bicycle riders wear helmets.[9] In each of these cases, the claim for exemption was dismissed with few reasons given. In R v Locke, however, the provincial-court judge, when rejecting the conscience claim, observed that "Mr. Locke's belief that wearing a seatbelt may cause him more harm than good is not of the same order

---

8   2002 FCT 69. In R v Chan, 2005 ABQB 615, a prisoner had a right to receive
    vegetarian meals for religious reasons.
9   See, for example, R v Dubbin, 2009 BCPC 164; R v Locke, 2004 ABPC 152 [Locke];
    and R v Warman, 2001 BCSC 1771.

as the comprehensive value system protected by section 2(a) . . . ."[10] Mr Locke's opposition to the legislation was based not on a commitment to a different set of values (concerning personal safety or physical integrity) but instead on a different judgment about the safety consequences of (not) wearing a seatbelt. He believed that he would be safer if he did not wear a seatbelt. The legislature, though, had specifically addressed this question and, relying on empirical evidence, had determined that the safety of passengers will be better protected if they wear seatbelts. In most of the other lower-court seatbelt cases, the individual's objection to the law seemed to be based on a libertarian view that the state has no right to regulate self-regarding behaviour. The opposition to the law in these cases, then, was based on a deeply held moral view that is in tension with the state's justification for the law. The difficulty with the accommodation claim, though, is that it represents a general challenge to the legitimacy of paternalistic laws and perhaps state authority more generally. The conscientious objection is based not on the value the objector attaches to the particular practice (of not wearing a seatbelt) but instead on the value of liberty and autonomy and the illegitimacy of state power. Such a claim may be too sweeping for the court to contemplate under section 2(a).

D. CONSCIENTIOUS OBJECTION TO MILITARY SERVICE

In Upper Canada, the *Militia Act, 1793* exempted Quakers, Mennonites, and Brethren in Christ from compulsory military service.[11] The exemption was intended to encourage the members of different pacifist groups to emigrate from the United States following the American Revolution. In the late 1800s, Mennonites, Doukhobors, and Hutterites were encouraged to settle in Canada with the assurance that they would be exempted from military service. The exemption granted to these groups was extended by the Government of Canada after Confederation to the members of any religious group that objected to the bearing of arms. This exemption was maintained during World War I until its cancellation near the end of the war. Despite the cancellation of the exemption, no conscientious objectors were called for active service. Compulsory military service was last imposed in Canada during World War II. The members of two categories of conscientious objectors were granted a postponement of military training and service: (1) Mennonites and

---

10   *Locke, ibid* at para 25.
11   (UK), 33 Geo III, c 1.

Doukhobors who had been exempted from military service by orders in council when they had come to Canada in the late 1800s, and (2) other conscientious objectors who were prohibited by their religion from bearing arms. Individuals who were excused from military service were generally required to perform some form of alternative service. During World War II the postponement for conscientious objectors was not extended to Jehovah's Witnesses, a group that was subject to a legal ban during much of the war.[12]

More recently, in *Prior v Canada*, a Quaker who was opposed on religious grounds to government expenditures for military purposes sought to withhold a percentage of her income tax that corresponded to the percentage of the general federal budget allocated to military purposes.[13] The Federal Court of Canada (Appeal Division) rejected her claim. The court found that the connection between the taxes she was required to pay and the money allocated by the government to the military was too remote to support her claim that the compulsory payment of taxes interfered with her religious freedom.

Conscription was last imposed in Canada in the 1940s, when the exemption to military service was limited to conscientious objection on religious grounds. The situation, though, is different in the United States, which invoked the draft during the Vietnam War in the late 1960s. The US Supreme Court, in its application of the religious exemption from compulsory military service in the *Universal Military Training and Service Act*,[14] has adopted an approach to freedom of conscience that is similar to the approach I have attributed to the Canadian courts. The statutory exemption from military service, although confined to "religious" objections, has been interpreted by the Court as encompassing objections to military service that are more often considered non-religious or "conscientious" in character.

The US statute exempts from military service those who by reason of their "religious training and belief" are "conscientiously opposed to participation [in military service] in any form."[15] In the statute "religious

---

12   For a more detailed account of this history, see Janet Epp Buckingham, *Fighting Over God: A Legal and Political History of Religious Freedom in Canada* (Montreal; Kingston: McGill-Queen's Press, 2014).

13   (1989), 44 CRR 110 (FCA), leave to appeal to SCC refused, [1989] SCCA 441. A complaint by Prior against the Government of Canada to the UN Human Rights Committee under the *International Covenant on Civil and Political Rights* was dismissed in *Dr JP v Canada*, Communication No 446/1991, UN Doc CCPR/C/43/D/446/1991 (7 November 1991).

14   50 USC App § 456(j) (1958).

15   *Ibid*, § 6(j).

training and belief" is described as "an individual's belief in a relation to a Supreme Being involving duties superior to those arising from any human relation, but [not including] essentially political, sociological, or philosophical views or a merely personal moral code."[16] The US Supreme Court in *United States v Seeger* noted that the section uses the expression "Supreme Being" rather than God and decided that "the test of belief 'in a relation to a Supreme Being' is whether a given belief that is sincere and meaningful occupies a place in the life of its possessor parallel to that filled by the orthodox belief in God . . . ."[17] It is not necessary, said the Court, that the individual believes that God has forbidden him to participate in war but only that he believes that he is bound by a rule or command beyond his will not to participate in war in any circumstance. This reading of the exemption, said the Court, "embraces the ever-broadening understanding of the modern religious community."[18]

The Court in *Seeger* sought to distinguish the "religious" objections to military service that fall within the scope of the exemption from those objections that are not exempted because they are part of the individual's personal morality or based on "political, sociological, or economic considerations."[19] It is difficult, though, to make sense of the distinction between, on the one hand, a duty or obligation that fills the same role in the individual's life as a religious duty and, on the other hand, a personal moral commitment, since the latter, as a moral commitment, must be understood by the adherent as external to her will, binding upon her, and even universal in its application. It is unclear what work the modifier "personal" does here—how it affects our understanding of the individual's moral commitment. The more substantial limitation identified by the Court is that the objection to military service must not be based on economic, political, or social factors. The obvious consequence of this limit is that an exemption will not be granted to an individual who objects to participation in a *particular* war for social, political, or economic reasons. Political judgments of this kind, said the Court, have historically been reserved for the government. It appears, then, that the exemption from military service, as defined by the US Supreme Court, will apply when an individual holds a profound belief

---

16   *Ibid.*
17   380 US 163 at 165–66 (1965). In that case, the Court found that the exemption did apply to Mr Seeger, and several other applicants, who the Court (citing the appeal court) accepted may have been "bowing to 'external commands' in virtually the same sense as is the objector who defers to the will of a supernatural power" (*ibid* at 186).
18   *Ibid* at 180.
19   *Ibid* at 173.

that he must never go to war.[20] The individual's conscientious objection must be peremptory in the sense that it does not depend on the contextual application of more abstract principles about which there might be reasonable debate among citizens. Either one accepts that war is wrong (or that it is wrong to take a life, even in self-defence) or one does not accept this and believes that "it all depends" or that "it is a complicated matter." A circumstantial objection may be rooted in either a secular or a religious morality.

Part of the motivation for the US Supreme Court's broad reading of the conscientious objection exemption in the military service legislation may have been to ensure that a law that is intended to protect the "free exercise" of religion does not at the same time breach the establishment clause of the First Amendment. The argument, sometimes made, is that when the state exempts a religious practice from the application of ordinary law without also exempting a similar nonreligious practice, it is preferring religion over nonreligion, contrary to the establishment clause.[21] However, religious accommodation is based not simply on the deep significance of religion to the individual and group but also on the particular vulnerability of (minority) religious practices to political restriction. The exclusion of religion from politics may lead to religious beliefs, and more particularly minority religious beliefs, being overlooked in the legislative process. When the state "accommodates" a religious practice, it is not preferring religious over secular beliefs. It is simply maintaining the separation of religion and politics, which involves both the exclusion and the insulation of religious practice from political action.[22]

The fact that an individual is deeply committed to a particular principle, such as non-violence, may not be enough to justify an exemption from a state law that is enacted in the public interest. Military service is not a personal matter like diet or dress. An exemption from service for some individuals or groups on grounds of religion or conscience will place a greater burden of public service on other members of the community. Yet even if compulsory military service,

---

20   See also *Gillette v United States*, 401 US 437 (1971) [*Gillette*].

21   This argument was made in *Gillette*, ibid.

22   Conscientious objection has been an issue in a number of recent European Court of Human Rights decisions involving Jehovah's Witnesses in Turkey and Armenia. See, for example, *Savda v Turkey*, Application no 42730/05, Eur Ct HR, 12 June 2012, in which it was held that the state had a duty under art 9 of the *Convention for the Protection of Human Rights and Fundamental Freedoms* [*European Convention on Human Rights*] to establish a system for determining whether an individual has a conscientious objection to military service.

particularly during wartime, is seen as essential to the security of the nation, it is an extraordinary intervention into the life of the individual. Conscription raises significant questions not just about moral duty and the sanctity of life but also about the authority of the state to compel a citizen to participate in war—to kill others. There may also be a pragmatic concern behind the recognition of a religious or conscientious exemption, which is that coerced military service may result in acts of civil disobedience. In time of war the risk of civil disobedience may be particularly destabilizing. The fear of instability may outweigh concerns that the burden of military service will be unevenly distributed.

E. FREEDOM OF CONSCIENCE AND AUTONOMY

Freedom of conscience was employed in a very different way by Wilson J in *R v Morgentaler*.[23] In her concurring judgment, she held that the *Criminal Code* ban on abortion breached section 7 of the *Charter* because it deprived a woman of her liberty and security of the person in a way that was not in accordance with principles of fundamental justice. To interfere with the decisions a woman makes concerning her body, and more particularly concerning reproduction, would be to deprive her of her liberty and security of the person. Furthermore, such a deprivation would interfere with her freedom of conscience, a principle of fundamental justice. According to Wilson J:

> [T]he decision whether or not to terminate a pregnancy is essentially a moral decision, a matter of conscience. I do not think there is or can be any dispute about that. The question is: whose conscience? Is the conscience of the woman to be paramount or the conscience of the state? I believe, for the reasons I gave in discussing the right to liberty, that in a free and democratic society it must be the conscience of the individual.[24]

In Wilson J's decision, conscience refers to a sphere of autonomous judgment. The individual has the right to make decisions about deeply personal matters such as reproduction. This, I think, is different from the standard section 2(a) freedom of religion or freedom of conscience claim. The standard claim is not that the state should refrain from regulating a particular matter (that all persons should be exempted from legal regulation) but rather that those individuals, and only those

---

23   [1988] 1 SCR 30.
24   *Ibid* at 175–76.

individuals, who have a deep moral commitment that is inconsistent with the law should be exempted from its application. It may be that an exemption will be granted only if the (religious) practice is sufficiently "private" (i.e., limited in its impact on the rights and freedoms of others), but that is not the same as defining a sphere of autonomous judgment that applies to all persons.

Despite their formal claims, the courts have not done much to accommodate religious practices and, unsurprisingly, even less to accommodate nonreligious practices. A nonreligious belief or practice that is fundamental to the individual, does not directly address civic or public concerns, and rests on moral premises that are not widely shared in the community may be insulated from political action. It might then be said that when "religion" looks like civic morality, it will be subject to the give-and-take of ordinary politics, and when "conscience" (secular morality) looks like religion, it will fall within the protection of section 2(a). Cases in which the courts find a breach of freedom of conscience will, I suspect, continue to be rare and will occur only when the restricted practice is similar in structure and content to familiar religious practices.

CONCLUSION

The foundations of religious freedom are both principled and pragmatic. According to the courts, section 2(a) of the *Charter*[1] protects the individual's freedom from compulsion by the state to participate in religious practices and her freedom to hold religious beliefs and to engage in religious practices subject only to restrictions in the public interest. The courts, though, have said that section 2(a) protects more than individual liberty and establishes a form of religious equality. Section 2(a) requires that the state remain neutral in religious matters. The state should not support or favour the practices of one religious group over those of another, and it should not restrict an individual's religious practices except for compelling public reasons. The requirement of state neutrality toward beliefs and practices that are the subject of disagreement in the larger public sphere rests on concerns that religious contest in politics and the alliance of state and religion may undermine social peace and contribute to the marginalization of some groups within the community.

Because religious beliefs are deeply held and because they have sometimes given rise to social and political conflict, the courts have said that the state should remain neutral in spiritual matters. The state should take no position on the truth of religious beliefs, because (or even though) they address matters of the utmost importance to the individual. Yet, at the same time, the courts seem to recognize that religious

---

1   *Canadian Charter of Rights and Freedoms*, Part 1 of the *Constitution Act, 1982*, being Schedule B to the *Canada Act 1982* (UK), 1982, c 11.

beliefs involve contestable claims about truth and right that sometimes relate to or touch on civic concerns and so cannot simply be removed from the political sphere. State neutrality is possible only if religion can be viewed as distinct from the civic concerns addressed by the state. Religious belief systems, however, often have something to say about the way we should treat others and about the kind of society we should work to create. Because religious beliefs sometimes address civic concerns and are often difficult to distinguish from nonreligious beliefs, they cannot be fully excluded or insulated from political decision making. Religious adherents may seek to influence political action—to support state policies that advance their religious views about what is right and just. At the same time, the state may pursue public policies that are inconsistent with the practices or values of some religious belief systems.

The Canadian courts' formal commitment to state neutrality in religious matters has resulted in a series of decisions under section 2(a) that seem difficult to reconcile. Sometimes religious belief is excluded or insulated from state action, and other times it is treated as an ordinary part of political decision making. The courts have said that the state has a duty to make space for religious practices, and yet they have been unwilling to require the state to compromise its policies in any real way. Accommodation takes place at the margins of law and involves at the most only minor and pragmatic adjustments to public policy. The courts have said that the state should remain neutral in religious matters, and avoid supporting the beliefs or practices of a particular religion, and yet they have accepted that religious values may play a role in political decision making.

The courts have required the state to remain neutral toward what may be described as the "private" or spiritual dimensions of religious practice. The "public" elements of belief that address civic concerns or the rights and interests of others in the community remain subject to the give-and-take of ordinary politics. This distinction, although not expressly made by the courts, underlies the different treatment the courts have given to religious "practices," which the state is precluded from favouring, and religious "values," which the courts have said may play a role in political decision making. This distinction between public and private religion may also play a role in the courts' accommodation decisions and account for their weak or selective protection of religious practices from state interference. Where the line is drawn between the civic and spiritual spheres will reflect the courts' assumptions about ordinary religious practice and appropriate state action. Because the civic and spiritual spheres of life are not always easy to separate, the process of drawing a line between them will often seem political and pragmatic. And because the line is not drawn explicitly but is instead framed as a (natural) distinction between practice and value in state support cases and buried within the formal section 1 balancing of interests in religious accommodation cases, the courts' assumptions about the nature of religious practice and state action are concealed from scrutiny.

Behind the courts' uneven application of the religious neutrality requirement lies a complex conception of religious commitment in which religion is viewed both as an aspect of the individual's identity that should (sometimes) be excluded and insulated from politics and as a set of judgments made by the individual about truth and right that should (sometimes) be subject to the give-and-take of politics. Religious belief is not simply a fixed attribute or characteristic; nor is it simply a personal choice or judgment. The challenge for the courts is to fit this complex conception of religion into a system of constitutional rights that distinguishes between immutable or deeply rooted traits that must be respected by the state as part of a commitment to human equality and choices or commitments that are protected as a matter of human liberty but subject to laws that advance the public interest. Because religion can be seen through both lenses, as cultural identity and personal commitment, this shifting by the courts between equality- and liberty-based conceptions of section 2(a) may be unavoidable.

TABLE OF CASES

INDEX

ABOUT THE AUTHOR

Richard Moon is a professor at the Faculty of Law, University of Windsor. He has written extensively about freedom of expression and freedom of religion, publishing more than fifty articles and book chapters in Canada and abroad. He is also the author of *The Constitutional Protection of Freedom of Expression* (2000), editor of *Law and Religious Pluralism in Canada* (2008), and a contributing editor of *Canadian Constitutional Law* (2010).